THE FLIGHT FROM WOMAN

Books by Karl Stern

The Pillar of Fire

The Third Revolution

Through Dooms of Love

The Flight from Woman

KARL STERN

The Flight from Woman

Paragon House
NEW YORK

Reprinted 1985 by
Paragon House Publishers
2 Hammarskjold Plaza
New York, N.Y. 10017

First published 1965 by
Farrar, Strauss and Giroux

Selections from the following books are used by the kind permission of the publishers: *Sonnets to Orpheus* by Rainer Maria Rilke, translated by M. D. Herter Norton; copyright 1942 by W. W. Norton & Company, Inc. *A Short Life of Kierkegaard* by W. Lowrie; copyright 1942 by Princeton University Press. *Nausea* by Jean-Paul Sartre, translated by Lloyd Alexander; all rights reserved; reprinted by permission of the publishers, New Directions. *Goethe's Faust*, translated by Philip Wayne ©1959 by Philip Wayne, and reprinted by permission of Penguin Books, Ltd. "Hedda Gabbler" from *Three Plays* by Henrik Ibsen, reprinted by permission of Penguin Books, Ltd.

Library of Congress Cataloging-in-Publication Data

Stern, Karl.
The flight from woman.

Reprint. Originally published: New York: Farrar, Straus and Giroux, 1965.
Includes index.
1. Men — Psychology — Case studies. 2. Philosophers — Relationships with women — Case studies. 3. Authors — Relationships with women — Case studies. 4. Emotions — Case studies. I. Title.
BF692.5.S74 1985 155.3 85-19194
ISBN 0-913757-51-9 (pbk.)

Contents

ACKNOWLEDGMENTS

The following persons have had a hand, at one time or another, in the preparation of the manuscript: Miss Martina Boland, Mrs. Ursula Glashan, Mrs. Lee C. Hilgenberg, and Miss Margaret Anne Mackay.

Dr. Leo Bartemeier scrutinized it especially from the point of view of the psychoanalyst; Professor Storrs McCall from the point of view of the philosopher.

To all these I wish to express my heartfelt thanks.

K. S.

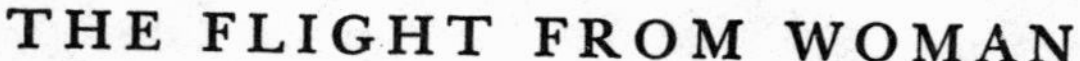

THE FLIGHT FROM WOMAN

ONE

Introduction

One way to start off a complex subject is to explain how it originated with the author. The present study was first prompted by clinical observations of certain abnormalities of character. The problem of activism—a lack of balance between action and contemplation—is said to be characteristic of our time. The man of restless energy, the hustler and go-getter, is a figure familiar to the popular imagination; one associates this kind of life with "organization men," "managerial" and "executive types." (The very fact that many terms are coined and freely bandied about is proof that a problem is genuine.) Now whenever we psychiatrists have an opportunity to observe this kind of person as a patient, we find at the bottom of it all a maternal conflict and a rejection of the feminine. The observation was first made in a peculiar and unexpected context—patients suffering from peptic ulcer of the stomach.[1] Many of these ulcer patients were found to be hard-working and spartan in their habits; they shied away from any pleasure of "receiving," from accepting tenderness, from all forms of passivity, even healthy ones. Yet deep down there persisted an extraordinary need to be mothered, to be fed. "Deep down" is the right term, because the conflict manifests itself literally deep down in the body, on an organic level. The patient protests in his life against "being fed," while his stomach revolts against "not being fed." However, feeding here means much more than the intake of nourishment; it means receptiveness in a large sense, receptiveness to love, and openness in a childlike attitude of trust.

Precisely the same attitude towards life occurs in many people who do not suffer from stomach ulcers, but whose underlying conflicts are the same. Psychoanalysts call conditions which are chiefly a matter of one's attitude towards life, and towards one's fellow men, *character neuroses*. The character neurosis of frenzied activism is not difficult to spot. There is an air of restlessness about such men—not necessarily the tension of subjective anxiety, but the tension of energy—an air of endless drive and ambition for which someone once used the term, "flight into work." On getting to know these persons more intimately, one notices an extraordinary denial of feeling, a shying away from tenderness, and a fear of dependence or passivity. Not to want to be dependent or passive is in itself healthy. In fact, it is well known that psychiatrists have to deal a lot with

---

1 Draper, S., and Tourraine, G. A. *"The Man-Environment Unit and Peptic Ulcer."* Arch. Int. Med., *49*, 616, 1932. Alexander, F., et al: *"The Influence of Psychological Factors upon Gastro-Intestinal Disturbances."* A Symposium. Psycho-anal., Qtrly. *3*, 501, 1934.

people who crave too much dependence and passivity. Nevertheless in a normal person one must allow for a need of dependence, passivity, and protectedness. The kind of individual I am talking about here is really in *terror* of dependence. The very possibility of being in the least dependent or protected, or even being loved, amounts to nothing less than a phantasy of mutilation or destruction.

A fear of being loved? The idea seems incongruous, and I can well imagine incredulity on the part of some readers. Yet it is much more frequent than one might assume. One of de Montherlant's heroes expresses it this way: "Shame and embarrassment at the passive role a man assumes who is being loved. To be loved, he thinks, is a state appropriate to women, animals and children . . . " " . . . A man who is being loved is a prisoner. All this is too well known, let's not go into it."[2]

The denial of feeling is at times accompanied not only by undue activism but by undue intellectualism. Some psychoanalysts speak of the frigid character. The word "frigid" is here used not with its common sexual connotation but to designate a person "who avoids feelings altogether; instead he has developed a cold intellect."[3] Fenichel describes one of his patients who could be wholly at ease in life only when he did mathematics, because this was the one activity in which emotional relationships did not enter. In our experience such a "cold" rationalistic attitude towards life has a basis quite similar to the one found in the man of undue drive. In fact, hyper-activist and hyper-rationalist attitudes often go together. The man in

---

2 Henri de Montherlant, *Les jeunes filles,* Grasset, Paris, 1936.

3 O. Fenichel, *The Psychoanalytic Theory of Neuroses,* Norton, 1945.

power, the executive who manages not only things but also people; the man who approaches human relationships as if they were matters of engineering; the man who acts as though he were on guard against his own heart—these types are only too well known. It goes without saying that such people may be successful in life, if we take "success" to mean material advancement. But one can frequently observe that they allow their technical or scientific or business acumen to extend into areas of human life in which these techniques have no place. In other words, they shy away from all interior means of communion, and tend to be great believers in the mechanics and manageability of human relations. This is something difficult to describe to those who have never encountered it. If individuals like these have any philosophical convictions at all, they tend to be rationalist and positivist.[4] Of course, to be a rationalist or a positivist is not in itself a psychiatric symptom, but within the setting of the kind of personality I have tried to describe, it is. Moreover, this philosophy takes on a characteristic shade. For instance, one of my patients, the product of a conservative cultural and religious climate, was the son of European immigrants. His enthusiasm for all that is "smart" and "progressive" was associated with an impatient and angry rejection of the values of his tradition, values which were often based on simple wisdom. When it came to his personal relationships, the man literally used the same words as

[4] I am using the word "positivist" without regard to any particular school and only to designate, for the want of a better term, the widespread popular belief in the primacy and exclusiveness of scientific truth and the applicability of scientific techniques to those aspects of human life which, until now, have been subject to wisdom rather than science.

de Montherlant's hero. He acted like someone who *feared* tenderness. And when it came to faith, he refused to "swallow" anything which he could not rationally prove. However, his protest against matters of faith was too furious not to be regarded as part of the other problem—namely a fear of dependence.

The fact that an exaggeratedly rationalist attitude towards life means trouble is well known. To go into the clinical aspect of this would require a book by itself. For the purpose of this inquiry we merely summarize: an undue emphasis on the technical and the rational, and a rejection of what for want of a better term we call "feeling," go with a neurotic dread of receiving, a fear of tenderness and of protection—and are invariably associated with an original maternal conflict. The poet Novalis made this confession after the death of his fiancée, in a letter to a friend: "Born with a softness of character, my intellect expanded more and more, and gradually displaced the heart from its domain. It was Sophie who returned to the heart its legitimate throne. Her death might bring back the reign of the usurper (the intellect) who would kill the heart in revenge."[5] This is not just a pretty metaphor of mourning. Psychoanalysis speaks, in the structure of a man's character, of an "armor," and Novalis observes that he had developed a cold rationalist attitude as an armor against a feeling of defencelessness. He had regained his equilibrium in the fusion with woman. His observation shows, with poetic intuition, that "intellect" and "heart" stand in

[5] Friedrich Hiebel, *Novalis; der Dichter der blauen Blume,* A. Francke, Bern, 1951.

antithesis, and that in this antithesis the "heart" is linked to the feminine.

The female counterpart to all this is frequently encountered today in the woman who finds it difficult to accept her womanly role. This is quite independent of the injustices imposed on women in many societies: it is rather an over-evaluation of masculine achievement and a debasement of values which one commonly associates with the womanly; a rejection, often unconscious, even of motherhood; an aping of man, associated with an unceasing undertone of envy and resentment. In either case, whether of the man or of the woman I have just sketched, there is a flight from the feminine.

If we assume, as many people do, that these disturbances are widespread today in comparison with other times in history, they entail far-reaching implications. Rationalism and positivism have influenced our Western civilization during the past three centuries to an extraordinary degree; yet the rich benefits of technology inspire a widespread alarm that *human affairs* will be increasingly more programmed, and not in Marxist countries alone. And if we equate the one-sidedly rational and technical with the masculine, there arises the ghastly spectre of a world impoverished of womanly values.

Such a summary formulation over-simplifies the complexity of the problem, and I have an abhorrence of sweeping theories. The pitfalls are innumerable; many of the most celebrated works on *Kulturphilosophie,* re-visited today, are like the ghost-towns of an era of feverish speculation. Yet the problem is too interesting not to be explored. Here, for once, one may take recent knowledge of the nature of man and apply it to an anthropology of the Hellenic and the Judaeo-Christian tradition. This is a reciprocal test, and it promises mutual enrichment. But just because of the danger of idle speculation, of the "big sweep," one has to go about it cautiously. This means that, before we do anything else, we have to go into the question of the polarity of the sexes. Secondly, we have to examine the validity of an antithesis which in philosophy is referred to under different aspects—namely of "analysis" and "intuition," or "science" and "wisdom," or the "scientific statement" and the "poetic statement," or of *homo faber* and *homo sapiens,* and so on. Thirdly, since this book is concerned with the ontological significance of psychological observations, we must also examine the relationship between psychoanalysis and metaphysics. Finally, we shall trace the "male-female" conflict in the lives of men who are representative of the modern era. For phenomenology and existential philosophy have taught us once more something that classical philosophers knew long ago: if one wants to get closer to the ontological mystery behind the facts of nature, there is only one reliable place to go—to the hearts of men.

TWO

Womanhood

All views of the role of the sexes follow, in essence, one of two possible lines: either one assumes a fundamental duality which remains immutable at the bottom of all cultural variants; or one regards the idea of an immutable duality as a myth, and considers cultural variability as the only provable fact.

The sex organs and the sex cells manifest a polarity and complementariness in morphology and in function. In the act of sexual union the male organ is convex and penetrating and the female organ is concave and receptive; the spermatozoon is torpedo-shaped and "attacks," and the ovum is a sphere "awaiting" penetration. That this polarity and complementariness should not be confined to the physical but also be reflected in the character of man and woman, is a view as old as history. As a matter of fact, in ancient religions and philosophies, sexual polarity and complementariness did not stop at the psychological. Human duality and human mating expressed an antithesis at the very heart of things, an antithesis striving for synthesis unceasingly, eternally—in an act of anticipation and restitution of unity. This tradition is so ubiquitous and abundant that one could not possibly present it here in detail. The most remarkable thing about it is perhaps the fact that it is expressed in religions and philosophies widely separated in time and place. We find the idea clearly expressed in Taoism and in the Sohar, in the Upanishads and in Christianity. Events in nature and in human history are explained by two principles. In Taoism these are *Yin*—the feminine which is calm, dark and receptive, and *Yang*—the male which is active, light and generative. An eternal movement of reciprocity between the two is safeguarded by a higher principle of oneness, the *Tao*. The rich erotic mysticism of the Kabbala shows a striking resemblance to the Chinese tradition.[1] Heaven as *Tiph'ereth* is the male principle which, through the arms of the world, is in union with earth as *Malchuth,* the womanly principle. Unity arises out of polarity. The highest expression of this is the idea that man is androgynous (male-female) in his origin and his final destination. The most famous presentation of this idea is found in Genesis when God created man in His image, "male and female"—*before* the separation of Eve out of the body of Adam. This, according to Christian tradition, indicates the androgynous nature of the Godhead Himself—meaning, again, that here *polarity in union* is the expression of the fullness of being.[2] No less famous is

[1] Langer, G. *Liebesmystik der Kabbala.* Otto Wilhelm Barth, München-Planegg, 1956.

[2] For the development of this thought in the history of Christianity, compare: Evdokimov, P., *La femme et le salut du monde. Etude d'anthropologie chrétienne sur les charismes de la femme.* Casterman, Paris, 1958.

the development of the same idea in the speech of Aristophanes in Plato's *Symposium*: man and woman, in the sexual embrace, restitute the primary unity of the human person in its fullness, a unity which has, at one time, been broken. It is remarkable that here for once, before the Christian epoch, Greek and Jew agree. The same idea had already been presented in the Upanishads: "But He, too, Athman (soul, God) had no joy, for He was as big as Man and Woman are together when they unite. Then his substance was divided into two parts, from whence came Man and Woman. Hence the body, too, is a 'half.' "[3] There exists a similar Assyrian version.[4] Indeed, it would not be surprising to find that this is, among esoteric traditions, the only universal one. Of course, if it were so it could easily be explained: the very existence of men and women is the one invariant in all civilizations. Our metaphysical sense tells us, with the irreducible immediacy of sensory perception, that this invariability *means* something, apart from all shifting contingencies. However, nowadays our thinking is so adapted to the tests of veracity applied by the cumulative sciences that we regard such language as that quoted, at best, as a pleasing poetic metaphor. For the time being we must, for the sake of a fair argument, grant the possibility that at one time men did have such immediate metaphysical sense and that in the existing multiplicity they beheld essences, with an irreducible simplicity which has to us become suspect. Whatever the truth may be, there is no doubt that today, for the first time in history, there occurs a trend which runs completely contrary to all

[3] G. Langer. Loc. cit.
[4] Ibid.

this. Not only is the metaphysics of sexual polarity regarded as a residuum of prescientific superstition, but even the belief that anatomical complementariness expresses psychological complementariness is no longer taken for granted. This is implied in many recent anthropological and sociological writings. Margaret Mead[5] comes to the conclusion, on the basis of anthropological observations, that the roles assumed by man and woman in life depend to a large extent on the notions implanted in the child at an early age, and that apart from the specific role in the function of reproduction, sexual difference is an outcome of social and cultural constellations.

The question is, of course, to what extent the physiological role in the function of reproduction does not penetrate and color functions seemingly unrelated to it. Erikson (1951) concluded from experimental observations of the playing of pre-adolescent children that there are two distinct psychological trends which are determined primarily *biologically,* and only secondarily by the child's expectation of its social role. "For it is clear that the tendencies governing these constructions (i.e. buildings and scenes made out of toy materials) closely parallel the morphology of the sex organs: in the male erectible and intrusive in character, serving highly mobile sperm cells; internal organs in the female, with vestibular access, leading to statically expectant ova."[6] Similar observations can be found in a remarkable study on the phenomenology of the womanly by Buy-

---

5 Mead, Margaret, *Male and Female.* Mentor, New York, 1955.

6 Erikson, E. H., "Sex differences in the play configurations of preadolescents." Am. J. Orthopsychiat. *21,* 667, 1951.

tendijk.[7] As a matter of fact Margaret Mead herself comes to the conclusion that there may be gifts, seemingly not connected with the physiology of reproduction, which are nevertheless fundamentally male and female.

George Sand[8] remarked a hundred years ago, in a letter to Flaubert, that one is generally inclined to overestimate the difference of the sexes, merely on the basis of anatomical differences. In our days Simone de Beauvoir has devoted an erudite study to the same idea.[9] To her the very sense of *otherness,* usually expressed by men, implies *alienation,* even reification of woman, and with this a loss of value. This come out most clearly in her analysis of diverse authors. From the most pathologically mysogynous texts of the Church Fathers to the most beautiful lines of a Breton or a Claudel, every word is interpreted as though man's very gaze were enough to lower the dignity of woman. No matter what way he looks at her, she cannot win. The potentially androgynous nature of Man which, according to Judaeo-Christian tradition, is more fully restituted in the marital act and eschatologically perfected, here loses all significance. It is replaced by some androgyny which is actually a dialectical construction. In the end one gets the impression that some villain arbitrarily divided humanity into two camps. Behind it all is the following idea: it is wrong to view the two halves of mankind as convex-penetrating and concave-receiving in equilibrium,

---

7 Buytendijk, F. J. J., *La Femme*. Desclée de Brouwer, Brussels, 1954. This study also contains important references to the literature on experimental psychology.

8 Deutsch, Helene. "Ein Frauenschicksal: George Sand." Almanach für das Jahr 1929. Internat. Psychoanal. Verlag. Vienna, 1929, p. 150.

9 Beauvoir, Simone de. *The Second Sex*. Knopf, 1953.

because the concave-receiving quality in itself implies humiliation. The very posture of receptiveness means slavery. The irony of it all is that with this point of view the author inadvertently, takes an androcentric position. None of the most mysogynous ancient texts imply such complete degradation of woman as de Beauvoir's book.

The roots of all this are very complex. For millennia women have suffered atrocious forms of social and legal injustice. It is no exaggeration to say that they have been, and often still are, the victims of a kind of interior colonialism. However, since the French Revolution and the rise of the feminist movement, the cry for *equality* has changed into an assertion of *sameness.* Any view of dissimilarity smacked suspiciously of injustice. It is characteristic of our time that the word "discrimination," which originally means "sorting out," has often acquired the meaning of hate, and in works like those of Simone de Beauvoir and others any attempt at making *distinctions* is branded as an act of *discrimination* in the derogatory sense. Ironically, with the social movement that developed from the declaration of the Rights of Man there arose a Cartesian view of the nature of the human person. The idea that anatomical differences are nothing but a matter of accidental implements of the body, interchangeable, as it were, is a touch of Cartesianism—something that imperceptibly creeps into many of our modern views of people and the world. Moreover any metaphysical dimension which we are inclined to add to the natural data is suspect of magic thinking, and held to be open to correction by scientific inquiry. The fact that we sense an immutable core behind the incessantly shifting social, cultural, psychological constellations is viewed as a prescientific tyranny of thought. In the end the very idea of sexual polarity is regarded, in relation to the findings of the social sciences, as a pre-Copernican universe would be in relation to the findings of astronomy. "There are different kinds of myths," says Simone de Beauvoir. "This one, the myth of woman, sublimating an immutable aspect of the human condition—namely the 'division' of humanity into two classes of individuals—is a static myth. It projects into the realm of Platonic ideas a reality that is directly experienced or is conceptualized on the basis of experience; in place of fact, value, significance, knowledge, empirical law, it substitutes a transcendental idea, timeless, unchangeable, necessary."[10] This statement is typical of the author's thinking as a whole. We shall remark a similar quality in the writings of Sartre: the writer borrows the terms of phenomenology and existentialist philosophy, but presents something altogether different—namely a thesis reminiscent of scientific positivism. Thus in spite of her wealth of knowledge, scientific and literary, the final result of de Beauvoir's thesis is an extraordinary impoverishment. What began in feminism as a movement of liberation is bound to end in a slavery worse than the first. For if there really existed a world in which "sexual characteristics" are the mere "product" of "culture," in which Mark might just as well have Martha's personality, and Antigone the personality of Achilles—persons would be reduced to fleshless ciphers, to mere intersection points in the graph of a social structure. Indeed, in such a world there are no Marks or Marthas, no Antigones or Achilles. That secret of freedom which lies at the depth of a man's

[10] Loc. cit.

or woman's personality would be conjured away, and would be replaced by a vastness of social entities, faceless and manageable. There is no doubt that the original Leninist doctrine of *sexual sameness* (since then modified and practically revoked, at least in the Soviet Union), was not only prompted by the motive of liberating woman but contained the hidden aim of depersonalization. And a lot of the relativism characteristic of the social sciences in non-Marxist parts of the world replaces the old concept of the person and his or her role by that of a social entity with *quasi-interchangeable parts.* In all this, behind an apparent process of unfettering, is hidden a preparation for potential enslavement.

A new way of looking at things is, of course, not wrong in itself. All advances in the natural sciences are based on thoughts which run counter to preceding millennia, and are first held only by a few, except that in our case it might be erroneous to take the matter entirely as a problem for the natural sciences. We have seen that there exists an indisputable scientific fact: the anatomical and physiological polarity and complementariness of the sexes. Throughout the ages the polarity and complementariness were assumed to apply also to the *person* of man and woman. Whether this assumption is justified, is a phenomenological problem. Therefore we begin with a phenomenological inquiry and first ask ourselves: what gives us that *sense of polarity?*

Maxim Gorki[11] tells in his *Reminiscences of Tolstoy* how one day a group of men, among them Chekov, were

[11] Gorki, Maxim, *Erinnerungen an Lew Nikolajewitsch Tolstoi.* "Der Neue Merkur," Munich, 1921.

sitting in the garden and talking about women. Tolstoy listened for a long time in silence, and then suddenly remarked: "I am only going to tell the truth about women when I am standing with one foot in the grave—I shall say it, jump into the coffin, pull the lid and then I'll say: 'Do with me what you want!' " This sounds as though the truth about women were something a man could not possibly say and stay alive. And this from the creator of Natasha and Marie, Anna and Kitty! However, though a joke, there is one thing the scene and Tolstoy's remark convey—a sense of mystery. If the truth about women is something a literary genius will keep until the moment of his death there must be, besides an old man's sly crack, another implication—the inexpressible, kind of *mysterium tremendum*. And this has been the feeling of man throughout history. That well-known enigmatic sense which people get by looking at the Gioconda is unthinkable in the case of a male portrait. The fact that in some civilizations women are veiled is not only due to jealous possessiveness on the part of the male. According to a contemporary woman writer, the element of the veiled and the hidden is associated with the very idea of womanhood.[12]

The alleged mysteriousness of the feminine is treated with benevolent jocularity in feminist literature. It is regarded as one of the numerous subtle ways in which men deprive women of club-membership. Yet, this should not prevent us from investigating. Though the definition of the mysterious is that we cannot explain it, we can eluci-

---

[12] Gertrude von Le Fort, *The Eternal Woman*. Transl. by Marie C. Buehrle with a preface by Max Jordan. Bruce, Milwaukee, 1954.

date the psychology of it. What gives us a feeling of the mysterious?

Woman, in the person of our mother, is the first being with whom we are in contact. "Contact" is not an adequate word, because there is no more intimate union than that which exists between the child and the mother who keeps it in the sheltering and nourishing womb. It all begins with a true *fusion* of being. That extraordinary oneness and communication continues for quite some time after birth. The infant is utterly dependent on the mother (or in case of absence or death on the substitute mother): he would starve if he were not fed, he would become sick if he were not cleaned. He is not only dependent for physical nourishment but also for mental nourishment, for love. He is as yet unable to give love, only to receive it. The baby's *love* for the mother is at this stage a *need* rather than a centrifugal movement, an *act*. The umbilical cord is cut and the child is physically severed from the mother, but psychologically the mother still *belongs* to the child. The baby has not found his own center of gravity as it were. Psychoanalysis has shown that the sum of the baby's psychic experiences is identical with the image of his body, and this world of the body extends without clearly defined border into the mother. We can also reverse the statement and say that the child is an extension of the mother, without clearly perceptible border. There exists a *participation mystique*,[13] a psychic flow from child to mother and from mother to child.

---

13 The expression has originally been coined by Lévy-Bruhl to describe a phenomenon in the psychology of primitive peoples, but we use it here to connote something different.

The function of a mother is not exhausted with sheltering, protection and dependence. By the very act of birth she puts us into the world; you might almost say that the first encounter with her involves being pushed away by her. At birth the umbilical cord is severed, and if the mother's love for the child is healthy, a gentle process of severing continues, not only physically but mentally. The mother shows the child that he is not the exclusive recipient of her love. She teaches him to share her affection with others. She turns his gaze away from her. He has to face reality. Only the neurotic mother maintains her child in a state of dependence and fixation; the wise mother knows not only how to bind, but also how to sever. In fact, man is truly capable of loving only if the psychological bond of maternal fixation is disconnected. Only then are we able to face the world and the "other."

Today we know that this early drama, more than anything else, is decisive for the formation of character. Yet all this occurs before there is conscious reasoning. There are several elements of paradox. Man's earliest love story takes place before the advent of reason; yet it is more profoundly experienced than anything he experiences later. It is a story of love but strangely intermingled with a story of severing, of gently pushing away, of farewell. It is not merely a story: it sets a pattern for all stories to come. Our experiences with father and with siblings enter into that pattern, of course, but the drama of "mother-child" leaves traces at the rock-bottom of the human condition.

Since our study is concerned with ontological problems, we should like immediately to draw attention to two particular aspects of all this. Firstly, man, the "king of creation," the being endowed with reason, is at birth more helpless than other mammals. He continues for a long time in a state which in many ways is close to the intrauterine. The anatomist Portmann has shown that the human baby's growth after birth, contrary to that of lower animals, presents for some time a continuation of the fetal growth curve. Even newborn anthropoids are less helpless than newborn humans, and anyone who observes a calf or a colt after birth is struck by the independence of the young animal in comparison to a newborn baby.

According to Bowlby,[14] man is more dependent on motherly care than the lower primates. In lemurs the mother is a "moving milk tank with plenty of fur to cling to," and the baby has to fend for himself. The chimpanzee mother is more gentle and responds to the baby's cry. Harlow[15] separated Rhesus babies from their mother at birth and had them fed by an automatic feeder which for one group of babies was mounted on soft rags, for another group on wire. Although there was no difference in the mechanism of nutrition, the babies of "wire mothers" were stunted in their mental growth, and the males, when grown up, were inhibited in their emotional development.

The second observation we have to add here concerns the experience of time. Everybody knows that with advancing age our subjective experience of duration becomes compressed. For the child, two consecutive summers are

---

14 Bowlby, John, "The Child's Tie to His Mother." Internat. Journ. of Psychoanalysis. *39*, 350, 1958.

15 Harlow, H. F., "Love in Infant Monkeys." Scientific American *200*, 68, 1959; and Harlow, H. F., and Robert R. Zimmermann, "Affectional Responses in the Infant Monkey." Science, *130*, 421, 1959.

separated by an eternity; for an old man, the summers seem to follow each other with accelerating speed. There are indications that the speed of cellular mechanisms is inverted to time experience; as the stretches of subjective time are long in the child, tissue reactions such as the healing of wounds are rapid—and vice versa in the aged. As we extend this back into infancy, it is obvious that we once inhabited a vast time universe; and there we lived in an intimate physical and mental fusion with another being.

From all this it is more understandable why woman imbues us with a sense of the mysterious. However, there is something else. We have already admitted that woman's role and position vary considerably in the course of history, and that anthropological observers confirm a common experience: what we call "womanly" does depend, in part, on cultural and social circumstances. In order to find the invariable, the common denominator, we have to go right down to the biological characteristics of woman, to her "nature." Her uniqueness, that which distinguishes her *absolutely* from man, lies in the biological. The point is that, contrary to what George Sand or Simone de Beauvoir believe, biology is not a matter of an instrumentarium of circumscribed purpose.

Just as in sexual physiology the female principle is one of receiving, keeping and nourishing—woman's *specific* form of creativeness, that of motherhood, is tied up with the life of nature, with a *non-reflective bios.* Helene Deutsch,[16] who has written some of the most perceptive pages on the subject of womanhood, observes

[16] Deutsch, Helene, *The Psychology of Women.* A Psychoanalytic Interpretation. Grune and Stratton. New York, 1945.

that "the most intuitive and introspective women shy away from observing their own psychic processes during pregnancy; one might almost say that they are deliberately trying not to observe them. This profoundly motivated behavior is one of the reasons why we have so little information about the psychic life of the pregnant woman." A remarkable phenomenological study on womanhood by Sister Thoma Angelica Walter is characteristically entitled "Seinsrhythmik",[17] "the rhythm of being." Indeed, the four-week cycle of ovulation, the rhythmically alternating tides of fertility and barrenness, the nine months of gestation which can be neither prolonged nor hurried—all this ties woman deeply to the life of nature, to the pulse beat of the Cosmos. What Goethe calls the law of *systole* and *diastole* enters more into her life than into man's.

How deep that *sense of time* reaches into the woman's body can be illustrated with another example. We not infrequently see that in those cases in which a woman commits an artificial abortion, let us say in the third month of pregnancy, the act seems to have no psychological consequence. Yet, six months later, just when the baby would have been due, the subject breaks down with a serious depression or even with a psychosis. Now there are two remarkable features about this. First, the woman is not necessarily conscious of the time incidence. The depression occurs without any conscious awareness of "this is the time when my baby would have been due." Moreover, the patient's philosophy is not necessarily such that she would

---

[17] Sister Thoma Angelica Walter, *Seinsrhythmik: Studie zur Begründung einer Metaphysik der Geschlechter*. Herder, Freiburg, 1932.

have morally disapproved of the act of interruption of pregnancy. Yet, her profound *reaction of loss* (not necessarily even with a conscious preoccupation with the missed birth) coincides with the time of the birth which did not take place. The mechanism of timing is similar to the one we observe in people who are able to wake up at any given hour without setting an alarm clock—so deeply is the unconscious of the subject linked with the tides of the body. Woman, in her being, is deeply committed to *bios,* to nature itself. The words for *mother* and *matter,* for *mater* and *materia* are etymologically related.

Let us, in contrast to this, look at the life of man. Quite independently of sociological and cultural shifts of emphasis, there exists an aspect of life which is forever associated with the masculine principle. Just as in the function of the spermatozoon in its relation to the ovum, man's attitude toward nature is that of attack and penetration. He removes rocks and uproots forests to make space for agriculture. He dams rivers and harnesses the power of water. Chemistry breaks up the compound of molecules and rearranges the position of atoms. Physics *overcomes* the law of nature, gravity, first in the invention of the wheel—last in the suprasonic rocket which soars into the stratosphere. Even in the realm of thought, in philosophy and in pure mathematics, the "nature" of things is being "pierced." It is noteworthy that even with a relativist anthropological point of view one arrives at such a basic dichotomy inherent in the sexes. Margaret Mead suggests the possibility that such activities as we have just indicated are basically "male," independent of cultural factors. According to W. I. Thomas[18] the matriarchal phases of history were those with little movement of population, a conservative, watchful attitude over things to grow, and specifically male abilities came into the foreground when climatic and other conditions made for more expansion, aggressiveness, and movability.[19] Whether rocks are blasted to gain more soil or matter itself is destroyed (as in atomic fission) to gain more energy—man's activity is always in a sense directed *against* nature.

Thus we see that the polarity of the sexes is based on body build and organ function but not confined to it. The male principle, according to Helene Deutsch[20] enables us to master our relationship with reality, to solve our problems rationally. Woman, wherever she is different from man, "acts and reacts out of the dark, mysterious depths of the unconscious, i.e. affectively, intuitively, mysteriously. This is no judgment of value but a statement of fact." Commenting on Kant's famous statement that "women don't give their secret away," Helene Deutsch states that "they don't because they don't know it themselves." Margaret Mead expresses the same idea, though more cautiously: "We may well find that there are certain fields such as the physical sciences, mathematics and instrumental music, in which men by virtue of their sex, as well as by virtue of their qualities as specially gifted human beings, will always have that razor edge of extra gift which makes

---

[18] W. I. Thomas, *Sex and Society, Studies in the Social Psychology of Sex.* Fisher Unwin, London.

[19] To present all this in detail would go beyond the framework of the present study. Readers interested in phases outside modern occidental history (including Bachofen's theory of the early matriachate and similar subjects) are referred to the vast technical literature in this field.

[20] Deutsch, Helene, *Ein Frauenschicksal: George Sand, loc. cit.*

all the difference, and while women easily follow where men lead, men will always make the new discoveries. We may equally well find that women, through the learning involved in maternity, which once experienced can be taught more easily to all women, even childless women, than to men, have a special superiority in those human sciences which involve that type of understanding which until it is analyzed is called intuition."

The dualism as expressed by Helene Deutsch and Margaret Mead is confirmed by everyday experience. It is confirmed by numerous observers of extraordinary divergence, such as a poetess of mystic leanings (LeFort) and a scientist and phenomenologist (Buytendijk).[21] Perhaps the most felicitous expression was found by Ortega y Gasset:[22] "The more of a man one is, the more he is filled to the brim with rationality. Everything he does and achieves, he does and achieves for a reason, especially for a practical reason. A woman's love, that divine surrender of her ultra-inner being which the impassioned woman makes, is perhaps the only thing which is not achieved by reasoning. The core of the feminine mind, no matter how intelligent the woman may be, is occupied by an irrational power. If the male is the rational being, the woman is the irrational being." The word "irrational" does not go well in this context since in English it often has the connotation of "foolish" or "stupid". There should be another word, such as "trans-rational," because Ortega, just like Helene

---

[21] Some of the most remarkable formulations of these insights are to be found in thinkers quite "outside the mainstream," such as Jakob Böhme or Franz von Baader.

[22] Gasset, Ortega y, "Landscape with a Deer in the Background." In *On Love: Aspects of a Single Theme.* Meridian, New York 1957.

Deutsch and others, speaks of a form of *knowledge* or *awareness* which is not only independent of reason but goes *beyond* it. The sociologist Georg Simmel remarks that for woman "being and idea are indivisibly one" (*unmittelbar eines*).[23] This creates the impression, so often expressed in popular psychology, that women have no logic. This popular view expresses, according to Simmel, *a lack in man*: for him the idea can be conceived only as an outside and an above; it is not immanent. It is in a very similar sense that Jean Guitton observes that love, as a natural gift, is a characteristic element of all womanhood.[24] As we shall see, intuitive intelligence is more intimately tied up with love than analytical intelligence. Hence, woman's "strength is the intuitive grasp of the living concrete; especially of the personal element. She has the special gift of making herself at home in the inner world of others."[25] When Ortega states that a woman's love is "perhaps the only thing which is not achieved by reasoning," we are rather reminded of Dante's statement about women "who possess the spirit of love" (*"ch'avete intelletto d'amore"*).

The elusive and trans-rational in the core of womanhood, the fact that in the creativeness of feminine love and of maternity exists an element of hiddenness, anonymity,

---

23 Simmel, Georg. *Philosophische Kultur, Gesammelte Essais.* Alfred Kroner, Leipzig, 1919. The essay in question is entitled "Das Relative und das Absolute im Geschlechter-Problem."

24 Jean Guitton, *L'amour humain.* Aubier, Editions Montaigne, Paris 1955.

25 Edith Stein, *Problems of Women's Education.* In Writings of Edith Stein. Selected, translated and introduced by Hilda Graef. Newman Press, Westminster, Md. 1956.

something that resists geometrical definition; the fact that woman is not delineated as man is because her outlines blend mysteriously with the *chtonic,* all this may explain the well known paradox that in Freud's work woman has found only a negative definition. Much in female psychopathology can be explained from the fact that at a certain phase of her evolution the girl discovers that she is "not a boy" (castration phantasy, penis envy). Freud's theory of feminine psychology is largely based on this. This has led to the most significant disagreements in the history of psychoanalysis since the exodus of Jung and Adler. Even such orthodox followers of Freud as Ernest Jones saw a weakness in the fact that this was a psychology of women developed by men. Zilboorg[26] saw in it a manifestation of an androcentric bias, of the tacitly assumed male superiority. Freud considered libido as essentially male, obviously on account of its pushing and climactic character. However, does not the tenderness of receiving, the stillness of holding, belong to the libidinal just as much as the orgastic experience? We know from clinical experience that the desire for orgastic fulfilment *only,* neither preceded, accompanied nor followed by the desire to envelop and hold, indicates a profound psychic disturbance, a masked form of frigidity, irrespective of male or female. At any rate, there is no doubt that the mode of sexual encounter reflects the phases of development of the person.[27] The very word *libido* has, in its origin, a dual meaning: *desire* and

---

[26] Zilboorg, G. "Masculine and Feminine. Some Biological and Cultural Aspects." *Psychiatry,* 7, 257, 1944.

[27] Compare also observations on this in "Identity and the Life Cycle," by Erik H. Erikson. Internat. Univ. Press, N.Y. 1961.

the *fulfillment* of desire (Sterba 1942).[28] Thus the phenomenology of sexual experience in its normal fullness in man or woman reflects a bisexual polarity. We may also deduce this from the pathology of character disorders. Phallic women are aggressive-competitive, with a tendency to be crudely sadistic in vengeance—a mental caricature of "maleness." I have observed cases of men with serious disturbance of genitality whose attitude toward life was one of hoarding and retentiveness, with a tendency to unproductive accumulation, a kind of un-ending pregnancy of material inflation which never came to creativeness or "birth." In these men, a pregenital "anal" structurization presents a caricature of femininity. Just as the aggressive drive of the phallic woman is frequently devoid of creativeness, in the case of such men inceptiveness and interior growth is imitated by *accumulation without issue.*

Karen Horney emphasized a primary character in the joyful experience of motherhood which resists all further reduction. Indeed, clinical observation suggests that the "concave" aspect of libido, the desire to receive, to hold and to nourish is as primary and irreducible as the phallic one. For example, the frequent dream symbols in women, referring to the act of nourishing, sheltering and warming seem to be deeply rooted in the primary process and the body image, and can hardly be explained on a *minus.* One of my patients, a woman in her menopause who had been frustrated by an impotent and mentally sadistic husband, produced a dream in which she was just about to close her summer cottage with the advancing autumn when un-

---

28 Sterba, R., *Introduction to the Psychoanalytic Theory of the Libido.* Nerv. & Ment. Dis. Monograph Series, New York 1942.

expected guests arrived and she was obliged to open the cottage once more and get out the food and blankets she had just put away. The house (the womb) to be closed for the approaching winter is, in my experience a not infrequent dream symbol in menopausal women. The wish, in her state of sexual frustration, to produce food and warmth once more is evidently just as primary as the wish for orgastic fulfillment would be.[29] Freud's own view that libido itself by its very nature is male, has an androcentric touch and disregards the other side of the coin. Nevertheless, a lot of what appears as androcentric in the psychoanalytical theory may be explained out of the hiddenness in the nature of the feminine. There is an analogous aspect of "femininity" to the male character for which the schema needs to be modified—the creative act of genius.

Since the rise of feminism, it has often been suggested that woman has been forcibly kept away from the peaks of creativeness in the arts and sciences only by cultural and social restrictions. One can easily see the fallacy here. If there had been female Bachs or Newtons, no power on earth could have kept them from producing. Having been barred from the basic training is no argument. In many civilizations of the past women made music or painted or wrote poetry. The best women writers or scientists since the emancipation are still far from the class of such giants. What is of interest here is the phenomenology of creativeness of the genius. We observe that the genius brings into the world something which has that irreducible quality of *it-*

---

29 Compare also the observation of Erikson on the play patterns of preadolescent children (loc. cit.) in which there is in girls an emphasis on the interior of the house, the peace of sheltering; in boys on the exterior of the house, and on mobility.

must-be-so. A sonata by Mozart or a painting by Giotto lack arbitrariness; there is nothing *voulu* about them. The greater the genius, the greater is this element of the unconscious. What Helene Deutsch said about the psychology of pregnant women—namely that even the most intuitive and introspectives ones "shy away from observing their own psychic processes" so that "one might almost say that they are deliberately trying not to observe them"—holds also for the male genius. Fancy interviewing Bach about the psychic process at work in creating the cantatas. All he might have been able to tell you is that he had a commission to put out one a week. Somebody once calculated that even for a copywriter to *copy* the works of Mozart would be difficult within a span of thirty-five years. And yet every one of these works has an earmark of perfection which no years of *calcul* could achieve. "The great and central virtue of Shakespeare was not achieved by taking *thought,* for thought cannot create a world."[30] All this suggests that the genius' work comes to us *through* him, not *made* but *born.* This incidentally pertains also to the greatest works in the field of mathematics (which is more closely related to the arts than one commonly thinks). The suddenness and spontaneity of coming-about has been recognized by people like Helmholtz and Poincaré, and it is characteristically preceded by an "incubation" stage wherein the study seems to be completely interrupted and the subject dropped.[31] Gauss' statement, "I myself cannot say what was the conducting thread which connected what

---

[30] Van Doren, Mark, *Shakespeare.* Holt, 1939.

[31] Hadamard, Jacques. *The Psychology of Invention in the Mathematical Field.* Princeton University Press, 1945.

I previously knew with what made my success possible" (speaking of a certain mathematical theorem) is reminiscent of Mozart's famous remark: "Then my mind seizes it (the work) as a glance of my eye takes in a beautiful picture of a handsome youth. It does not come to me successively, or with its various parts worked out in detail as they will be later on, but it is in its entirety that my imagination lets me hear it." If one wants to express the sense of marvellous completeness and perfection in a work such as the St. Matthew Passion or the Isenheim Altar, there exists in the German language the word *Wurf,* that is, something *thrown.* The same word is used for *birth* in the animal kingdom. Indeed, the greater the work of art, the greater is the element of the "thrown," of the *naïveté* and *anonymity* of the creative act which resembles that of conception and birth. In other words, it is only at the peaks of artistic creation (which includes certain aspects of philosophy and sciences) that man approaches the level of feminine creativeness, namely motherhood. Whether this observation is connected with that of Helene Deutsch and others, that in the intuitiveness of the artist his femininity is mobilized, is a question we do not want to pursue in this connection. The very fact that at the peaks of male creativeness the phenomenology reveals parallels with conception, gestation and birth will perhaps be better understood when man's androgynous nature is still more elucidated. Jung's theory of "Animus" and "Anima" touched some aspects of this problem. We shall encounter it once more in connection with a type of woman who refuses to be man's "Muse." Considering our present knowledge, that aspect of the problem lies in the area of the speculative.

To come back to the subject of feminine psychology, we have seen that, according to psychoanalysis, there exists an infantile preconceptual communication with the mother. Now this flux is by no means a one-way affair. The mother herself participates similarly with the child. An invisible cord persists, long after the umbilical one is severed. There exists a deeply *knowing* relationship between child and mother—a mode of knowledge which *precedes* the advent of reason and, in a sense, *transcends* it. What observers such as the ones quoted (Helene Deutsch, Ortega y Gasset and others) consider as the "male" component of intelligence does not participate in this. This is the reason why we find that the father does not have the same inner relationship to the newborn child as the mother. One must not be misled by feelings such as pride and happiness. The kind of inner communication the mother has, the father cannot share until the child himself communicates by signals, be they ever so primitive. Here are two passages from *Anna Karenina,* in which the relationship of Kitty and Levin to their small baby, Mitia, is described. First Kitty and her baby:

"I must run down to Mitia. Unfortunately, I haven't nursed him since breakfast. He is awake by now and must be crying." And she made for the nursery with a rapid step. She knew that the child was crying even before she got there, and indeed she had not been mistaken. It was a good hungry cry. "Has he been awake long, nurse?" Kitty asked, seating herself on a chair and undoing the bodice of her dress. "Give him to me quickly. How tiresome you are, nurse! Can't the cap be tied later?" The child yelled louder and louder. "It won't do at all, Katerina Alexandrovna," Agafia Mihailovna said, trying to soothe the child, and paying no further attention to the mother. The nurse carried the child over to Kitty; Agafia Mihailovna walked behind, her face full of tenderness. "I declare he knows me!" she shouted louder than the baby. Kitty paid no heed to her words; her impatience, like that of the child's, was increasing. Owing to their mutual impatience things did not go smoothly at first; the child had some difficulty in taking the breast, and grew angry. Finally, after a desperate cry, matters were satisfactorily arranged between them, and mother and child grew quiet simultaneously. "He seems all in a perspiration," Kitty said, feeling the boy. "What makes you think that he knows you?" she asked Agafia Mihailovna, looking sideways at the child's eyes, which seemed to her to peep out roguishly from beneath his cap. "It's impossible! If he recognized anyone at all it would be me!" She smiled to herself. *In her heart she knew that he not only recognized Agafia Mihailovna, but comprehended a whole lot of things that nobody ever knew, and that she was only just beginning to find out, thanks to him. For Agafia Mihailovna, for the nurse, for his grandfather, and even for his father, Mitia was only a weak little creature who demanded material attention, but for her he was already a human being, with a whole history of moral relations.* "When he wakes up, you will see for yourself," Agafia Mihailovna said. "When I do this, he beams, the darling. His little face looks as bright as the sky on a clear day." "All right, we shall see," Kitty said in a whisper. "You can go now, he is falling asleep."

And now Levin, the father:

Kitty, with her sleeves rolled up, was bending over the bath in which Mitia was kicking and splashing. When she heard her husband's footsteps she turned her face towards him and beckoned him with a smile. She was supporting the baby's head with one hand and sponging him with the other. "Just look at him!" she said when her husband came up. "Agafia Mihailovna is right; he is beginning to recognize people." An experiment had to be made. Levin bent over the bath, and the child seemed to know him. The cook was then called; she, too, bent over him and the child frowned and screwed up its face. Next Kitty bent over him and his face lighted up with a smile. He pressed his little hands against the sponge and made such a strange, satisfied sound that not only Kitty and the nurse, but even Levin was transported with joy. The child was taken from the bath, wrapped in a sheet, rubbed down as it yelled lustily, and turned over to his mother. "I am glad you are beginning to love him at last," Kitty said to her husband, as she sat down in his customary place with Mitia at her breast. "You always said you had no feeling for him, and it used to worry me." "Did I say that, really? I only meant that I was disappointed in him." "What! disappointed in him!" "Not exactly in him, but in my feeling for him; I had expected more. I had expected some new, pleasant feeling, but instead there was only a sensation of pity, disgust . . ." Kitty listened to him as she put on her rings, that she had taken off before bathing the baby. "There was more fear and pity than satisfaction. I never knew until today, during the storm, how I loved him." Kitty's face grew radiant.

Levin and Kitty represent perfect examples of the father's and the mother's relationship to the child. All this illustrates how the father develops an inner relationship to the baby properly when the baby just begins to come out of that primeval world which he shares with the mother, from that *participation mystique* which we encounter in the first quotation. How decisive that maternal *participation mystique* is for the future life of the baby has been first pointed out by Freud. He made his discoveries in grown-ups, and his work was like that of an archaeologist who, from bricks and shards, builds up a vanished civilization. I remember how some of my teachers in psychiatry used to scoff at Freud's notion that depressions occur in early infancy. Moreover, the idea that schizophrenia or certain forms of melancholia might go back to early maternal deprivation or rejection or merely to conflicts *within* the mother, seemed preposterous. The point of Freud's critics was, obviously, that to appreciate loss or conflict your intellect has first to be developed. To get depressed by loss you have to be pretty smart; this was the implied argument. The Freudian discovery meant no less than that man's modes of *knowing* and of *loving* arise out of a preconceptual, pre-rational and pre-verbal world—a world inhabited by mother and child together.

Freud was vindicated by direct observations of infants. René Spitz has proved by direct observation of babies, long after Freud's first hypotheses, that separation from the mother (or the maternal love object) during infancy produces emotional and intellectual defects which can never be completely made up for. Before the age of six months, the child is not yet able to identify the loved person. The most critical period for bereavement is the age between six months and eighteen months.[32] Infants, be-

---

[32] Spitz, René A. "Hospitalism. An enquiry into the genesis of psychiatric conditions in early childhood." The Psychoanal. Study of the Child, *1*, 53, 1945. Anaclitic Depression. The Psychoanal. Study of the Child, *1*, 313, 1945. Compare also the same author's film: "Grief—A Peril in Infancy."

reaved of their mothers during that phase, go through the most extraordinary reaction of mourning. Even under the best conditions of child-care, nutrition and hygiene, they regress in their mental development, lose weight and are susceptible to infections. Their facial expression and attitudes bear a startling resemblance to those encountered during psychotic depressions and other serious psychoses in adults. Indeed, Helene Deutsch has shown that inexplicable depressions in grown-ups are repetitions of such early experiences of grief.[33] The unwanted child, long before there could be any conceptual knowledge of such unwantedness, grows up with a wound quite similar to the one sustained by absence or loss of the mother. It all comes down to something which was already implied in the observations of comparative zoology quoted above: if we look over the animal kingdom and distinguish between impersonal factors decisive for the baby's future, facts of nature as a whole (weather, vegetation, herd) and individual factors, we see that man's fate is shaped from the beginning by a *personal relationship.*

Incidentally, the fact that the experiences most decisive for our entire life stem from a preverbal, preconceptual and prelogical realm, accounts much more for the original resistance of academic psychiatry to Freud than does his emphasis on sex. Three centuries of rationalistic thinking so conditioned scientists that they shied away from the acceptance of "causes" which were not causes in a mechanistic sense. In the light of our thesis, it is no coin-

[33] Deutsch, Helene. "Absence of Grief." Psychoanal. Quarterly, *6,* 12, 1937.

cidence that so much of that from which discursive reasoning recoiled was of the world of the maternal.

The most obvious scientific argument against all sexual duality is the fact that none of the many different "male" or "female" characteristics established by numerous authors has ever been found in pure form in one individual. We know that a man may look after babies, and a woman scale mountains—without being perverted. This, however, does not speak against the existence of sexual characteristics. We know that every person harbours his contra-sexual *anlage*, and trouble does not occur as long as M and F remain integrated within the individual. The bisexual nature of man is a vast subject, and for our purpose we must limit ourselves to a few points. First, anatomical and physiological observation arrived at conclusions at which psychoanalysis had arrived quite independently. Secondly, this is one of the few points in which those disciples of Freud who parted from him at an early phase, namely Jung and Adler, remained in some agreement, although their elaborations led them in widely different directions. It is impossible to outline here in detail Jung's theory of "Animus" and "Anima."[34] Nowhere is the original relatedness as well as the difference between Jung and Freud more apparent than here. A lot of what is implied in the Animus-Anima concept is contained in Freud's observations on man's latent femininity and woman's latent masculinity. But since Freud's interest is primarily clinical and Jung's generally symbolic the points of

---

[34] Certain aspects of this theory are outlined in: Emma Jung, *Animus and Anima*. Two Essays. The Analytical Psychology Club of New York, Inc., 1957.

concordance are not obvious. To the clinician, skipping the biological is always suspect. Adler's concept of the "masculine protest" overlaps to a considerable degree with Freud's observations on phallic women.

However, the most striking feature is the fact that here, for once, modern science confirms notions which go back to ancient nonscientific traditions. Let us recall once more the very first account of the creation of man in Genesis, *before* Eve is taken out of the body of Adam. "And God created Man to His own image: to the image of God He created him, male and female He created them" (Gen. 1, 27). As we have said, this was interpreted, long before the advent of modern science, to mean that *Man in his fullness is bisexual.* We do not need to quote verbatim the famous passage in Plato's *Symposium* in which Aristophanes makes the same affirmation, and explains the mutual attraction of the sexes out of the need to restitute a whole: man and woman, in the sex act, are two halves which fuse in order to restitute the original fullness of Man. A Platonist might say that our bisexuality is a shadow of all this, sketched into the human image. Anatomically, the morphology of the external genitalia of woman represent rudimentary tracings of the male genital organs, and the residual of Müller's duct (utriculus masculinus) are the feminine traces in man. Endocrinology also proves our bisexual nature. The findings of psychoanalysis have again been summed up by Helene Deutsch: " 'Woman' and 'Man' have, at one time, arisen out of a common origin which is still living on in the bisexual *anlage* in all human beings. They have differentiated in the course of development without ever being completely separated from one another. . . . The quantity of contrasexual residuals (*gegengeschlechtliche Reste*) differs with each person. *In the psychic budget of the individual the two components, male and female, must be linked in harmony.*"[35] What "linked in harmony" actually means cannot be easily explained without going into a great amount of clinical observation.[36] At any rate, lack of integration, unbalance of the two principles leads to a "troubled destiny" (*gestörtes Lebensschicksal,* Helene Deutsch). The significance of this observation can hardly be exaggerated. It is not only confirmed in everyday clinical experience but also in fields of psychiatry to which, at first sight, it does not seem to apply. Now we ask ourselves: does it have implications *beyond* psychology? To the philosopher, nothing is purely psychological or purely biological. The very fact that through the entire history of human thought, from Greek to contemporary philosophy, the theme of "existence" versus "essence" has occupied the minds of men, means simply that there is no empirical observation which does not give us at least the *sense of wider implication.* Every empirical fact contains its "beyond." This is particularly true about our subject. The body of science, like those corpses in ancient legends, is always in search of a *supplément d'âme.*

---

[35] Deutsch, Helene, *Ein Frauenschicksal.* Loc. cit. (The italics are mine.) Coleridge made the statement, amazing for his time: "The truth is, a great mind must be androgynous." This holds for everybody, not only "a great mind," but in a way which we cannot yet define with clinical precision.

[36] Compare Erikson, E. H., *Childhood and Society.* Norton, New York, 1950.

THREE

Scientific Knowledge and Poetic Knowledge

In the preceding chapter we have pointed to a remarkable concordance of the most divergent authors, from Dante to contemporary psychoanalysts, concerning "maleness" and "womanliness." According to this notion the polarity of the sexes corresponds to a polarity in human intelligence—that of "discursive reason" versus "intuition." At first sight this appears one of those stereotypes with which all writing on the sexes abounds. The polarity of "male" and "female," once we leave the firm ground of anatomy and physiology, resists Euclidian definition. So do the concepts of "discursive reason" and "intuition." If we line up the four concepts in two pairs the impression of vagueness is so heightened that we arrive at what looks like a compounded cliché.

In order to get a clearer view of the matter let us take

one of the pairs, namely "discursive reason" and "intuition" and consider it by itself, quite apart from any relevance it may have to sexual polarity. At first we are discouraged because there exists no one definition of the term "intuition." A recent investigator[1] distinguishes at least seven meanings of the term, and it seems that such meanings as "hunch" and "extra-sensory perception" do not come into the issue under discussion. They are quite heterogeneous to other forms of intuitive knowledge, all of which have one thing in common: knowledge by union, contrary to knowledge by disassembly.[2] Hence it is best to restrict our field of vision, exclude such meanings as the "hunch," and limit ourselves to the Bergsonian notion of analysis and intuition which I shall outline presently. Simple self-observation shows that there exist two modes of knowing. One might be called "externalization," in which the knowable is experienced as an *ob-ject*, a *Gegen-stand,* something which stands opposed to me; the other might be called "internalization," a form of knowledge by sympathy, a *"feeling with,"*—a union with the knowable. Of this distinction there is no doubt. Whether the terms "analysis," "scientific knowledge," "discursive reason" are perfectly synonymous or refer only to phenomena with a common denominator does not concern us here. The same is true about the terms "intuition," "poetic knowledge,"

---

1 Herbert Feigl, "A Critique of Intuition from the Point of View of Scientific Empiricism." In *Philosophy East and West,* University of Hawaii Press, 1958–59.

2 Feigl's remarkable discussion suggests to me that even the "hunch" aspect of intuition comprises different phenomena, and that the "hunch" of the creative scientist (which precedes experimental-analytical procedure) belongs actually to the category of 'knowledge by union.' This question would be worth further phenomenological investigation.

"knowledge by connaturality." The only thing of importance in the present context is a basic duality in the mode of knowing.[3]

Let us start with the most famous example. Bergson begins his *Introduction to Metaphysics*[4] with the statement: "A comparison of the definition of metaphysics and the various conceptions of the absolute leads to the discovery that philosophers, in spite of their apparent divergencies, agree in distinguishing two profoundly different ways of knowing a thing. The first implies that we move round the object; the second that we enter into it. The first implies that we move around the point of view at which we are placed and on the symbols by which we express ourselves. The second neither depends on a point of view nor relies on any symbol. The first kind of knowledge may be said to stop at the *relative;* the second, in those cases where it is possible, to attain the *absolute.*"[5] After having elaborated on these two modes of knowing Bergson continues: "It follows from this that an absolute could only be given in an *intuition,* whilst everything else falls within the province of *analysis.* By intuition is meant the kind of *intellectual sympathy* by which one places oneself within an object in order to coincide with what is unique in it and consequently inexpressible. Analysis, on the con-

---

3 Feigl, in the investigation quoted above, is inclined, from an empiricist point of view, to reject the idea of intuition as a separate mode of knowing, and to regard it as a kind of sub-liminal form of discursive reason, based on previous experiences. This, I feel, is possibly due to the fact that he puts the main emphasis on the "hunch" aspect of the concept of intuition.

4 Bergson, Henri. *An Introduction to Metaphysics.* Putnam, New York and London, 1912. (Originally published in "Revue de Métaphysique et de Morale," January, 1903.)

5 Italics in the original.

trary, is the operation which reduces the object to elements already known, that is to elements common both to it and other objects." Bergson affirms that what he calls analysis produces a ceaseless variety. It has to proceed by symbol formation and by "a representation taken from successive points of view," and it multiplies its number of points ceaselessly, "so that it may perfect the always imperfect translation. It goes on, therefore to infinity. But intuition, if intuition is possible, is a simple act."

Edmund Husserl, the father of the phenomenological school, was preoccupied with the same distinction in most of his work, although he did not use the same terms. He regarded what he called *Wesensschau* as a form of insight fundamentally different from discursive reason. *Wesensschau* means an immediate beholding of essences as opposed to insights obtained by analysis. Husserl found that we have now come to a point at which even the naive thinker who lacks scientific training is no longer capable of thinking of his experience as other than part of an "objectivity," that is, "a totality which wears geometrical, mathematical relationships like some sort of a dress." "If we want to go back to experience in its deep layer and origin, then we must come to an experience of life and the world which does not yet know such idealization, but (on the contrary) represents its very fundament."[6] Husserl elevated intuitive knowledge, in its own domain, to the same validity as analytical knowledge, but never meant to imply by this distinction a hierarchy, as one above the other. "This is not meant as a devaluation of exact knowl-

---

[6] Husserl, Edmund, *Erfahrung and Urteil. Untersuchungen zur Genealogie der Logik.* Academia, Verlagsbuchhandlung. Prag, 1939.

edge or of the apodictic evidence of logic. All it means is a lighting of the paths by which we may reach higher levels of evidence, and of the hidden conditions on which they rest, and which define and outline their meaning."

In 1913 Karl Jaspers, while still a psychiatrist, published a remarkable paper on "causal" versus "understandable" connections in the history of psychiatric patients.[7] He applied the duality of the modes of knowing to the field of abnormal psychology. "Understandable connections are something essentially different from *causal* connections. For example, we understand an action out of motivations, we explain a movement causally from the stimulation of nerves. We *understand* how moods arise out of affects, how out of moods certain hopes, phantasies and fears arise; we *explain* the development and disappearance of memory dispositions, of fatigue and of recovery etc. The understanding of the psychic *by* the psychic is also called *psychological explanation,* and those scientists who are occupied with observation and causal explanation, manifest an understandable and justified aversion to *psychological explanation* whenever it is supposed to *replace* their method. Understandable connections within the psychic have also been called *causality from within;* this indicates an unbridgeable abyss between this kind of causality on the one hand and causal connections on the other—i.e. the *causality from without.*" Incidentally, a lot of needless and confused controversy in psychiatry could have been avoided if Jaspers' statement had been understood and heeded. What he meant was the following.

---

[7] Jaspers, Karl. "Kausale and verständliche Zusammenhänge zwischen Schicksal and Psychose bei der Dementia Praecox (Schizophrenie)." Z.f.d. ges. Neurol. und Psychiat. *14,* 158–263, 1913.

Imagine a psychiatric institution in which two men are, independently of one another, engaged in research on psychoses following childbirth. One, a psychoanalyst, investigates the early history of the afflicted mothers and the kind of relationship they had with their own mothers. The other is engaged in observation on the pituitary hormone, the adrenal hormones, the alkalinity of the blood, etc. before and after delivery in the psychotic mothers, compared to women normal after childbirth. Each of the two investigators wants to go to the bottom of the thing. Each asks *why,* and comes up with a *because.* However, their *whys* and *becauses* belong to two different chains of connection. To speak in philosophical terms they belong to two different roots of the axiom of the efficient cause. When the psychoanalytical observer finds that the patient suffers from a psychosis following childbirth because she herself had been not desired by her mother, he *com-prehends* ("takes into") in the sense of "intellectual sym-pathy" (feel with).[8] In finding out that the patient was deficient in a certain ion in the blood, the other observer *ex-plains* ("lays outside," the movement opposite to comprehend), and no act of intellectual sympathy is involved. We see from the examples of Bergson, Husserl and Jaspers that the dualism of knowing has metaphysical as well as psychological implications. Even the terms these authors used were similar. Jaspers' "causality from without" and "causality from within" correspond to Bergson's "moving

[8] The fact that psychoanalysis uses the imagery and language of *mechanisms* should not mislead us. Jaspers was the first one to point out that although Freud borrowed his terminology from the natural sciences (chemistry and physics) the true method of his discoveries was that of the *empathic* genius.

around the object" and the "entering into" it. Later on, in the same study, Jaspers speaks of *"external"* and *"internal meaning."*

Jaspers, like Husserl, was careful not to make one method appear superior to the other. In fact, human knowledge seems to have the greatest chance to arrive at truth when the two methods are at a perfect balance. Bertrand Russell put it very aptly, in spite of a somewhat unfortunate use of terms:[9] "Metaphysics, or the attempt to conceive the world as a whole by the means of thought, has been developed, from the first, by the union and conflict of two different human impulses, the one urging men towards mysticism, the other urging them towards science. Some men have achieved greatness through one of these impulses alone, others through the other alone: in Hume for example, the scientific impulse reigns quite unchecked, while in Blake a strong hostility to science coexists with profound mystic insight. But the greatest men who have been philosophers have felt the need both of science and of mysticism: the attempt to harmonize the two was what made their life, and what always must, for all its arduous uncertainty, make philosophy, to some minds, a greater thing than either science or religion." Except for the strange use of the term "mysticism" and the banal confrontation of "science" and "religion," this statement conveys the *balance* we need between the two "impulses."[10] The word "mysticism" is here used loosely, and unhappily, to summarize all non-analytical modes of knowledge.

---

9 Russell, Bertrand, *Mysticism and Logic*. George Allen and Unwin. London, 1951.

10 Incidentally, Bertrand Russell undoes this effect later in the same essay by leading up to the primacy of the scientific-analytical method and by debunking the Bergsonian notion of intuition.

In fact, there is a looseness and fluidity of terms throughout the vast literature on the subject. One might, of course, contend that the variety of terms and the fact that the concepts are not accurately identical but roughly overlap, is against the validity of the entire distinction. I would argue precisely the contrary. If there exists a non-analytical mode of knowing it would be, by its very nature, more difficult to define than the analytical one. If it has relevance in metaphysics, in the understanding of men, in the realm of moral and aesthetic truths—it might well be varied depending on the theme. If you use telescopic lenses to watch the opera, a battlefield, or the moon, you need a different kind each time, but the optic principle is the same. To distinguish, say, between the Bergsonian intuition of duration and Jaspers' empathic knowledge would make an interesting study. To do this would lead us too far away from our subject. All we need to keep in mind is that these methods have a common core which distinguishes them from the analytical-scientific one.

Dilthey, for example, who was one of those who anticipated the controversy, spoke of poetic insight very much in the way in which Bergson spoke of intuition: "Ever since the ascent of the mechanical sciences it has been the function of poetry to uphold the great experience of life in nature, that mysterious experience which is forever closed to all analysis. Poetry protects, as it were, all that which can be experienced but not explained so that it will not vanish under the dissecting operations of an abstract science."[11] I. A. Richards as well as Carnap, inde-

---

11 Dilthey, Wilhelm. *Einleitung in die Geisteswissenschaften. Versuch einer Grundlegung fur das Studium der Gesellschaft und der Geschichte.* I. Duncker und Humblot, Leipzig, 1883.

pendently of each other, also contrast poetic statements with scientific ones. Scheler[12] devoted an entire study to the problem of empathic knowledge. Maritain in his *Science and Wisdom*[13] outlines two realms of knowledge and their respective validity. We quote these sources not for the sake of completeness. After a careful study of all the evidence adduced it appears highly probable that the notion of "analysis" versus "intuition" is not a popular cliché but based on a reality.

Since there exist two modes of knowledge, the best attitude is, as we have just seen, to refrain from a judgment of value, and to watch out when to use which. For most of the trouble comes when people do not keep their methodological powder dry (e.g., when poetic knowledge was applied to scientific problems, before the rise of modern science—or scientific knowledge is applied to domains reserved for wisdom, as people are inclined to do in the social sciences today). Indeed some thinkers are capable of maintaining such an unprejudiced stand. The best example is Jaspers, in the study quoted on scientific versus empathic investigation in psychology. However not all philosophers, after having stated an objective polarity, are capable of acting like well-trained referees. They feel they have to take sides, even where there is no side to be taken. Some thinkers, for example Maritain and before him Dilthey, go about the problem with caution, and try to find out just where and in what way these modes of knowing are relevant. Dilthey, in an attempt to sum up the fallacies,

[12] Scheler, Max. *Wesen und Formen der Sympathie*. Schulte-Bulmke, Frankfurt a-M., 1948.

[13] Maritain, Jacques. *Science and Wisdom*. Geoffrey Bles, London, 1940.

states: "It was the fundamental error of the abstract School to neglect the relationship of abstracted partial content and living whole, and finally to treat abstracted partial contents as if they were realities. The scholars of history made the opposite, no less fatal, error to escape from the world of abstractions into the deep feeling of a living, irrationally powerful world with complete disregard of the axiom of the efficient cause."[14] In the same spirit of discernment, Dilthey is remarkably critical of the German school of the philosophy of nature: "All those popular presentations of nature which sentimentally project some makebelief of inwardness into the hard and clear concepts of scientific reason, play a foolish double-game; German Philosophy of Nature produced nothing but confusion in the realm of science—all it did was to lower the spiritual principle by some strange kind of contemplation of nature; only Poetry maintains its immortal task." Others *appear* biased on occasion. Husserl, in discussing psychology, seems to deny to the experimental-analytic method all relevance: "Even now we have enough reason to state that the psychic, seen in its own essence, has no nature, it cannot be conceived by itself in its natural meaning, it has nothing of space-time causality; it has nothing which could be treated ideally mathematically; it has no laws in the sense of the natural sciences; no theories are here possible with reference to an apprehensible world; no observations or experiments leading to a development of theory as in the natural Sciences—*notwithstanding all the self-deceptions of empirical-experimental psychology.*"[15] Such bias

[14] loc. cit.

[15] Husserl. loc. cit. Italics are mine.

can be explained either by the fact that the author happened to be acquainted only with the more sterile aspects of experimental psychology, or because he was carried away by certain motives to which we shall presently come back.

Others again, even more remarkably, seem to change their standpoint radically within a lifetime. "Professor I. A. Richards who at one time accepted the extreme opposition between scientific and poetic statements, classing poetic and ethical statements with the emotive, and the emotive with the non-meaningful, in his most recent work attributes both meaning and value to poetry. He even seems to be on the brink of awarding higher status to poetry than to science: 'Let us not suppose too lightly,' he says, 'that the business of distinguishing and relating poetry to science belongs to science.' "[16] As to the root of the present-day conflict about the relevance of the "poetic statement," I should like to offer a tentative hypothesis. The earliest and most indisputable concept of intuitive knowledge is the concept of *knowledge by connaturality*. Dionysius the Areopagite stated that, besides knowledge of external objects, we have a knowledge of things human—of virtues, vices and so on—because we are co-natured with other men. In other words, the fact that we share our human nature with other human beings, gives us a form of *knowledge from within*. Indeed, all non-scientific psychology—the psychology which the poet presents of an Oedipus, a Macbeth, or an Othello—is based primarily on his ability to *intuit* other human beings by

[16] Nott, Kathleen. "The Misery of Philosophy." *Encounter*, Vol. *VII*, No. 4, Oct. 1956. p. 45.

virtue of his connaturality, and only secondarily on a collection of the elements of external experience.

The difficulty comes with the application of poetic knowledge to things not human. Are we also co-natured with them, and in what way? When we behold the picture of a rabbit by Albrecht Dürer and compare the experience we draw from it with the experience we have in studying a scientific treatise on the rabbit (anatomy, physiology, embryology, biochemistry and so on) the distinction is literally the same as the one made by Bergson. Dürer presents, by "intellectual sympathy," all that is "unique" and consequently "inexpressible" in the rabbit. The scientist reduces the rabbit "to elements already known, that is to elements common both to it and other objects." The science of the rabbit proceeds "by a representation from successive points of view" and "goes on, therefore, to infinity." Dürer's presentation of the rabbit is a "simple act." Where then does connaturality come in? The artist's comprehension of the rabbit, unbroken by deduction, is close to the child's comprehension. And—even at the risk of begging the question—this form of comprehension implies a sense of creatureliness. Illusory or not, this sense of creatureliness is the connaturality which is at the basis of poetic grasp of all that is outside the human. With this we anticipate some of the things which we shall touch upon in subsequent chapters. Here we limit ourselves to a simple observation: while positivist philosophers may grudgingly admit the revelance of poetic statements concerning man (based on the validity of empathy), they will reject all poetic statements about the non-human. Yet there are indications that the artist has a form of *knowledge,* bound up with love, which is derived from the fact that we are co-natured with everything that *is*.

We mentioned in the beginning of this chapter that the distinction between the two forms of knowledge is nothing new. Saint Thomas Aquinas took the idea of knowledge by connaturality from Dionysius. Moreover, Saint Thomas' dichotomy of *ratio* and *intellectus,* Aristotelian in origin, anticipates the Bergsonian division which we put at the beginning of this chapter. It seems a mark of true genius that Francis Bacon, who is today generally credited with the introduction of experimental criteria in Science, separated "Poesy" from Science as another approach to truth, with other areas of relevance—and that he, too, did so without any judgment of value. Descartes declared poetic knowledge to be highly relevant. As we shall see, he made this declaration under strange, personal circumstances—almost solemnly, like an act of abjuration.

Many contemporary rationalist philosophies (of the positivist, empiricist, naturalistic variety) imply that non-scientific thinking is archaic, and is being outstripped by evolution which will lead to an ultimate triumph of discursive thought. Indeed, we are inclined to bracket different phenomena such as "poetic insight," "intuition" etc., because these forms of thinking have one thing in common: they are supposed to be close to the world of the child and the primitive while scientific thinking belongs to the world of the adult and of advanced civilization. According to Piaget[17] the child reaches fully the *cogito* of rational thinking only at the age of twelve. And one of the

---

17 Piaget, J. *La Représentation du Monde chez l'Enfant.* Alcan, Paris. 1926.

reasons why we associate all praeter-rational thinking with womanhood is that the knowledge by connaturality originates in the child-mother relationship. All *knowledge by union;* all knowledge by incorporation (incorporating or being incorporated); and all knowledge through love has its natural fundament in our primary bond with the mother. The skeptic warns the believer not to "swallow" things and not "to be taken in." And from his point of view, he is right. Faith, the most sublime form of non-scientific knowledge, is (if we consider its natural history, independent of all questions of grace) a form of swallowing or of being taken in. It goes back to an infantile, oral form of union. This is also true about Wisdom. *Sapientia* is derived from *sapere,* to taste, and *Sophia* is the she-soul of Eastern Christendom. However, does the fact that the rationalist *cogito* appear ontogenetically and phylogenetically late in the game mean that earlier forms of knowledge are mere rudiments cluttering up the basement of the human mind? "The unsophisticated thinking of our earliest years remains an indispensable acquisition underlying that of maturity, if there is to be for the adult one single intersubjective world," says Merleau-Ponty.[18] "My awareness of constructing an objective truth would never provide me with anything more than an objective truth for me, and my greatest attempt at impartiality would never enable me to prevail over my subjectivity (as Descartes expresses it by the hypothesis of the malignant demon), if I had not, underlying my judgments, the primordial certainty of being in contact with being itself, if before any

18 Merleau-Ponty, M., *Phenomenology of Perception.* Routledge, Kegan Paul, London 1962.

voluntary *adoption of positivism* I were not already *situated* in an intersubjective world, and if science, too, were not upheld by this basis. With the *cogito* begins that struggle between consciousnesses, each one of which, as Hegel says, seeks the death of the other. For the struggle ever to begin, and for each consciousness to be capable of suspecting the alien presences which it negates, all must necessarily have some common ground and be mindful of their peaceful coexistence in the world of childhood." Thus we see that the phenomenologist, without any bias, states that a later level of thinking is not *higher* than an earlier one, but that the two must be harmoniously combined to form an undistorted view of reality. Indeed, we may assume that praeter-logical thinking puts in two appearances, as it were, during early childhood in the form of the "primary process" (imagery and affect unstructured), and later wedded to the structure of discursive reason, as an alloy. In the latter form it appears most clearly in the mind of the artist, the poet and the mystic. Imagery and affect, untempered by reason, and rationality unfettered by the heart, are both, each in its own particular way, manifestations of trouble.

What then has made the entire problem acute in our time? Why have many minds become so intensely preoccupied with a distinction which is as old as the history of philosophy? The answer is obvious. With the development of the scientific method, with the industrial revolution and the triumph of technology, human values become threatened. In the beginning only a few individuals here and there were bothered: Goethe and Blake at the end of the eighteenth century who dreaded, under the impact of scientific rationalism, the rape of Wisdom; or Ruskin who, at the end of the nineteenth, nursed a sense of aesthetic nostalgia like a cold. These are scattered exponents of something which has by now become universal, a conflict in which every one of us in involved. For if the scientific-technological approach succeeded in objectifying man and society, man would cease to be man and become something for which no word has yet been coined. Man as a pure object, *reified* Man, ceases to *be.*

C. S. Lewis picked up a seemingly innocuous statement of linguistic positivism—some author had "demonstrated" that the sentence "the waterfall is sublime" is nonsense—and showed in a remarkable *tour de force* that the devaluation of poetic truth leads to a society in which a small minority of men will run mankind as if it were a compound of so many objects. The essay is characteristically entitled "The Abolition of Man."[19] If the entire world were objectified—and science, which until now handled only things, would also handle man and society—everything would become object, *Gegen-stand,* that which stands opposed to me or that to which I stand opposed. Love would cease to be. Kierkegaard, whose insights were not unlike those of Goethe and of Blake, only perhaps with a greater sense of fearful apprehension, said: "In the end all corruption will come about as a consequence of the natural sciences . . ." But lest anyone thinks that Kierkegaard had an axe to grind against science as such, this is what he really meant: "The scientific method becomes especially dangerous and pernicious when it encroaches on the realm of the spirit. Let science deal with plants, and

19 C. S. Lewis, *The Abolition of Man.* Macmillan, New York, 1947.

animals and stars; but to deal in that way with the human spirit is blasphemy."[20] In an entirely objectified world we would end up (to borrow terms which Gabriel Marcel used in another context) by *having* everything, and *being* nothing. For Science enables us to *have* more, while poetic knowledge enables us to *be* more. In the end that "dress" of scientific relationships of which Husserl spoke becomes a straight-jacket. The universal appeal of Kafka and Huxley and Orwell is precisely this: while you and I stand in awe of unheard-of machinery, we are suddenly seized by the eerie feeling that we might be part of the machinery ourselves, part of something, some *thing* that can be run.

Thus we see why the duality with which we dealt in this chapter has occupied the minds of so many modern thinkers. Behind a philosophical question of apparently academic interest lies a profound sense of dread.

---

[20] S. Kierkegaard, *Concluding Unscientific Postscript,* translated by David F. Swenson, introduction and notes by Walter Lowrie, Princeton University Press, 1944.

FOUR

Psychoanalysis and Metaphysics

In the following chapters we shall frequently be talking about a man's creative thought in the context of his personal history. We shall be skipping back and forth between things transcendental and things historical. Whether we are dealing with Goethe's view of the world in connection with his love affairs; or with Descartes' philosophy in connection with the story of his childhood—we must first ask ourselves: what is the nature of this connection?

When one walks through the bedroom of a great man of the past to peek into hidden closets or enters his study to look at manuscripts, one does so in a spirit of reverent affection. Thousands of people have walked through historical places and hundreds of biographies have been written with this attitude. We want to be there when Rembrandt paints Saskia, or Brahms writes the Alto Rhapsody.

Biography, in this sense, is a labour of love. In the case of negative subjects—the lives of dictators or swindlers or gangsters—it is a matter of fascination. Both love and fascination feed our curiosity, and the matter of psychology comes in only secondarily.

Not so in the case of psychoanalysis. There exists a link of motives between a man's life and his work, and this link can be traced. This principle is an extension of the psychoanalytical method into the field of history. Thus the biographical gains a new dimension: the creative act itself is open to *Deutung* (interpretation).

The idea that spirit and nature should not be two airtight compartments, independent from one another, is very old. It is implied in Greek and in Hebrew-Christian thought. However, with the advent of psychoanalysis, something has been added. The most striking and dramatic aspect of the psychoanalytical method is that metaphysics seem to be *reduced* to psychological mechanisms. This approach is not entirely new with Freud, and has its roots in nineteenth century German philosophy. Thinkers as disparate as Schopenhauer and Feuerbach, Nietzsche and Marx, began to scrutinize things of the spiritual order as to their natural origins.[1] Once the natural determinant,

[1] There is the remarkable case of Swift, who anticipated all this much earlier: "Such Order from confusion sprung, / Such gaudy Tulips rais'd from Dung." Swift was in horror that "everything spiritual is really material; Hobbes and the Scientists have proved this; all religion is really a perversion of sexuality." His attitude was ambivalent: he was obsessed with this kind of thought due to his mental state; yet as a believing Christian he was able to satirize it. Cf. Norman O. Brown, "The Excremental Vision," in *Swift,* a collection of critical essays, Prentice-Hall, 1964. Also William Empson, *Some Versions of the Pastoral,* Chatto & Windus, London, 1935.

usually psychological, was ferreted out, the spiritual was shown to be spurious. Or this, at least, was implied.

To take a well-known example, according to Nietzsche, Christianity is based on the *ressentiment* of the weak against the strong, an envy of have-nots towards haves. Nietzsche maintained that during the time of the Roman Empire, the scum of society, the poor, the sick and the weak eagerly seized on the Gospel because it elevated sickness and weakness into virtues. The weak gained a subtle victory over the strong, that ruling class of *Herren* (masters) of the Roman Empire. In other words, Christians debunked human strength and earthly achievement out of envy. Here a phenomenon of the supernatural order, namely faith, is reduced to its psychological substratum by exposing hidden motivation and self-deception. This trend in philosophy is called *psychologism,* because the psychological is allotted a position of absolute primacy. Nietzsche's verdict on Christianity was harsh: it represented "the pessimism of the weak, the vanquished, the suffering, the oppressed." "Their (the Christians') mortal enemies are 1) power in character, spirit and taste; 2) the classical (concept of) happiness, noble lightness and scepticism, the hard pride, eccentric debauchery and cool self-restraint of the wise, Greek refinement in gesture, word and form. Their mortal enemy is the Roman as well as the Greek."[2] Nietzsche's argument has one weak point: it would not be difficult to beat him at his game. By using this method one could, from a study of his life, discover the psychological mechanism which made *him* evolve *his* philosophy. As a

---

2 Nietzsche, Friedrich. *Der Wille zur Macht.* Alfred Kroner, Leipzig, 1923.

matter of fact, in his case no great scrutiny is required. Those weaklings who elevate oppression into a virtue, and those hard and noble pagan *Herren* are figures of the philosopher's inner world, and largely fictitious. Nevertheless we must admit that in individual cases suffering and submission may be employed as perverted means to power: here Nietzsche's psychological intuition anticipated psychoanalytical observation. But such an observation tells us nothing about the truth or untruth of the Christian doctrine. And this is the general fallacy of all reductive methods. If I find out that a man denies the existence of God because he lost his father early in childhood, I contribute an interesting observation on the psychology of the atheism of that man, but the statement "There is no God" might still be true. If all atheists were found to have lost their fathers in early childhood, we would not be one bit closer to the truth or falsity of an atheist philosophy. If all God-seekers were found to have lost their fathers early in childhood—God might still exist.[3] Karl Marx's celebrated statement about religion as the opium of the masses is quite similar. Here, too, something which until then had had its autonomous core, namely faith, is explained away on the basis of hidden motives. And just as in Nietzsche's case, there is an element of truth in the observation: frequently in history religion has been abused by individuals as a means of exploitation.

The arguments against such *psychologism* are very simple. Firstly, the investigator is, before he even starts, limited by a premise: metaphysical truths are no truths,

---

3 Freud himself put it very neatly when he remarked (without realizing what the statement meant when applied to his own writings on religion): "The polemical use of analysis obviously leads to no conclusion." (Freud, S. *Female Sexuality*. Internat. Jnl. of Psychoanalysis *13*, 1932.)

and if I show their purely *conditional,* i.e. psychological or historical roots, I add proof to my statement. The fallacy is more obvious when we look at a field outside metaphysics. It is conceivable that Newton, in demolishing ancient physics, was under the influence of an unresolved father complex but nobody in his right mind would ever use this as an argument against Newtonian physics.

Secondly, just as it is easy for me to show why Nietzsche reduced Christianity to *ressentiment,* it would be equally easy to show why *I* reject his theory. But of the one who dissects *my* motives thus, it can be shown, from his own personal history, why he does so. And so on, *ad infinitum.* Indeed it has been pointed out that for the outcome of this game it all depends who is quicker on the psychological draw. In other words, with this attitude carried to its logical conclusion, there exists an endless number of psychological truths (plural) but truth (singular) does not exist. This can be illustrated by the incongruity between the results of the reductive procedure on the Marxist side and on "ours." One should expect—and the claim is often made—that with science as the only criterion of truth there should be one global body of truths, acceptable to all men. Dialectic Materialism explains the story of the human spirit on the basis of economic factors, and the reductive method is in principle the same as the one frequently used in the social sciences and humanities hereabouts. Yet those popularized philosophies on either side of the Iron Curtain are opposed to one another except on certain points, and even on these points they meet with mental reservations. Only one thing is certain: the custom of reducing the ontological to the conditional, as it first began with German Philosophy in the nineteenth century on an esoteric level, has percolated down and contributed to that hollowness to which the masses on either side of the Iron Curtain are condemned.

Thirdly, there is that *fascination by the genetic*—a kind of mentality which belongs to the climate of a scientific age. It means that by accumulating causalities we arrive at essences. Nobody in his right mind would say that a lily *is* soil and air and water and that's all there is to it. To many people the psychoanalytic concept of sublimation has that limited meaning. It may be recalled that an unconscious conflict can be solved so that a crude instinctual drive is "lived" in a masked, refined form as it were, to meet with the approval of society. Thus, we may find that a great schoolmaster is, unconsciously, homosexual. He has channelled this drive into a socially acceptable activity, the education of youth. Sublimation, as a "mechanism of defence" (against the socially inacceptable) is a partial, inadequate "explanation" of the creative act. It is good strictly for clinical use. We marvel how out of the soil of instinctual energies the Sistine Chapel paintings or the Unfinished Symphony emerge—but we know for certain that they do not do so because society has prohibited the manifestation of crude drives. We marvel how lilies grow out of soil, mineral, water and air but we know that the lily *is* not a chemical mechanism. Entelechy is not something which stands at the right side of an equation. Yet the two ends, soil and flower, are linked by mysterious causality. Sharpe[4] has demonstrated in a remarkable psy-

[4] Ella Freeman Sharpe, *Francis Thompson: A Psychoanalytic Study*. (British Journal of Medical Psychology *5*, part 4. Author's abstract in Int. J. of Psychoanalysis *8*, 81, 1927.)

choanalytical study of Francis Thompson how Thompson the religious seer and Thompson the opium addict present two poles of human existence. The shorthand of clinical terminology can do little to disguise this observation: "Sublimation of his unconscious conflicts resulted in the greatest verse of the Nineteenth Century. Failure of sublimation resulted in the ineffectual, irresponsible Thompson who became an outcast and an opium drinker." No theologian could formulate more clearly the polarity between the childlikeness of faith and the infantile dependency of neurosis than a clinician does here empirically. The two ends of the "equation" are linked by the irreducible phenomenon of entelechy, or by the mystery of grace. But not to the philospher of psychologism. He must worry metaphysics and theology, as a dog worries a bone. He cannot leave things alone. However, with all this we are anticipating one aspect of the present study; therefore let us here merely summarize: with the victories of the experimental sciences in full view, the philosophers went to their laboratory benches and proceeded to boil things down. And we know today, in the drab laboratory of naturalism, what things boil down to: all that remains is a little psychological or economic or sociological residuum at the bottom of the flask.

Such a summary would be unjust if we did not look at the positive side of the matter. Life in Europe in the nineteenth century had many aspects of complacency and hyprocrisy. And those who looked into the motives "behind" faiths and philosophies were often moved by a need for purity and truthfulness. They were great purgers, and their ruthlessness was the ruthlessness of the prophets.

They shook us up, and due to them, self-deception has become much more difficult than before. Nietzsche was right: one must not exploit one's suffering to exert power over others. Marx was right: woe unto those who use religion as opium for the people. Freud was right: faith devoid of the primacy of love is a compulsive-obsessive neurosis. In other words: Nietzsche or Marx or Freud were heirs of an aristocratic humanism to whom the reductive method was a means of exhortation and an expression of ascetic courage. However, in the eighty years since Nietzsche, the reductive approach has developed into an epidemic. The social and psychological disciplines have become so adept at this game that in the minds of many people they are about to replace philosophy. All this is facilitated by a general "loss of metaphysical sense." Whereas thinkers like Nietzsche and Marx and Freud were still working in the tradition of such artistocratic humanism, the procedure has in our time become incredibly vulgarized. The psychology of philosophies and faiths is being studied today as if it were a question of market research. I suspect that in some cases it is just that. All you have to do is to open any journal of sociology or anthropology or psycholoanalysis, and you will find at least one reference in every issue concerning "the mechanisms behind" a cultural phenomenon. The very procedure has something inflationary. There is no end to insights. You can get rich quick. And the entire thing creates an alarming sense of *hubris*. To the one who looks through the psychoanalytic or sociological field glass at the pilgrims to Chartres or Mecca, to find out what makes them go, the pilgrims become amoebas. With such "motivational" know-how, reality is destroyed. One perceptive psychoanalyst made a similar observation: "And we were dismayed when we saw our purpose of enlightenment preverted into a widespread fatalism, according to which man is nothing but a multiplication of his parents' faults and an accumulation of his own earlier selves. We must grudgingly admit that even as we were trying to devise, with scientific determinism, a therapy for the few, we were led to promote an ethical disease among the many."[5]

Now the psychoanalytic interpretation of religious concepts is not merely based on the search for unconscious motivations. In order to illustrate this let us take another example. Freud explains the origin of the idea of God in the following way. To the child the first image of the father is one of omnipotence and omniscience. As the child matures he is compelled to correct this image: the father is neither omnipotent nor omniscient. However, such phantasies are not easily given up. Thus the lost father-image is beamed towards the sky, as it were, and the omnipotent and omniscient father is preserved in the person of God.

Here, besides the genetic explanation, something has been introduced which was not apparent in the preceding examples. Between the "real" something (father) and the "phantasy" something (God) exists a nexus which one might call the analogical link. The entire theory just outlined is only justified because the two images—father and God—have common features. The entire psychoanalytic method of *Deutung* (interpretation) is based on such kinship. Moreover, while the genetic part of the argument is

---

[5] Erik H. Erikson, *Young Man Luther. A Study in Psychoanalysis and History.* W. W. Norton & Co., N.Y. 1958.

shaky (even if the psychological observation is true it does not, of course, disprove the existence of God) the kinship is an unshakable fact. We call God "father," and He has paternal qualities.

This particular aspect of the argument—the analogical link between things immediate and things transcendental—is essential to the Hellenic and the Jewish-Christian tradition. We can follow it through centuries. Saint Paul claims that all fatherhood on earth is *named* after God. Goethe says that "all that is passing is merely a parable" (of the eternal). Charles Williams talks boldly of "the identity of the image with that beyond the image."[6] The examples could be infinitely multiplied. Williams makes his remark about Beatrice, but he obviously implied (as did Goethe) that this kind of sense of metaphysical reality is at the basis of all poetic knowledge. In this particular context the difference between the Platonic and Aristotelian tradition is irrelevant. Whatever the absolute valency of the image may be, in either case it possesses further dimensions.

Freud, as is well known, was in his youth decisively influenced by Goethe's philosophy of Nature, and if one took the trouble one would probably be able to find a link between the world of Goethe and Carus on one hand, and Freud's discoveries on the other—not necessarily a concrete tie but one of "climate." Only that Freud, as a clinician who *had* to reduce symptoms to their biological substratum, and worked under the influence of the natural sciences, knew only one nexus between image and "beyond"—the genetic mechanism. But if we disregard that

[6] Charles Williams, *The Figure of Beatrice. A Study in Dante.* Farrar, Straus, New York, 1961.

part of it, then the entire procedure of *Deutung* is one aspect of a great current, a movement to re-establish a sense of metaphysical realism. Then Freud appears as a contemporary of Bergson and of Husserl rather than of those materialistic debunkers of the nineteenth century. For *Deutung*, exegesis as a method by which we point out links between different levels of occurrences, is nothing new. The fact that a story is relevant on different planes is the basis of all interpretation. All Scriptural exegesis is based on this method. Even the concept of over-determination (relevance on more than two planes) has always been known. Dante[7] picked a sentence from the Bible ("When Israel went out of Egypt, the house of Jacob from a strange people; Judah was his sanctuary, and Israel his dominion") and considered it on four different levels of meaning: "If we consider the literal sense alone, the thing signified is the going out of the children of Israel from Egypt in the time of Moses; if the allegorical, our redemption through Christ; if the moral, the conversion of the soul from the grief and misery of sin to a state of grace; if the analogical, the passage of the sanctified soul from the bondage of the corruption of this world to the liberty of everlasting glory." Innumerable examples could be added to this one, from the Midrash as well as from the Fathers of the Church. This kinship by analogy, this parallel of significances has been re-introduced into the method of *Deutung* by Freud, in his concept of over-determination. A dream can be interpreted not only in one way but in a

[7] Letter to Can Grande della Scala. Quoted by Williams, loc. cit. Some Dante scholars question the authenticity of this letter, but the passage quoted here is characteristic of Dante's spirit and of an entire tradition behind it.

number of ways, all of them being perfectly valid: the various interpretations refer to various layers of personal evolution.

When we study the Fathers of the Church and follow their way of reading multiple meanings into the stories of Scripture—how a seemingly naive story of a few protagonists is meant to prefigure the destiny of entire nations, we have at times the impression of something arbitrary. It looks like a game any number can play. And yet we are apt to forget that those men were deeply imbued with a sense of universal order and inter-relatedness which we have lost. We have lost it because for the purpose of scientific investigation phenomena had to be isolated. However, the nexus between the ontological and the psychological cannot be investigated without an assumption of the order and interrelatedness of spheres. In the light of this order of spheres the drama of man's life—say, in our context, Descartes' or Goethe's neurosis—is related to the world of ideas not only conditionally. The subject of "Neurosis and Genius" has a striking popular appeal. There are various reasons for this, but one of them is a dim awareness that our troubles (not only those of geniuses) are signposts towards the untroubled; the creative solution of the neurotic conflict is a proof that the psychological does not stand by itself but has its *beyond.* We have only to read the poems of Hölderlin or look at the paintings of van Gogh to realize that the meaning of the psychological discord is not exhausted by psychology. "Being is sensible only in becoming; in the latter, rather, it is itself posited as eternity. But in the actualization (of being) through opposition there is necessarily a becoming. Without the conception of a humanly suffering God—a conception common to all the mysteries and spiritual religions of the past—history remains wholly unintelligible."[8] Schelling's statement implies that human suffering too is a clue to the intelligibility of history. The stories of our insufficiencies point to a sufficiency. All the disorders in the microcosm of personal lives prove, paradoxically, that there must be a universal order.

To the ancients, actually to all philosophers from antiquity until the end of the Renaissance and the beginning of the time of which we are talking here, the relationship between things human and things beyond the human was part of an *intrinsic order* of the world. If one could conjure up the ghosts of Plato and Aristotle or of Shakespeare and Milton and propose to them that Nature and Reason at war are reflected in a disharmony between the sexes, they (the ghosts) would understand. They went much further, and I am not sure whether their view of relevance was not right. To them the principle of the world was an *order* in which Angels and stars, Nature and Society, and each human soul participated—and disorder in one sphere was reflected in the others. The Elizabethans[9] had a keen sense of this: a famous statement of it is Ulysses' speech on "degree" in *Troilus and Cressida.* Hamlet's first reflection, on hearing of his family's tragedy, is: "The time is out of joint." We could use the

[8] Schelling, K. F. A. *Über das Wesen der menschlichen Freiheit.* Schelling's Werke, edit. by A. Weiss, *3*, 499, 1907.

[9] Tylliard, E. M. W. *The Elizabethan World Picture. A Study of the idea of order in the age of Shakespeare, Donne and Milton.* Vintage Books, N.Y. 1961; and Theodor Spencer, *Shakespeare and the Nature of Man.* Macmillan, N.Y., 1945.

same metaphor when we see the ravenous women and passive men in the world of Strindberg or Tennessee Williams; or Faulkner's juxtaposition of the doctor as abortionist and the murderer as midwife. "The time is out of joint" is a naive metaphysical statement. All it means is that between the spiritual order and order in the human family, between things ontological and the microcosm of everyday life, there exists a correspondence.

Thus the lives of men are related to the order of ideas by a relevance which is more than psychological. All tragedy of the contingent and haphazard is a mysterious signpost towards the meaningful, the immutable and the harmonious. Hence we shall see in the following pages that the character and history of a man can be related to his ideas in two ways: *genetically,* as a merely accidental element, as a condition; and by way of an *inner relevance* by which spheres, the historical and the trans-historical, are related to one another. To consider the first kind of relationship as the only possible one is the basis of all *psychologism.* In the following pages we shall frequently give the impression that we have succumbed to the temptation of psychologism. Indeed, there is no getting away from the world of personal motives as a conditional cause. Schopenhauer would not have developed a certain set of ideas if his mother had been a different person. This is psychologically interesting but not more; we shall always be aware of its relative significance. The deeper relevance is by its very nature mysterious. And yet to point it out is necessary for the plenitude of insight. Jaspers emphasizes the necessity of knowing one's entire position, including one's personal psychological background, to give fullness, as it were, to one's philosophy. He speaks, in this context, of *Existenzerhellung* (the illumination of existence). Jaspers was particularly wary of the pitfalls of psychologism, and his statement does *not* imply a simple reduction of philosophical ideas to conscious or unconscious motives, as it had with Nietzsche. It rather implies an added dimension, a rounding-off of insight.[10] Jaspers also speaks, in another context, of metaphysics as a reading of "ciphers." Anything in inanimate and animate nature and in the life of man can be a "cipher" which stands for a vast reality. In this sense, phenomenology and even certain trends in existentialist philosophy are about to close a ring. We are rejoining, after many peregrinations and adventures of the human mind, the *philosophia perennis*. For what else has been the meaning of classical philosophy than the deciphering of given data? To be more specific, we are rediscovering a relationship between psychological phenomena and metaphysical realities.

---

[10] One phenomenologist, Merleau-Ponty, goes so far as to absolve Marx and Freud from the error of the reductive fallacy by pointing out the obvious, namely that a link between economics and history or between sex and creativeness does not mean a one-way reduction. However, *de facto*, the motive (to debunk) was there.

FIVE

Descartes

At the threshold of modern philosophy stands Descartes. There are those, for example Hegel and Schelling, who regard him as the father of modern philosophy. For just as the Church passed through a patristic period, the universal Non-Church had its time of the fathers. And among these Descartes is the prince; he is the Saint Augustine of the Age of Reason. The comparison is not specious; it is justified on various grounds. And here we encounter a paradox: Descartes' philosophy, with its crystalline lucidity, with that "pre-eminently aesthetic" sense of pleasure which, according to Thomas Mann, all great philosophical systems convey, hides a dark area of personal conflict.

Before we get to that let us first take a look at the Cartesian system. Decartes' philosophy comprises so many subjects that, for the purpose of our study, we confine ourselves in the beginning to one aspect, namely the so-called Cartesian *dualism*—a total split of the universe into two, as it were: a *res cogitans* (a thinking something which has no spatial extension) and a *res extensa* (a spatial something which has no psychic qualities). If one stops there and regards the split as the basic premise for all scientific investigation, it is quite legitimate and there is nothing wrong with it. On the contrary, it was only by this radical severance between observing subject and observable object that the exact sciences could be developed. The subject must first leave the stage of the world so that the world can be mathematically elucidated. In medieval and other civilizations, as long as man conceived of himself as imbedded in nature and intrinsically united with what he beheld, scientific objectivity was impossible. Without the Cartesian dichotomy that wonderful burst of human creativeness which we witness in modern technology could never have come about. In other words, as a *methodological basis* for the exact sciences, Cartesian dualism was a prerequisite.

Where it goes beyond that, however, it develops into a disastrous fallacy. For one thing, it implies a fearful estrangement. Just think of nature as nothing but a huge, vastly extended soul-less machine which you can take apart experimentally and analyze mathematically, which you can run—but with which you have lost all oneness!

Thus Cartesianism provides the first example of an error which is typical in the entire history of modern thought: namely that a methodological principle which works for a circumscribed problem is expanded into a philosophy with universal claims. What happened in the case of Descartes has happened many times since. If you asked me to state quickly what is wrong with "modern thinking," I would say that methods become mentalities. This happened, for example, in the case of Darwin or of Freud. The method, with its pristine clarity and compactness, is processed and diluted into something penetrating and pervasive which makes up a climate.

What is the Cartesian mentality (for which Descartes himself is only partly to blame)? First of all, it is the idea that there exists, about phenomena around us, only one criterion of truth—the scientific one. The devaluation of poetic knowledge, i.e. knowledge by interiorization, goes back to the Cartesian split. From here to the view of the modern positivist (Carnap) that the poetic statement has only emotive and no cognitive validity seems to be only one step. This, incidentally, illustrates a point we have made before—that all rationalist philosophies are linked. Symbolic logic could not have developed as it has without the rationalism of the seventeenth century.

People simplify matters when they say, as they often do, that the pre-Galilean era was unscientific. There have always been attempts—in ancient Babylon, Egypt, Greece—to know the world scientifically. But as a matter of preponderance we can say that, before the modern era, man's view of nature has been "poetic" (in the sense in which we have just been using the word) rather than scientific. As we have pointed out, the words for *mater* and *materia, mother* and *matter,* are entymologically related in more than one language. The sense of mystery which the poet and the contemplative have towards nature; the sense of imbeddedness, of a personal relationship of protectiveness or cruelty, of the familiar or the awe-ful—all this is not a matter of animism or of a vague sentiment which will eventually be repealed by scientific elucidation. Quite the contrary; if a kind of Cartesian ideal were ever completely fulfilled, i.e. if the whole of nature were only what can be explained in terms of mathematical relationships—then we would look at the world with that fearful sense of alienation, with that utter loss of reality with which a future schizophrenic child looks at his mother. A machine cannot give birth.

This is the point at which we come to Descartes, the man. For our remarks served not so much as an outline of Cartesian thought, but to bring us closer to a startling puzzle: Descartes conceived his system not, as one might expect, as a mere *calcul,* but with a sense of foreboding and ecstasy. We are bewildered to learn that a mathematical genius should conceive his philosophy with the sense of a haunting personal drama. Yet this is precisely what happened. There was one memorable night (November 10, 1619) which Descartes always regarded as the turning-point of his life.[1] He gives us many indications that his *méthode* was then in its incubation period. On the day preceding that night of dreams he was in a state resembling inebriation. The *scientia mirabilis* seemed within grasping distance. He must have been in that phase close to parturition which we know from the self-observations of great mathematicians, composers and painters. He was aware of the global character of his discovery. Indeed this *scientia mirabilis* seemed a matter of limitless relevance. All exponents of scientism today, all believers in the religion of progress, whether of the Marxist or the Western

---

1 Adam, Charles, *Descartes, sa vie et son oeuvre* (Paris: Boivin et Cie., 1937).

variety, should celebrate the 10th of November as their feast day. That night was, as Maritain[2] put it, the Pentecost of Reason. Yet, paradoxically enough, the illumination appeared in the guise of something dark. The door to the Castle of Reason was opened with a sense of the shadowy and oppressive. And the victory of abstraction was initiated by imagery. If a pre-Freudian scholar set out to demonstrate the haphazardness of dreams, if he tried to concoct a maximum of absurdity to prove his point, he could do no better than invent the dreams of that night. Yet the man who gave the scientific method its permanent basis regarded those dreams as replete with special significance. He woke up and, as though to banish dreads emanating from the strange illumination, he vowed a pilgrimage to Our Lady of Loretto.

At the time of that famous night, Descartes was twenty-three years old and found himself in Ulm, in Bavaria. He was taking part in the campaign of the Duke of Bavaria, apparently without quite knowing what it was all about. When he found out that they were marching against Frederic, the king-elect of Bohemia and champion of Protestantism, he quit. Descartes' entire situation was somehow typical of that chaotic century. He had left France on a trip which was supposed to take him to Denmark. All we know for certain is that at one point he landed in Frankfurt, for we have his eye-witness report of the crowning of the Emperor Ferdinand in that city in the late summer of 1619. And then we find him again in Ulm, in the winter quarters of the Bavarian army. What made the frail and sickly young scholar seek a non-commissioned

---

2 Maritain, J. *Le songe de Descartes.* Correa, Paris, 1932.

officership in an army in the field is hard to guess. The question is related, as we shall see, to the psychological riddle of Descartes. Be this as it may, we find him whiling the cold, damp months away, snuggling up "in a stove" as he put it. It was in this unlikely setting that he made some of his most important mathematical discoveries and that the outline of his philosophical system began to take shape. And it was here also that the three dreams occurred. Winter quarters in Ulm were anything but cheerful. It is the more remarkable that Descartes states explicitly that, on the day preceding the dreams, he was filled with enthusiasm about his discovery of a *scientia mirabilis.* He noted the dreams of that night in detail but the original is lost, and we have to rely on the description of Baillet,[3] his first biographer:

The moment Descartes had fallen asleep he believed he saw certain phantoms and was frightened by their appearance. He believed he was walking in the streets and was so terrified by the apparition that he bent over (*renverser*) to his left side to get to the place he was heading for, because on his right side he felt a great weakness and he could not stand upright. Embarrassed by having to walk like this, he made an effort to straighten himself out, when he felt a strong wind. The wind seized him like a tornado, so that he whirled three or four times on his left foot in a circle. But even this was not the thing that frightened him. To advance was so difficult that he expected to collapse at each step. At last he noticed on the road a *Collège* which was open, and he entered to find refuge in his trouble. He tried to reach the church of the *Collège* and his first thought was to say a prayer, when he suddenly noticed he had passed an

3 Baillet, Adrien. *Vie de Monsieur Descartes,* I, Paris 1691.

acquaintance without greeting him and wanted to turn back to show his politeness. However, he was prevented forcibly by the wind which blew in the direction of the Church. At that moment he saw in the middle of the courtyard of the *Collège* another man. This one addressed Descartes politely and amicably by name, and told him he had something to give him to take along in case he was going to see Mr. N. Descartes believed it to be a melon which someone had brought from an exotic country. He was most astonished to see that the people who had gathered around him with this man, to chat, were all able to stand upright and firmly on their feet while he was still bent over and staggering, although the wind which had threatened to knock him over had diminished considerably.

With this he woke up and at the same moment experienced a real pain, and he was afraid all this might be the work of evil spirits who wanted to tempt him. He immediately turned over to the right, for he had been asleep on his left side, and it was while lying on the left that he had had that dream. He prayed to God and asked Him to protect him from the evil effect of his dream and from all misfortune which might come over him as a result of his sins. He realized that his sins were serious enough to draw the lightning of heaven on his head, although until now, in the eyes of men, he had led a spotless life. And for two hours, after having had all sorts of thoughts about good and evil in this world, he fell asleep again.

He presently had a second dream. He believed he heard a violent, loud noise. He took this to be thunder (*coup de foudre*), was frightened, and immediately woke up.

As he opened his eyes he saw many fiery sparks in the room. This had happened to him at other times; it was nothing out of the ordinary for him to wake up suddenly at night and have sufficient vision to be able to see objects close to him. But now he wanted to come back to explanations which philosophy offered to him and as he opened and closed his eyes and observed things as they presented themselves to him, he drew conclusions favorable to his insight. Thus his fear vanished and, with a sense of peace, he fell back into sleep.

Soon he had his third dream, less terrifying than the first two. In this dream he found a book on his table without realizing who had put it there. He opened it and, when he saw it was a dictionary, was delighted, for he hoped it might be very useful to him. At the same moment he discovered another book under his hand; this too was unknown to him and he had no idea where it had come from. He noticed that it was a collection of the poems of different authors under the title *Corpus Poetarum* (divided into five books, printed in Lyon and Geneva, etc.). He was curious to read something from the book, and on opening it he came across the verse, *"Quod vitae sectabor iter?"* At the same moment he noticed a man whom he could not identify, who handed him a poem which began with the words *"Est et non,"* and who praised it as excellent. Descartes told him he knew the poem, that it was one of the "Idylls" of Ansonius, and that these "Idylls" formed part of the book that lay on the table. He wanted to show them to the man and began to leaf through the book the order of which he prided himself on knowing. While he was looking for the place in the book, the man asked him where he had got the book, and Descartes answered that he could not tell how he had obtained it but that one moment ago he had held another book in his hand which had immediately disappeared without his being able to tell who had brought it or who had taken it away. He had hardly finished talking when the book appeared again at the other end of the table. But he was able to observe that the dictionary was no longer as complete as he had seen it before. In the meanwhile he found the poems of Ansonius in the anthology through which he was leafing but he was unable to find the poem beginning with *"Est et Non"* and he told the man that he knew a poem still more beautiful, by the same poet, which began with *"Quod vitae sectabor iter?"* The man asked him to show him the poem and Descartes was about to look for it when he found in the book several small portraits in copper engraving. Whereupon he remarked that he found this book very beautiful but it was not the edition he knew. He was still occupied by all this when the books and the man disappeared without his waking up. It cannot but seem remarkable that, while he was still in doubt whether what he saw was dream or vision, he not only decided, while still asleep, that it was a dream but even began to interpret the dream before waking up. He thought that the dictionary meant the interconnectedness of all sciences and that the poetic anthology, *Corpus Poetarum,* very clearly signified the intimate connection of all philosophy with wisdom. For he believed that one should not be surprised to find in poets, and all those who seem to be given to foolish leisure, much more serious, reasonable and better expressed thoughts than in the writings of the philosophers. Divine enthusiasm and the power of imagination worked this miracle. They make the seed of wisdom (which is hidden in every man's spirit as the spark is in a pebble) grow more easily and abundantly than through the reasoning of philosophers. As Descartes continued to interpret his dream while still asleep, he came to the conclusion that the poem which was concerned with what kind of life to choose and which began with the words, *"Quod vitae sectabor iter?",* signified the good counsel of a wise person or moral theology itself. Still uncertain whether he was dreaming or meditating, he awoke without being at all upset. Awake, he continued the interpretation of the dream and his trend of thought.

The poets assembled in the anthology he interpreted as the revelation and enthusiasm which he had experienced. The

"Est et Non," which is the "Yes and No" of Pythagoras, he regarded as Truth and Error of human knowledge and the profane sciences. When he realized that the application of all this went so well, according to his desire, he dared to assume that the spirit of Truth itself had wanted to reveal the treasure of all knowledge to him through the dream. And since there were only those copper-engraved portraits left to explain, which he had discovered in the second book, he did not seek any further interpretation of them after an Italian painter had paid him a visit the following day.

Before we make any attempt to find a link between these dreams and the person of the dreamer, we must pause to give thought to Descartes' own interpretation. This occurred right after the dream about the dictionary and the book of poetry. Even before fully awake, Descartes pondered the meaning of the dream and he made his observations on the importance of poets who only "seem to be given to foolish leisure" but whose insights are more weighty than those found in the writings of the philosophers. To those used to the observations of psychoanalysis, these remarks seem to be an intellectual aside, a marginal note on the manifest content of the dream rather than free associations leading to a deeper understanding.

However, let us not judge too rashly: even in these remarks—though they seem to take us from shadow and image towards the reassuring light of the intellect—we are made to feel a remarkable anticipation. For today we know something which Descartes could not have known then except by a vague sense of premonition: namely that the *scientia mirabilis* implies a dreadful devaluation of *poetic knowledge,* taking the term in its broadest sense. As we have seen, this is the chief characteristic, not of Descartes' philosophy but of the Cartesian *climate*. The climate created by a philosophy, the smoketrail which follows it, makes its universal impact, that which contributes to the "outlook of the common man." As Jaspers[4] has justly put it, never has there been, in the entire recorded history of man, such depletion of Faith. Our point is that for this to happen there had first to occur a complete severing of the aesthetic from the scientific continuum. This entire process has affected everybody, on both sides of the Iron Curtain. It is a matter of belief even with the "man in the street." If philosophy were a matter of voting, one would obtain a landslide in favour of: "*Resolved that,* all truth will eventually be attained by scientific exploration." Strangely enough, the makers of the scientific image of the world did not quite see it this way. This is why Descartes' own immediate interpretation of his dream is so remarkable. When Francis Bacon, who is commonly considered an initiator of experimental criterion in the natural sciences, speaks of "poesy"; when Descartes speaks of "the poets" of his dream, these two thinkers do not merely refer to a verbal embroidery with which you can or cannot cover the practical furniture of this world. They were still aware, from the ancient tradition in which they had been raised, of poetry as a form of *knowledge*. Poetic knowledge was on the same level of veracity as the scientific, although not applicable to the same questions, and its way of demonstrating truths was different. With the progress of the industrial civilization, Beauty and Truth became increas-

[4] Jaspers, Karl. *Descartes und die Philosophie* (Berlin: de Gruyter, 1956).

ingly more compartmentalized, but it had all begun with the Cartesian split. In the end, the nineteenth century bourgeois listened to the poet's words ("Beauty is Truth and Truth Beauty") with that tolerance one displays when one is tired of the practical workaday world and doesn't mind being entertained by arbitrary statements. A severance had occurred. Today when people (the people we canvass in our philosophical opinion poll) say that something is "unscientific," they mean to say that it is not true.

What interests us here is the phenomenology of the modes of knowledge. And in a previous chapter we have already indicated two significant differences: firstly, poetic knowledge is acquired by union *with* and attachment *to* the object; scientific knowledge is acquired by distance and detachment *from* the object. The poetic relation to nature is one of imbeddedness, the scientific one is that of confrontation. Scientific knowledge is associated with disassembling and breaking-up. The poet knows the object by an act of fusion which cannot be reduced to anything more basic; the scientist knows the object by an act of piercing which can be broken into steps. In the present context one thing is remarkable: to Descartes himself the conception of his method seemed like an *incantation.* Its results, the primacy of the scientific over the aesthetic continuum, the faraway ideal of a "mathematization" of all knowledge with an eventual complete *Entseelung,* de-animation of the knowable[5]—all this would later come to

[5] Goethe describes the first impact of the Cartesian philosophy of nature. He was a young student in Strasbourg and got to know all this through a book, freshly imported from France, *"Système de la Nature,"* the author of which he does not mention. "It seemed to us so grey, monstrous and death-like that we could hardly stand it; we shuddered as though facing a ghost." (*Dichtung und Wahrheit,* Third Part, Eleventh Book.)

brood like a spell over the world. And those first dim thoughts of the half-awake dreamer in Ulm sound like exorcism and a plea of "not guilty."

The fact that Descartes related those three dreams in such detail and that he gave them so much significance has roused the curiosity of psychoanalysts.[6] Curiously enough Freud himself, when asked by Leroy to comment on Descartes' dreams, was hesitant. He felt that, without having the subject freely associate on the dream content, one could not say much. His first impression was that Descartes' dreams seemed to be close to overt problems of wakeful thinking.[7] This reluctance is the more remarkable since Freud did not hesitate to draw far-reaching conclusions from fragments of other great men's lives, e.g., a brief childhood reminiscence of Leonardo. Indeed Leonardo's life is less well documented than that of Descartes, though we must keep in mind that in the case of Leonardo there exists a rich documentation of his inner life in his works.

Freud's hesitancy seems justified when we see that the interpretations from various authors vary considerably. Hence their points of agreement seem the more significant. And they all agree—not only the three Freudian an-

---

[6] Schönberger, Stephen. "A Dream of Descartes: reflections on the unconscious determinants of the sciences." Internat. J. Psychoanal. *20*, 43, 1939.—Wisdom, J. O. "Three Dreams of Descartes." Internat. J. Psychoanal. 28, ii, 1947.—Lewin, Bertram D. "Dreams and the uses of regression." (New York: Internat. Universities Press, 1958).—The study with the most detailed biographical and historical documentation comes from a representative of the Jungian School: von Franz, Marie Louise. *Der Traum des Descartes.* In "Zeitlose Dokumente der Seele" (Zurich: Rascher, 1952).

[7] Freud, S. "Letter to Maxim Leroy on a Dream of Descartes." Gesammelte Schriften. Internationaler Psychoanalytischer Verlag. Wien, *12*, 403, 1934.

alysts among themselves but also the Jungian—that the chapel of the *Collège,* in which the dreamer seeks refuge in the first dream, stands for the mother. "Revelation, the authority of the Church, stood in his mind for a haven of refuge, the school in the dream, the mother in the infantile situation: reason, natural light, stood for independence of mind, pursuing philosophical truth for himself no matter where it led him, walking in the dream, reading Ansonius' poetry."[8] In fact the first dream conveys the image of a conflict between two sides. The symbolism of "Right and Left," so wide-spread in dreams and in psychotic symptoms, plays an important role in this dream. Right and Left have in many languages the dual meaning of the body image on one hand, and moral values on the other. Right also means "just, correct," and Left means "sinister." At the same time there are indications that the Right-Left symbolism refers also to the two sexes. Justice and correctness and the rational stand for the Father; the "sinister" left is the world of the unconscious and prerational—a world in which we are still at one with the mother. Therefore the interpretation of moral "right" and "wrong" (Lewin), and "male" and "female" (von Franz) is in this case only apparently contradictory. In my own experience, with schizophrenic patients in whom asymmetry of the body image is more frequent than one might think (particularly in the beginning of the psychosis, when these things are more easily verbalized) I have often had the impression that the symptom refers to bisexuality. When the patient remarks "my left side is bigger than my right,"

[8] Wisdom, J. O. loc. cit. von Franz (loc. cit.) agrees in principle with the interpretation of "school-church" as the maternal.

or "my left collar bone is lower than my right" etc., the symbolism seems to be the same as that of (illusory) asymmetries in the Rorschach Test. The latter have been shown to mean a breaking up, as it were, into a male and female half.

For the purpose of the present study it is not necessary to go further into the matter of those dreams. When we look at Descartes' origin, his genius and his work, we expect one of those neat and tidy biographies—a little colourless and uneventful perhaps. There is no reason why the man who conceived of all life as a precision watch should not have lived and died like Professor Kant who never in all his life left his native town, and by whose daily walk the people of Königsberg used to set their clocks. It is the more startling to realize how torn and jagged Descartes' life curve was. There is about the discoverer of the *méthode* an air of the unsteady and the adventurous. Certainly the stage appeared set for a conservative professorial life. He came from an old, rooted family of the provinces, a family of the lesser aristocracy. Among his ancestors were several prominent physicians. His father was a high-ranking civil servant, his mother, Jeanne Brochard, was the daughter of a high law officer. At the age of eight René entered the Jesuit College at La Flèche. He was one of the favorite pupils of Father Dinet who later became confessor of Louis XIV. When Henri IV was assassinated, Descartes was one of the boys at the school especially chosen to take part in the ceremony of the King's heart on the occasion of its burial. He could have ended his days at the University of Poitiers where he began.

There exists a similar contrast between the provincial

tradition-bound background on the one hand and a life without moorings on the other, in Nietzsche. However in Nietzsche the philosopher we would expect that air of flight and uprootedness—there is a parallel between his thought and his destiny. In Descartes—whose name is to us the very symbol of the ordered and the measured, of the *mathesis universalis*—that shadowy and fleeting quality, that life "without a lasting place" evokes a sense of paradox. Not that he despised the shelter of a conservative tradition. On the contrary, there are aspects of his everyday existence, particularly during his stay in Holland, when it is quite obvious how much he needed the accessories of a genteel life to make him happy. And yet there goes with it the unmistakable stigma of Ahasverus. In 1618 at the age of twenty-two he left France, ostensibly to go to Denmark, but we find him in the army of the Duke of Bavaria. How he came to land there remains obscure to this day. Italy he found too hot for his taste, Sweden too cold. Even in Holland, during the phase of his life which appears most settled, he changed his abode twenty-three times, for reasons no biographer can explain. Indeed Jaspers who, in his study on Descartes' philosophy,[9] makes a few marginal remarks on Descartes the man, speaks of the opaque and uncanny in Descartes' personality which stands in such striking contrast to the transparency of his thought:

"However, although Descartes is classical in form, although he was able to convey his ideas with the clarity of personal experience, he is anything but transparent in his character

[9] Jaspers, Karl. loc. cit.

. . . Descartes seems rather like hiddenness itself. It is not only on account of his cautiousness that he remains opaque. There is something weird about his hiddenness because it does not hide anything that one might reveal by interpretation. The very fact that Descartes' personality is not open to our eyes tempts us to seek the secret of his soul. But instead of finding it one feels compelled to look for hidden meaning in what he says, *only to find an ambiguity which actually does not hide anything but seems to be part of his own character.*"[10]

Descartes referred to himself as the "philosopher with the mask." When Jaspers speaks of a hiddenness which is the more weird because we are unable to interpret it, he is speaking of philosophical rather than psychological interpretation. In fact, there are some clues to the riddle of Descartes. What little we have said so far is enough to suggest a *Schicksalsneurose,* a neurosis of destiny. This is not a mere clinical label, a formula to banish the feeling of obscurity. That sense of the fugitive, of roaming impermanence in someone who, by the expectation of historical probability *might* have led a rooted life, who manifested all the yearning for rootedness and the paraphernalia of status—to the clinician this is all familiar.

Our search leads us still further into the past. And there we find that Descartes lost his mother when he was little more than a year old. She died in childbirth, and her newborn baby died with her. We can visualize the sickly schoolboy, with his chronic chest ailments, his need for prolonged sleep (the Jesuit fathers at La Flèche permitted him to stay in bed longer then the rest, at times until

10 Italics are mine.

eleven o'clock, an allowance for his sickly disposition—which earned him among his fellow-pupils the nickname of *chambriste*), and his general melancholia, which he later claimed to have overcome by an optomistic philosophy. The bereavement and grief of infancy impregnated his life with the permanence of a scent. (He remarked on several occasions, particularly in letters to Princess Elizabeth, that he had inherited his sickly disposition from his mother. We know today that such passing-on is much less through chromosomes or germs than through the experience of bereavement, at a time when the child's main implement to grieve is still his body). When I spoke of a sense of tragedy in his case, I extended the meaning of the word into areas to which it is not usually applied: into dim, poorly illuminated regions of origin—to fate indeed, but to fate in a sense unknown to the Greek.

Descartes' celebrated friendships with women were lofty, intellectual and platonic. But he kept a life-long affection, an attachment of the heart, for his wet-nurse, to whom he paid a yearly allowance and for whom he secured in his will continued support after his death. And the only woman with whom we know he had an affair, Helena Jans, seems to have been a domestic servant. From her he had a daughter, Francine, who died at the age of five. Thus we see in his life something which we shall encounter again in Goethe, something not infrequent in the lives of great men—the apparently total cleavage between the carnal and the spiritual in the image of woman. Psychoanalysts speak of the "prostitute-madonna" conflict when they refer to such inability to combine sexual relation and "higher friendship" in the same person. In Descartes we encounter the seemingly paradoxical: it was not in sexual adventure that danger lurked, but in the platonic woman friend, the cool goddess with whom he discussed matters of metaphysics and geometry. All these women—the Duchess of Aiguillon, Anne-Marie de Schurmann, Princess Elizabeth, Queen Christina of Sweden—were highly ambivalent in their relationship with him. (This comes out most clearly in Mlle. de Schurmann and in Queen Christina). To this kind of woman he was lured magically, as though to his perdition, and paradoxically enough she, while not the sexual object of his love, was his *femme fatale*. As a matter of fact, Christina became his fatal woman in the literal sense of the word.

But I am anticipating. The psychoanalytic term "prostitute versus madonna" is misleading in his case. One word is too derogatory, the other too lofty. There should be a more accurate way to describe Descartes' conflict. "Heart versus mind" might do, for the want of a better phrase. One is moved by the story of Helena and the child Francine much more than by those platonic adventures. Somehow he managed to have his illegitimate child close to him most of the time—quite a feat, considering circumstance and social prejudice. One of his landladies very charitably offered to take Francine in *with* him ("We won't need to worry about money," she said, "one more child around does not make any difference"), and Helena was to join them to work as domestic in the same household. He later made arrangements to have little Francine educated in France by one of his pious aunts, but the child died before this could be accomplished. He was inconsolable, and often remarked that this loss was the greatest sorrow of his life. On this occasion he showed extraordinary insight into the nature of mourning. "I noticed," he said, "that those who tried to prevent me from being sad, made me sadder, while those who were moved by my unhappiness, by their very kindness gave me relief."[11] And four months after the little girl's death: "I don't belong to those who claim that tears and sadness are something for women, and that to be a man of courage, one has always to keep a cool exterior." He warned Princess Elizabeth not to study his writings too much because "reading them is not conducive to gaiety but to sadness." In her letters she pours her heart out about an endless list of little ailments, and the advice he gives her often has a surprisingly non-Cartesian twist. She talks about a stomach ailment, and he recommends the waters of a certain spa—but it all depends *in what state of mind* one takes the water. On another occasion, when she talks about a low-grade fever and cough, he tells her that he inherited that very same thing from his mother, and that the only true cure for it is an optimistic outlook. It is in this connection that he talks of "having been used for a long time not to have any more sad thoughts, and that even in his dreams nothing distressing occurred anymore." (letter of September 1st, 1645).[12] All this could be part of a psychoanalytic paper on the somatic equivalents of grief. It is as though Descartes himself, whenever he let wisdom and intuition speak, skipped a few centuries of mechanistic thinking and became utterly non-Cartesian—less Cartesian,

[11] This is an anticipation of Freud's famous observation that "grief must be lived."

[12] Adam, Charles. *Descartes: ses amitiés féminines* (Paris: Boivin & Cie., 1937).

at any rate, than a great many physicians still are today. Even Goethe in his most anti-rationalist mood might have hesitated to come out with statements such as that "even in gambling where it is all a matter of pure luck he found fortune always more favorable when he was in a happy mood, rather than when he was sad"[13]—this from the man who believed literally in the limitless relevancy of the mathematical method. One might be inclined to regard such remarks as small talk, the kind of little asides he indulged in when he was off-duty as a philosopher, were it not for the fact they all add up to a whole, to an aesthetic-affective view of life and nature which just does not fit into the precision grid. This conflict, the fact that Descartes may—on the psychological level—even have used the precision grid to screen off the world of feelings, is enough to explain the uncanny and veiled element that Jaspers perceives in Descartes' personality. That aesthetic-affective relationship to the world of nature in a philosopher who was apparently sincerely convinced that animals are machines comes out at the most unexpected moments, and is quite revealing. For instance Princess Elizabeth, who made certain objections to his philosophy—objections which he himself considered very clever—once asked him: how can a soul which is nothing but thought, act on a body which is nothing but matter? Does not the former have to have some kind of material extension? He counselled her not to spend too much time on questions of this kind. "It is healthier to spend most of one's time without reflection, just looking at the scenery, watching the birds and the

[13] Adam, Charles. loc. cit.

things of nature." This has a Goethean ring, but coming from Descartes, and as an answer to the question, it is a striking non-sequitur. As a matter of fact he did subsequently write the "Treatise on the Passions," especially for Elizabeth, and as an answer to that question. No genius is ever a true disciple of the "ism" which is named after him. And just as a camel loads its body with water for the long desert trip, Descartes carried enough *supplément d'âme* to last for the arid journey of a *mathesis universalis.*

There is only one thing we have to keep in mind. His was not that comfortable double-ledger to which we have become used since his time, for instance in the great scientists of the nineteenth century who managed to keep their Sunday Mind neatly separate from their Laboratory Mind. In Descartes' case it all indicates an area of tension, of dark conflicts. Here we must come back briefly to the psychoanalytic aspect. One of the possible results of early maternal deprivation is the breaking up of the image of Woman into two (we shall encounter this problem in subsequent chapters). It is quite possible, if one may judge from analogies, that those remote and lofty non-carnal women with whom he experienced spiritual exchange and challenge represented the remote mother, the one who had left him in the cold. Nietzsche, who anticipated so many psychoanalytic discoveries, spoke of *"das typische Erlebnis"* (the typical experience). He wanted to say that an experience in life which repeats itself with striking similarity is not accidental but is complementary to our character, and unconsciously sought by us. As is well known, Freud rediscovered the same phenomenon and named it "repetition compulsion." Particularly in cases in which we manoeuvre ourselves repeatedly into painful experiences, Freud admitted himself at a loss for an immediate explanation. With his customary caution he ventilated one possibility—namely that the patient who keeps coming back for a beating may unknowingly be coming back to an unresolved conflict in search of a solution. In the light of all this it is particularly revealing—and perfectly terrifying—when we think of the last one of Descartes' frigid associations, Christina of Sweden.

It is well known that Christina is one of the first great phallic women in modern history. She was meant to be a boy, according to the wish of her father, Gustavus Adolphus, and she grew up like a boy. She was masculine in her intellectual *and* physical ambitions. She would take books along when she went on a hunt. Chanut, the French envoy who acted as a go-between to get Descartes to Stockholm, was an excellent horseman, but she beat him in a race. There is no doubt that the only kind of relationship she could enter into with a man was one of competitiveness or of ownership. As though by some dark foreboding, Descartes hesitated for a long time when he was invited to the Swedish Court. But the idea that there should exist somewhere in Holland that frail little Frenchman with a superhuman intellect gave Christina no peace. In the end she sent an admiral with a ship especially to get him. In retrospect, it all sounds a bit like the fly-and-spider story. For the first few weeks she gave him full freedom from court obligations so that he would settle and acclimatize. The Swedish winter was cold, and Descartes seems to have regretted the step even before his duties began. The routine was bad enough. Christina made our poor *chambriste,* for whom long sleep was a vital necessity, report regularly at five o'clock in the morning, to talk to her on matters of philosophy and mathematics. Like so many people who have been traumatized in the early phase of infancy, he had special rituals of eating and a very cautious diet. Now he had to attend interminable court dinners, and he deferentially gulped the six courses of meat which he abhorred. On February 2nd, 1650, less than five months after his arrival, he fell sick, and on February 11th he died. This was obviously a case of exhaustion and lack of resistance, for his illness had actually begun as an ordinary cold. (Chanut had the same sickness around the same time, and recovered.) Not long before his death, Descartes had spoken to the Queen about some method by which one could calculate one's probable life expectation. After his death she facetiously remarked that he would have made a poor oracle.[14] However, she planned the erection of a vast temple as a special burial place for the famous man. Chanut objected that this would not go at all with his late friend's simplicity of heart. Thus Descartes was buried in an ordinary cemetery, in a burial plot for unbaptized children.[15]

Schicksalsneurose, neurosis of destiny! What appears as a clinical label becomes the expression of a haunting

---

[14] There is little doubt that unconsciously she made him die. The enormous sadistic impulses of this kind of woman towards the male object of envy came out overtly during the tragic life of Christina, most notably in that dreadful episode of the murder of Monaldeschi. The details make ghastly reading. The slow torture of the poor victim; the unrelenting avenger—all this is a clinical study of *une dame sans merci.*

[15] I could find no explanation for this; it may have to do with his status as a Catholic in a Protestant country. Incidentally, his body was later taken to his native country and given a tomb of honour.

reality. That this motherless, roaming spirit would finally succeed in manoeuvring himself inextricably into the hands of the Anti-Mother! Christina literally deprived him of the maternal triad, warmth and sleep and the proper food, and thus, with the uncanny sureness of her own unconscious, caused him to die. What made him seek this end? Why did he not, like Goethe, find a compromise in staying with that maidservant? He might, like Goethe, have settled down and reached a ripe old age. However, it is wrong to approach past lives with "ifs" and "mights." Finished lives are like the physiognomies of the dead: one feels the end is not an arbitrary break but a fulfillment.

If a clinical summing-up is permitted at this point, we see how through the entire work of Descartes the lines of personal conflict may be traced. Consider, for a moment, his way of thinking, outside the framework of the philosophical edifice, and you enter into a paradoxical world whose very genesis is intertwined with the sense of *loss*, whose *reality* is founded on *uncertainty*. Again and again in Descartes' writings, particularly in the *Meditations*, we find him, almost in a free association of thoughts, muse on the mysterious relationship between dream and wakeful reality, between the certainty of delusional insanity and the certainty of reason. "For example, there is the fact that I am here, seated by the fire, attired in a dressing gown, having my papers in this hand, and similar matters."[16] From here the thinker goes straight into the world of the insane who believe that they are kings clothed in purple, or think that their heads are made of glass! "At the same

[16] Descartes, R., *Meditations*. The Philosophical Works of Descartes, translated by Elizabeth S. Haldane and G. R. T. Ross. Vol. I, 1931.

time I must remember that I am a man, and that consequently I am in the habit of sleeping, and in my dreams representing to myself the same things or even less probable things, than do those who are insane in their waking moments. How often has it happened to me that in the night I found myself in this particular place, that I was dressed and seated near the fire, whilst in reality I was lying undressed in bed!" Take all this out of the philosophical context and you enter into a world which is only too familiar from clinical experience: the world of those to whom the certainty of being has early been shattered by maternal bereavement. For to all of us, the core and meaning of reality was at one time, before all cogitation, the certainty of carnal presence. Descartes, the adult and philosopher, postulates to "doubt sensible things because they have deceived us," and it is in this connection noteworthy that in French the word *déçu* has the double meaning of "deceived" and "disappointed." The certainty of the flesh which is the foundation of all certainty *had* to be conjured away—because it was here where the terror and pain of abandonment lurked. To the man who was to make an *act of doubt* the basis of all inquiry, doubt had supplanted trust a long time before conceptual thinking. "To those who thus resolve to doubt all, there is apparently no mark by which they can with certainty distinguish sleep from the waking state."[17] Reality, perceived primarily through the flesh, meant dread, and therefore ratiocination, the pure *cogito,* became an impenetrable armor. "As we have once upon a time been children and have judged the things presented to our senses in various ways, while we

---

[17] Ibid., *The Principles of Philosophy.*

had not the entire use of our reason, many judgements thus precipitately formed prevent us from arriving at the knowledge of the truth, and apparently there seems to be no way in which we can deliver ourselves from these, unless we undertake once in our lives to doubt all things in which the slightest trace of uncertitude can be found." He once introduced, playfully as it were, as a mere working hypothesis, the idea that the reasoning of wakeful reality is not to be trusted, in view of the possibility of a mocking demon deceiving us!

If we encountered such thoughts, not as a philosophical system, but as a mode of everyday experience of an "ordinary man," merely *in its psychology,* as it were—we would find that the ideal of the *cogito,* of the *mathesis universalis,* means *denial,* a defence against the flesh because the flesh is synonymous with anguish; and the clean fission between mind and body is an *isolation,* a setting-apart and rendering innocuous of all that which spells dread. As we have pointed out in the chapter on psychoanalysis and metaphysics, this has nothing to do with the problem of validity. All it shows is how the clinical element, the raw material of suffering, is assimilated by genius.[18]

What is the legacy of Descartes? In order to answer

---

18 Everything presented here on the drama of Descartes' life will be understood if the reader consults the original observations of René Spitz (loc. cit.) and others on early maternal bereavement. We purposely refrained from going into more "clinical detail"—for example the question of the rôle of his childhood nurse, whose person may have saved him from a more grave psychic injury and to whom, incidentally, he remained devoted all his life. What interests us here mainly is the metamorphosis which the neurotic dynamics undergo when that mysterious element of genius is added to the inner constellation. Here something manifests itself in an eminently creative form which otherwise might have come out as a serious hiatus.

this question we must simplify matters. We must disregard the glittering ambiguities in his writings and the fascination of his character, the richness and colorfulness of Descartes, the man and writer, because the historical impact of Cartesian thought has little to do with all that. First of all there is modern scientism. The naive and dangerous belief in an absolute manageability; the absolutism of the scientific method, with a devaluation of wisdom; the optimistic belief in the solubility of all problems, with a scotomization of the mystery; the sense of organization taking precedence over the sense of organism. All this would be impossible without the impact of Descartes. Of course there are others, for instance Hume, also responsible for the rise of scientism. Moreover, Descartes himself failed to adhere to the scientific method which isolates one problem at a time and tackles it. (His statement, for example, that the pineal gland was the seat of the soul is as naïve as any of the wildest pre-scientific claims which Aristotle made in the field of natural history.) But just *because* he created a kind of scientific scholasticism, a naive *Summa Scientifica,* his influence became so penetrating. Eighteenth century enlightenment, the Goddess of Reason, the nineteenth century absolutism of thought in Hegel (with Marxist dialectics as a derivative), and our present-day positivism, the religion of progress—none of this would be possible without the Cartesian *cogito.*

He still believed in God. But even in the Cartesian philosophy, God is already expendable. He is relegated to the drawing room, a good piece of furniture which the philosopher dusts from time to time.

Descartes made an act of doubt the basis of all inquiry.

And what we have said in the beginning of this study about Cartesian dualism is also about Cartesian doubt: as a springboard for scientific objectivity it is necessary and legitimate. To take nothing for granted—this is essentially the meaning of doubt in Descartes' system—is one of the prerequisites of scientific procedures. However, here again a *methodology* turned into *mentality*. The necessity of doubt as a circumscribed tool, as a first step in the method of scientific inquiry, grew into the significance of *doubt as basis and condition,* a primary doubt which usurps the place of faith. "Doubt is a threat and enemy to the soul," says Ernst Cassirer,[19] "for its weakens and undermines its (the soul's) true strength, the strength of faith which unites it with God. Whoever yields to doubt becomes unstable and shiftless. For Descartes, however, who acknowledges no guidance of the spirit from without, who knows no passive *illuminatio* or *informatio,* the radicalism of doubt becomes the only and true source of all knowledge."

Jaspers comments on Descartes' fleeting and seemingly playful hypothesis of reality as a mirage presented by a mocking demon: "He who makes this hypothesis into a conviction—one does not even need the assumption of a creating demon, and needs only to leave, as the only form of reality, this world as an infinitely ambiguous and deceptive creation, as it actually appears in certain ideas of Nietzsche—not only loses his faith in reason but falls into a bottomless abyss, because there is no other bottom but reason to hold him."[20] This is precisely what happened in the

[19] Cassirer, Ernst. *Descartes: Lehre—Persönlichkeit—Wirkung,* Stockholm: Berman-Fischer.

[20] Jaspers, K. loc. cit.

case of contemporary nihilism, as we shall see in the chapter on Sartre.

Several authors have drawn attention to the un-historical nature of Descartes' philosophy. The optimism of science, the philosophy of technology knows only the future, and the future beckons with infinite possibilities. A great workman of modern technology, Henry Ford, made the famous statement: "History is bunk." In a more veiled and refined form, by implication, this statement is already contained in Descartes' philosophy.[21] In such a world there is infinite space to penetrate and explore but no soil to be rooted in. I feel that Hegel's idea of history as a kind of jellied thought is an attempt to save history from the vacuum into which it fell with the triumph of rationalism. But history as the living drama of revelation is unthinkable in Descartes' linear picture of the world. With the possibility of a *mathesis universalis,* the I of the *cogito* being reduced to a Euclidian point, reality becomes a formula, Man is made flesh-less, as it were, and the Incarnation as the pivotal point of history becomes a meaningless myth. This wave of the Cartesian tide has left its stain everywhere, even on Christianity—as we witness in certain trends of present-day theology.

From what we have seen in preceding chapters, it becomes quite clear that we encounter in Cartesian rationalism a pure *masculinization of thought.* There is nothing childlike left in man's gaze. The hand of Wisdom, *Sophia,* the maternal, is rejected, and a proud intellect lays claim

---

21 It is well known how he made fun of the study of ancient languages. (In doing so, he used to draw upon himself the wrath of his intellectual lady friends.)

to omnipotence. Goethe was to perceive the craze and destructiveness in all this: modern man, the un-historical, uprooted self-reliant victor, is a haunted fugitive. The march of conquest is actually a flight in perpetuity, and the only resting place, the haven of delivery, is the Eternal Feminine.

As we have pointed out, the "ism" in Cartesianism is a simplification, and it is in this simplified form that Descartes exerted his permanent influence. However, for the understanding of the entire phenomenon the interstices in the scaffold are just as important as the structure which he left behind. The uncharted dark chasms become illuminated when we look at Descartes' philosophy within the context of his personal conflicts. And although he was undoubtedly the greatest exponent of that rationalist fallacy which Goethe fought throughout his life, there are numerous hints here and there that Descartes hid unawares, in the depth of his person, the mystic antithesis to which Goethe attained poetic insight. During a religious controversy with a Huguenot minister he once remarked, perhaps facetiously, that he could not possibly abandon the faith of his nurse. When he woke up from his famous dream, at the birth of his method, possibly shivering at the stove in Ulm from the interstellar coldness of a Cartesian system, he vowed a pilgrimage to Our Lady of Loretto. It is too easy to speak of such apparent trivialities in terms of infantile regression. I, for one, cannot help feeling that the Faustian pilgrim to Loretto was not only Goethe's antipode but also his brother.

SIX

Schopenhauer

In order to understand the significance of the Cartesian mentality better, we must realize that Cartesian dualism was not as new as it appears. A total opposition between spirit and nature had occurred in other philosophies before. Only there it had not been stated for the sake of scientific clarity, as in the case of Descartes. It was rather an emotional and moral matter—a matter of enmity, a hate of the flesh as imbued with evil, intrinsically opposed to the spirit. This has been the case in Manichaeism and in certain neo-Platonic trends. The voice of Mani can, every once in a while, be heard rumbling in the subterranean caves of Christianity. Strangely enough, by one of those coincidences of which one never knows whether they *are* pure chance, a countryman and contemporary of Descartes, Bishop Jansenius, was the last great exponent of a revival of Manichaeism in the history of the Church. There is evidence that Descartes had some personal contact with some of the Jansenists, but not more than an important French philosopher of that time might have had with any of the exponents of that dynamic group. That Cartesianism and Jansenism sprang up at the same time in the same country is a matter of the *zeitgeist* rather than of direct influence. In fact, in the Protestant countries around that time, similar trends made themselves felt.

At any rate, when one comes to look for what warps the minds of many Western Christians today, it is not hard to trace it all to that double dose of Descartes and Jansenius which France got in the seventeenth century. Just as in the Cartesian concept of the world, nature can be entirely understood *more geometrico* as an apparatus, in the Calvinistic and Jansenistic religion God becomes a retribution machine which works with mathematical precision. Justice is autonomous, and severed from charity. All motherliness is taken away from the relation to God. The word of Isaiah, "I shall comfort you as a Mother comforteth," is as alien to this form of spirituality as though it came from some dead ancient religion.

Nor did the Manichean current remain confined to Christianity. In 1818 a young German philosopher, Arthur Schopenhauer, published the first part of his famous treatise, *The World as Will and Idea.* This and Schopenhauer's subsequent works were to have far-reaching influence on the thinking of the most diverse minds, and like all forceful ideas, influenced the course of history. One must stress this, for today it seems to many of us that Schopenhauer is a philosophical museum-piece, quite unlike his contemporary, Hegel, whose influence on the course of history is so evident. The word "Will" in the title of Schopenhauer's main work is not to be confounded with the common meaning of the word, namely as conscious, intentional volition. In Schopenhauer the word "Will" could be replaced by "Life." It comprises all drives—all forces of nature that make up the will to live—even blind and unconscious ones, from the growth of plants to the hunger and sex instincts of animal and man. Opposed to this world of "Will" is the "Idea"—the world of pure reflection. And the *Idea* will never come to complete realization until Nature is entirely overcome and negated. The ascetic ideal is not merely a matter of discipline that enables us to foster the life of the Spirit—it amounts to complete and utter obliteration of Nature, attaining a state of nothingness, very much as in the Buddhist religion. Indeed Schopenhauer was the first European scholar with strong Buddhist and Hindu sympathies and considerable knowledge of Vedanta and the Upanishad, the holy books of the Hindu religion.

One does injustice to the rich mind of a genius whenever one tries to summarize his ideas. For our purpose we want again to emphasize only certain aspects of Schopenhauer's work. Schopenhauer's dualism is not one so much of *res cogitans* and *res extensa* but of *res cogitans* and *res concupiscens,* as it were. Instead of *logos* versus *materia* it is more a question of *logos* versus *bios.* Contrary to Descartes whose dualism is necessary and justified as the basis of scientific method (for, as we have seen, the observer really *has* to be totally excluded from the observed if exact sciences should succeed) Schopenhauer's thesis is primarily a moral one. And while for the Frenchman the *res extensa,* the universe around us, could be elucidated as a crystalline mathematical pattern, to the Teutonic mind it became a huge dark vortex of insatiable forces which surely devour us unless the spirit is able to reduce them to a void. The flesh cannot be spiritualized. The only solution is the utter denial of that which to the Christian is the natural soil of human love—life itself. From this it will not surprise anyone that to Schopenhauer sex is the evil lying at the very centre of nature:

"It follows that the genitals are the real focus of the will, and consequently the opposite pole of the brain, that representative of perception and as such, of the other side of the world, the world as idea. The genitals are the life-preserving principle, ensuring time its eternal life. In this capacity they were revered by the Greeks in the phallus, by the Hindus in the lingam, which are thus symbols of the affirmation of the will. Knowledge on the other hand, makes possible the annulment of the will, redemption through freedom, conquest and annihilation of the world.[1]

If in our view of the world we take the thing in itself, the will to live, as our point of departure, then we shall find its essence, its greatest concentration in the act of procreation: that is primary, that is the point of departure: it is the *punctum saliens* of the egg of the world and its main concern.[2]

On more than one occasion Schopenhauer compares sexual intercourse to a criminal act:

The act through which the will affirms itself and through which man comes into being is an act of which all are ashamed in their most innermost heart, which they, there-

---

[1] *The World as Will and Idea.*
[2] *Parerga and Paralipomena.*

fore, carefully conceal; yes, if they are caught at it, they are frightened, as if they were caught in a crime. It is an act which, on somber reflection, one usually recalls with repugnance, in a more exalted mood even with abhorrence. . . . A strange sadness and remorse follow the performance of the act, a remorse which is most keenly felt after the first time, and generally is the clearer the nobler the character of the person.[3]

From what we have learned in preceding chapters, we should not be surprised at Schopenhauer's attitude towards womanhood. As we have seen, that which we call womanly in the human psyche has a deep kinship to the unconscious "natural," as opposed to the conscious "rational."[4] Schopenhauer has anticipated this observation. He draws attention to it again and again in various contexts. The remarkable thing is that he does so with hate and contempt. Never since the early Fathers of the Church fifteen centuries before (who had been very much under the influence of the Manichaeism) has there been voiced such abominable hate of woman. One can also find some grim misogynous texts in scholastic philosophy. While womanhood was extolled in the Blessed Virgin and in woman saints, women as such were presented as inferior. The attitude is reminiscent of that neurotic cleavage of which we spoke in connection with Descartes. The misogynous statements of scholastic philosophy sound as though spoken with the voice of adolescent ambivalence. Not so

---

[3] *The World as Will and Idea.*

[4] cf. chapter 2 and the references to Helene Deutsch, Ortega y Gasset and others.

with Schopenhauer. It seems as though no ambivalence had to be resolved because there was none:

> For, as Nature has endowed the lion with claw and fang, elephant and boar with tusks, the bull with horns and the jelly fish with obscuring liquid—in the same way she has endowed woman with deceit, for her protection and defence; all the power which (Nature) has given to Man in the form of physical strength and reason, she has lent to woman under the guise of that gift (of deceit). Deceit is inherent to woman, almost as much to the stupid as to the clever. To use it on any occasion comes as naturally to her as it comes to those animals to use their weapons, and she considers it as her right. Hence an entirely honest woman without deceit is probably impossible. This is the reason why they look through the deceit of others so easily that it is advisable not even to try it on them. From this basic fault and its concomitants spring falseness, unfaithfulness, treason, ingratitude, etc. Women are much more frequently than men guilty of perjury. In fact, one should ask oneself whether they should ever be put under oath.

This is taken from the second part of *Parerga and Paralipomena.* Such a ghastly view of woman's soul is not enough; here is a picture of her body: "Only the male intellect befogged by its sexual urge could regard as beautiful the undersized, narrow-shouldered, broad hipped, short-legged sex. Its only beauty lies in this urge. It would be more to the point to call this sex not the fair but the unesthetic sex." On one occasion Schopenhauer wrote to his disciple Frauenstaedt:

> A perfect woman is more beautiful than a perfect man—*quae qualis, quanta!* Here you have given an extremely naive

confession of your sexual urge . . . Wait until you have reached my age and see what you will then think of these short-legged, long-torsoed, narrow-shouldered, broad-hipped, teat-bedecked creatures; even their faces are nothing compared to those of the most handsome youths, and their eyes are listless.

Although Schopenhauer was no overt homosexual this is, as Hitschmann[5] justly pointed out, a homosexual evaluation of the womanly body. However I should like to draw attention to the similes Schopenhauer uses in the quotation on woman's deceit. The lion's claw and fang, the elephant's and wild boar's tusks, the bull and the jelly fish —there is a wealth of imagery referring to the phallic and the oral-sadistic. It seems to be a matter of speculation to equate the evil dangerous image of nature with an orally sadistic mother, the mother ever ready to destroy and devour, but from countless clinical experiences the link is quite evident. To illustrate its relevance I should like to quote a view of mother nature presented by the Marquis de Sade:

Nature averse to crime? I tell you, nature lives and breathes by it; hungers at all her pores for bloodshed, aches in all her nerves for the help of sin, yearns with all her heart for the furtherance of cruelty. Nature forbid that thing or this? Nay, the best or worst in you will never go so far as she would have you; no criminal will come up to the measure of her crimes, no destruction seem to her destructive enough. We, when we would do evil, can disorganize a little matter, shed a little blood, quench a breath at the door of a perishable

5 Hitschmann, E., *Great Men: psychoanalytic studies.* Edited by S. G. Margolin. Foreword by Ernest Jones. Int. Universities Press, New York, 1956.

body; this we can do, and can call it crime. Unnatural is it? Good friend, it is by criminal things and deeds unnatural that nature works and moves and has her being; what subsides through inert virtue, she quickens through active crime; out of death she kindles life; she uses the dust of man to strike her light upon; she feeds with fresh blood the innumerable insatiable mouths suckled at her milkless breast; she takes the pain of the whole world to sharpen the sense of vital pleasure in her limitless veins; she stabs and poisons, crushes and corrodes; yet cannot live and sin fast enough for the cruelty of her great desire. Behold, the ages of men are dead at her feet; the blood of the world is dead at her hands; and her desire is continually toward evil, that she may see the end of things she hath made. Friends, if we would be one with nature, let us continually do evil with all our might. But what evil is here for us to do, where the whole body of things is evil? The day's spider kills the day's fly, and calls it a crime? Nay, could we thwart nature, then might crime become possible and sin an actual thing. Could but a man do this; could he cross the courses of the stars, and put back the times of the sea; could he change the ways of the world and find out the house of life to destroy it; could he go into heaven to defile it and into hell to deliver it from subjection; could he draw down the sun to consume the earth and bid the moon to shed poison or fire upon the air; could he kill the fruit in the seed and corrode the child's mouth with the mother's milk; then had he sinned and done evil against nature. Nay, and not then: for nature would fain have it so, that she might create a world of new things; for she is weary of the ancient life: her eyes are sick of seeing and her ears are heavy with hearing; with the lust of creation she is burned up, and rent in vain with travail until she brings forth change; she would fain create afresh, and cannot, except it be by destroying; in all her energies she is athirst for mortal food, and with all her forces she labours in desire of death. And what are the worst sins we can do—we who live for a day and die in a night? a few murders. . . .[6]

All this could be pure Schopenhauer; there are many parallel passages in the *The World as Will and Idea.* But the quotation comes from the man after whom Sadism is named, and the remarkable thing is that for long passages in this quotation you can replace "nature" by "woman" and you have a perfect replica of the orally sadistic mother, or the vagina dentata of psychoanalytic literature.

This becomes more dramatically evident if we hold the strange portrait of Mother Nature painted by Schopenhauer and de Sade up against the one presented by Goethe in his celebrated essay on "Nature":[7]

She plays with them (all men) a friendly game, and is happy if one wins against her. She plays her game so discreetly that she's won before they become aware of it . . . She enjoys illusion. Whoever destroys this in himself or in others, she will punish like a severe tyrant. Whoever follows her with confidence, she will take to her bosom like a child . . . Her spectacle is ever new. Life is her most beautiful invention, and death is her trick to achieve more life . . . She rewards herself and punishes herself, makes herself happy and tortures herself. She is rough and gentle, sweet and terrible, weak and all-powerful . . . She has neither language nor speech; but she creates tongues and hearts through which she speaks. Her crown is Love . . .

---

[6] Marquis de Sade, *Justine ou les Malheurs de la Vie.* Préf. de Georges Batailles. Paris 1950.

[7] It is noteworthy that this essay had a decisive influence on the young Freud in his choice of Medicine as a career.

Goethe, on rereading this manuscript as an old man, forty-two years later, noticed in it a "tendency to a kind of Pantheism."[8] What interests us in the present context is the fact that nobody, not even the most rigorously trained scientist, can think of Nature as a whole without lending it a meaningful image. We are able to confine ourselves to the objective framework of the categories of discursive reasoning only if we examine a sector of the material world. The moment we try to conceive of it wholly we have a "view" of it. We endow it with qualities which relate it mysteriously to the personal. The validity of such experience is not under discussion here. Nevertheless we must keep two important points in mind. Firstly, the "views" of Nature presented here are relevant—positively or negatively—to the Christian belief in the potential holiness of matter. Secondly, the sadistic destructive mother in Schopenhauer's and de Sade's image is closely linked up with that estrangement from Nature of which we spoke in connection with Cartesianism. The irredeemably evil and cruel Matter of Schopenhauer's "Will" is the corollary of that machinery of Descartes which stares coldly and indifferently at the *res cogitans.* Quite in contrast to this Goethe made, as we shall see, a vain attempt to re-establish a cosmology which his critics call "medieval." Indeed his *Weltgefühl*—as one may guess from the few quotations here—is closely related to that of the Book of Wisdom, the Psalms and to Franciscan spirituality.

Schopenhauer was born in 1788 in Danzig, the son of Heinrich Floris Schopenhauer who was then forty-one and

---

8 See appendix to "Die Natur," in Goethe's *Werke,* Cotta, Stuttgart and Berlin, *15,* 253.

Johanna Trosiener who was twenty-two years old. When Arthur was born the parents had been married for three years. Heinrich Schopenhauer was a tall, broad-shouldered man of severe discipline. He was a successful, wealthy businessman. Johanna had married him, who was nineteen years her senior, on the rebound, after an unhappy love affair. There are many reasons to believe that this was a marriage without love. Heinrich, at the age of forty-eight, fell through an opening in one of his warehouses into a canal and was drowned, and there was a suspicion of suicide. Heinrich's widow became one of the celebrated women of the time, the first of the great literary bluestockings, the German counterpart of Madame de Stael or George Sand. She wrote several books, among them novels—none of which withstood the test of time. However her salon in Weimar and her "teas" were famous in the literary Germany of the time. This is the way L. Feuerbach described her: "A rich widow, she makes a profession of being erudite. A writer. She talks a great deal and very well; is sensible; but has no heart or soul. Self-satisfied and eager for applause, smug."

She was probably less gifted than her French opposite numbers but even more under a violent phallic drive. To women of this kind their own son is often an added glory, even more than to healthy mothers. Not so Johanna Schopenhauer. She was competitive and castrating even towards her son. This may be illustrated by a few examples. Arthur who was very musical (which is also borne out in his writings) had in his youth one great wish—namely to learn to play the flute. The father was agreeable to buying him the instrument but, as Schopenhauer later wrote, "My poetic mother, the *bel esprit* of Weimar was opposed to my desire: 'Someday he will have enough money to have somebody play the flute for him.' " After Arthur had completed his first great philosophical work (which happened to be his thesis for the Ph.D.) he presented a copy to his mother. This work is called "The Four-fold Root of the Axiom of a Sufficient Cause," and the mother's only comment was a sarcastic remark about the title. She said that it sounded like something written for pharmacists.

After her husband's death, when the *salon* was in full flourish, Johanna Schopenhauer began a lasting friendship with a man, a Herr Müller who was about twenty years her junior. Arthur made no attempt to conceal his disapproval. And it seems to be on one of those occasions that the final break occurred. After that mother and son did not meet again for the remaining twenty-three years of her life.

It is obvious that, but for a twist of fate, Schopenhauer might have been a Christian, and his ingenious mind might have provided the most powerful buttress for the Christian edifice. To see this more clearly we must take another look at Schopenhauer's philosophy. The "Will," as we have seen, is unreflective nature. This will precedes all reflection, all idea. It is the fundamental datum, indeed antedatum of being, and with its imperious demand, its ravenous insatiability, it is the very image of infinity. Neither time nor space can hold it. Even the idea is, to begin with, its servant. For in the ascending animal scale the gradual appearance and differentiation of the nervous system has only one purpose: to aid the instinctual drives in an ever more refined fulfillment. The same holds true of man. Only in man something entirely new and unexpected is added. Reason is capable of refusing to be the servant of nature and, instead, become its master. This happens on two possible planes: the aesthetic and the ethical. The artist and the saint are the only two who have the power to bring the eternal, ceaseless movement of the "will" to a standstill. All true art is pure contemplation. Here nature, in all its merciless insatiability finds its antithesis and, in a sense, its abolition. The same is true in the case of sanctity. There exists a mysterious polarity about the will: in its ceaseless groaning and travail it is huge and monolithic; at the same time, however, it seeks individuation so that each single one among the myriad of organisms represents a microcosmos of appetites, and has neither eye nor ear for the labour and pain of the individual right at its side. However with man for the first time the possibility of *compassion* arises. In certain individuals this gift of compassion, of "suffering *with*," reaches such a high level that they become truly self-less, i.e., able to overcome "Will" in an act of love. This, in brief, is an outline of Schopenhauer's aesthetic and moral philosophy.

To the Christian all this sounds familiar. But for a slight difference it might be an outline of the gospel. What is the difference? Why did Schopenhauer start out with all the ingredients, and yet not arrive at the Bread of Life? One might possibly see the reason in the fact that he, like so many other "modern" thinkers, wanted to have the ethical pure and devoid of all myth and dogma.[9] I believe the reason to be deeper. Schopenhauer's ethics had to remain

[9] This seems also to be Thomas Mann's explanation. (Cf. Thomas Mann, *Essays*. Vintage Books, New York 1958.)

in a non-historical vacuum because there is no place in his system for the Incarnation. Ever since the birth of Jesus the mystery of love has been inextricably bound up with the mystery of the God-Man. If nature is evil *per se,* the Word cannot become Flesh. With Schopenhauer nature cannot possibly be ennobled—it can at best be negated. No blessing can ever come from motherhood, for conception and birth serve only one purpose—the perpetuation of a curse. Nothing in nature can ever partake of the redemption—this would be, in Schopenhauer's system, a contradiction in terms. No Mother can bear a Saviour. And with this Christianity must fall.

Among Schopenhauer's many hatreds there was one remarkable one—the Jewish people. And besides all possible accidental personal factors there is a hidden reason for that. The Jews are the live testimony of the Incarnation. No matter how many philosophical systems may come and go—the Jews bear witness to something which defies all systems: *the drama of history.* Moreover the Jews are earthy. I do not mean this at all in the sense of materialism. If there has ever been a people in whom reason was nuptially bound to nature, it is the Jewish people. It often appears as if the Jews (contrary, for instance, to the Greeks) had no sense of the transcendental. It only seems so because to them the transcendental is literally in the blood; it "comes naturally." Whenever Schopenhauer does not indulge in antisemitic diatribes this point comes out quite clearly. To him Christianity has a dual aspect: in its pure ethical content it is akin to the Vedas, but its association with Jewry is an unpleasant encumbrance—an historical freak. It is in this connection that he calls the Old Testament "optimistic" (which with him amounts to a dirty word)—and never has he been more accurate.

It is, incidentally, remarkable that Schopenhauer's ethics of compassion was not reflected in his personal life. He died in crotchety self-isolation, an embittered old bachelor, full of a thousand pet hates (of which misogyny and antisemitism are only two) and full of personal resentments. He held the poor in disdain and he watched the first signs of the rise of the working classes with a jaundiced eye. It is noteworthy that he bequeathed his money to a fund for the invalids of the revolution of 1848 and their families—not the poor rebels, but the soldiers who had shot them! None of all this should be understood as an *argumentum ad hominem*. There have been many defenders of good causes who in life manifested the opposite of their teaching. The remarkable thing about Schopenhauer's philosophy is that, with all its lofty ethics, so close to the idea of the gospel—it somehow never inspired love in the hearts of men.

On the contrary. Schopenhauer opened up that vast unredeemed world of the irrational which gave birth to Wagner and to Nietzsche. The latter tried to turn the tables but, in some subtly perverted way, remained Schopenhauer's disciple to the end. In vain do you seek the warmth of love in that world. There is an eerie oscillating light, a light of weird fascination—not the calm Sun of Reason as we experience it in ancient philosophy. What is so eerie, cold and yet so seductive about it all? We can only attempt to explain it. In the preceding chapter we have dealt a lot with the intellect cut from its moorings, and the destructive element inherent in rationalism. Here we are dealing with the opposite which is no less dreadful. *Bios* without *logos,* the forces of *chthone* unredeemed and unredeemable, are destructive in a magic way.

Fascism, in contrast to Communism, never had any well-defined philosophy. Its ideology was based on mood rather than thought. And this mood arose out of those dark recesses of a German movement which began with Schopenhauer. We encounter such affirmation of blind forces elsewhere in the nineteenth century, in a Gobineau or a Sorel. But in the *mystique* of "blood" and "soil" a disgruntled *petite bourgeoisie* finally overcame its sense of weakness by identification with an irrational something of unlimited power with sadistic devouring features. Indeed, one can trace a direct descent from the irredeemable non-reason of Schopenhauer's "Will" to that incomprehensible phase of madness in this century that nearly succeeded in destroying the world.

SEVEN

Sartre

At first sight the world pictures of Descartes and of Schopenhauer look like two sides of the same coin. Here is the duality and cleavage between Reason and Nature that impresses us. The two philosophies seem to have, each along its own subterranean bed, descended from ancient sources of Manichaeism. Only in Descartes nature shows the face of a cold and estranged mother, and in Schopenhauer that of an inimical and dreadful one.

And yet, this is not merely the same thing seen from two angles. A downward movement is implied: from the crystalline geometrical pattern of the *mathesis universalis* we *descend* to the dark maelstrom of the "Will." The *res extensa* of Descartes exhibits a harmony which is not only in opposition to the beholding subject. Its mathematical order is intrinsically related and exists in resonance with the reason of the observer. Gaston Bachelard, in one of his studies on the philosophy of science,[1] observes that in all classical physics, up to and including the theory of relativity there exists from subject towards object a "passivity of the human spirit," a "Platonic realism" in the face of "operating ideas." In other words, underneath the mathematical detachment of Descartes' philosophy there is alive a spirit of contemplation. Newton and Kant were still inspired, by the laws of stellar movement, to a faith in God.[2] It is interesting in this connection that one of the very few open references which Einstein made to religion was that he could not believe that God played dice with the universe. This is the more interesting since he remarked it in connection with the later development of quantum physics—a phase of which Bachelard claims that it presents a break from the "contemplative" attitude of classical science. At any rate, Cartesianism is *not* alienation pure and unadulterated. The very structure of the *res extensa* denotes an element of the divine. There exists a Pythagorean analogy between celestial mechanics and the music of Bach: in both cases harmony and counterpoint sing a hymn to the creator. It is the music of the spheres.

Yet a process of alienation was initiated. No Pythagorean harmonies were enough to maintain the experience of the world as a shelter. In Pascal we become aware of *cold abandonment* evoked by immense interstellar spaces. This is the first step towards alienation. Now in the im-

---

1 Gaston Bachelard, *L'expérience de l'éspace dans la physique contemporaine*. Alcan, Paris 1937.

2 The psychological analogue of this kind of *Naturgefühl* is, no doubt, the "fatherly." This is a evident from many passages in poetry, the Psalms, etc. It is also suggested by the features of order and ruling rather than those of imbeddedness, growth and nourishment which we rather encounter in the "nature" of immediate experience.

mediate experience of the world and of nature in everyday life not even the harmony of physical precision is evident. On the contrary, once the world around us is purely objectified and things are no longer beheld through the medium of trustfulness, its huge multiplicity and amorphousness, and the phenomena that clutch at us unceasingly and from all sides seem purely haphazard. Existence becomes synonymous with contingency. This is the world into which we are introduced by Jean-Paul Sartre.

Sartre is an aphoristic philosopher. Apart from his work *Being and Nothingness* which employs a system of sorts, at least in form, he has made numerous statements which give the impression of purposeful scattering. Like Kierkegaard and Nietzsche he has used the poetic form, at times in fiction or in drama, and therefore one often is led, as at a masked ball, into corners in which it is difficult to identify one's man. Do the hero of *Nausea,* the hero of *The Flies,* and the author of *Being and Nothingness* represent three facets of the same person? There is the same hide-and-seek as in Kierkegaard, the same glitter of mirror effects as in Nietzsche.

We may take the novel *Nausea* as representative of the Sartrian mood. The story deals with one Antoine Roquentin, who is engaged in writing the biography of an eighteenth-century nobleman, the Marquis de Rollebon. We meet Roquentin in a small Norman town, doing library research on his subject, and at the same time we are witnesses of a most extraordinary philosophical journey. The story is very much like that of a religious evolution. The diary tone, the way in which encounters are interwoven with rumination, the atmosphere of places tinged with a metaphysical *modus*—it all reminds us of Kierkegaard. There is even the sudden experience resembling a conversion—if one may use the term. Indeed the way in which all this evokes Kierkegaardian associations is reminiscent of two mathematical formulas which are identical but for reversed signs. We even encounter that *tristitia* which is said to be characteristic of religious seekers. (The original title of the novel was *Melancholia.*) However the true feeling which pervades the entire story, a kind of sensory *leitmotif,* is that of nausea. The writer succeeds, with poetic deftness, in conveying nausea as if it were an inherent quality of the objects perceived. In the end the reader himself comes to see the entire world of lifeless objects and of plants, animals and persons as one encounters an infinite, slightly disgusting mass, not enough to make you retch, but just enough to maintain a nauseous sensation.

Before we go further, let us first look at an episode which comes rather late in the book, namely the one resembling conversion. Roquentin's entry marks, significantly, the hour of the day. It is 6 P.M.

"I can't say I feel relieved or satisfied; just the opposite, I am crushed. Only my goal is reached: I know what I wanted to know; I have understood all that has happened to me since January. The Nausea has not left me and I don't believe it will leave me so soon; but I no longer have to bear it, it is no longer an illness or a passing fit: it is I.

So I was in the park just now. The roots of the chestnut tree were sunk in the ground just under my bench. I couldn't remember it was a root any more. The words had vanished and with them the significance of things, their methods of use, and the feeble points of reference which men have traced on their surface. I was sitting, stooping forward, head bowed, alone in front of this black, knotty mass, entirely beastly, which frightened me. Then I had this vision.

It left me breathless. Never, until these last few days, had I understood the meaning of "existence." I was like the others, like the ones walking along the seashore, all dressed in their spring finery. I said, like them, "The ocean *is* green; that white speck up there *is* a seagull," but I didn't feel that it existed or that the seagull was an "existing seagull"; usually existence hides itself. It is there, around us, in us, it is *us,* you can't say two words without mentioning it, but you can never touch it. When I believed I was thinking about it, I must believe that I was thinking nothing, my head was empty, or there was just one word in my head, the word "to be." Or else I was thinking . . . how can I explain it? I was thinking of *belonging,* I was telling myself that the sea belonged to the class of green objects, or that the green was a part of the quality of the sea. Even when I looked at things, I was miles from dreaming that they existed: they looked like scenery to me. I picked them up in my hands, they served me as tools, I foresaw their resistance. But that all happened on the surface. If anyone had asked me what existence was, I would have answered, in good faith, that it was nothing, simply an empty form which was added to external things without changing anything in their nature. And then all of a sudden, there it was, clear as day: existence had suddenly unveiled itself. It had lost the harmless look of an abstract category: it was the very paste of things, this root was kneaded into existence. Or rather the root, the park gates, the bench, the sparse grass, all that had vanished: the diversity of things, their individuality, were only an appearance, a veneer. This veneer had melted, leaving soft, monstrous masses, all in disorder—naked, in a frightful, obscene nakedness.[3]

The haphazardness and impenetrability of the world around us is the mark of existence. Such degrees of haphazardness and opaqueness, in their stark inexhaustibility are well nigh unbearable.

> All these objects . . . how can I explain? They inconvenienced me; I would have liked them to exist less strongly, more dryly, in a more abstract way, with more reserve. The chestnut tree pressed itself against my eyes. Green rust covered it half-way up; the bark, black and swollen, looked like boiled leather. The sound of the water in the Masqueret Fountain sounded in my ears, made a nest there, filled them with signs; my nostrils overflowed with a green, putrid odour.[4]

The irreducible sensory data of experience are not only severed from a *res cogitans,* as they were with Descartes, they have achieved a position of primacy and dominance and reduce the rational to something secondary and shadowy.

Now when we consider the way in which the primary data of sensory experience are here presented we have no difficulty in identifying the phenomena. The two quotations are textbook examples of what Freud calls the *primary process.* Before the development of the ego—that is to say, before the child learns to master reality with the help of reason—thinking is dominated by the concrete-pictorial for which syntactic relations play as yet a feeble role. In the world of the primary process, the logical texture, the

---

[3] Sartre, J. P., *Nausea.* New Directions. New York, 1959.
[4] Ibid.

demands of reality and of order in time and causality either do not exist at all or are subordinated to the immediacy of imagery and affect. Images group themselves according to affective laws of condensation and displacement rather than logical coherence. One can reconstruct this early infantile thinking on the basis of psychoanalytic "archaeology." In the grown-up we encounter it only in dreams, in certain psychotic states—and through the ingenuity of poets and artists.

In the light of this, read the description which Sartre gives of a trolley-car trip.

> I lean my hand on the seat but pull it back hurriedly: it exists. This thing I'm sitting on, leaning my hand on, is called a seat. They made it purposely for people to sit on, they took leather, springs and cloth, they went to work with the idea of making a seat and when they finished, *that* was what they had made. They carried it here, into this car and the car is now rolling and jolting with its rattling windows, carrying this red thing in its bosom. I murmur: "It's a seat," a little like an exorcism. But the word stays on my lips: it refuses to go and put itself on the thing. It stays what it is, with its red plush, thousands of little red paws in the air, all still, little dead paws. This enormous belly turned upward, bleeding, inflated—bloated with all its dead paws, this belly floating in this car, in this grey sky, is not a seat. It could just as well be a dead donkey tossed about in the water, floating with the current, belly in the air in a great grey river, a river of floods; and I could be sitting on the donkey's belly, my feet dangling in the clear water. Things are divorced from their names. They are there, grotesque, headstrong, gigantic and it seems ridiculous to call them seats or say anything at all about them: I am in the midst of things, name-

less things. Alone, without words, defenceless, they surround me, are beneath me, behind me, above me. They demand nothing, they don't impose themselves: they are there. Under the cushion on the seat there is a thin line of shadow, a thin black line running along the seat, mysteriously and mischievously, almost a smile. I know very well that it isn't a smile and yet it exists, it runs under the whitish windows, under the jangle of glass, obstinately, obstinately behind the blue images which pass in a throng, like the inexact memory of a smile, like a half forgotten word of which you can only remember the first syllable and the best thing you can do is turn your eyes away and think about something else, about that man half-lying down on the seat opposite me, there. His blue-eyed, terra cotta face. The whole right side of his body has sunk, the right arm is stuck to the body, the right side barely lives, it lives with difficulty, with avarice, as if it were paralysed. But on the whole left side there is a little parasitic existence, which proliferates; a chancre: the arm begins to tremble and then is raised up and the hand at the end is stiff. Then the hand begins to tremble too and when it reaches the height of the skull, a finger stretches out and begins scratching the scalp with a nail. A sort of voluptuous grimace comes to inhabit the right side of the mouth and the left side stays dead. The windows rattle, the arm shakes, the nail scratches, scratches, the mouth smiles under the staring eyes and the man tolerates, hardly noticing it, this tiny existence which swells his right side, which has borrowed his right arm and right cheek to bring itself into being. The conductor blocks my path.

"Wait until the car stops."

But I push him aside and jump out of the trolley. I couldn't stand any more. I could no longer stand being so close. I push open a gate, go in, airy creatures are bounding and leaping and perching on the peaks. Now I recognize myself. I know where I am: I'm in the park. I drop onto a bench between great black tree-trunks, between the black, knotty hands reaching towards the sky. A tree scrapes at the earth under my feet with a black nail. I would so like to let myself go, forget myself, sleep. But I can't, I'm suffocating: existence penetrates me everywhere, through the eyes, the nose, the mouth . . . .

And suddenly, suddenly the veil is torn away, I have understood, I have *seen.*[5]

We can almost wander with the thinker from the world of the conceptualized (secondary process, Freud) to the world of the pre-conceptual (primary process). "I murmur: 'It's a seat,' a little like an exorcism. *But the word stays on my lips: it refuses to go and put itself on the thing.* It stays what it is, with its red plush, thousands of little red paws in the air, all still, little dead paws. This enormous belly turned upward, bleeding, inflated—bloated with all its dead paws, this belly floating in this car, in this grey sky, is not a seat. It could just as well be a dead donkey tossed about in the water . . ." Word and concept (*seat*) are considered, as though in order to release something which wriggles under the net of reality. And there is no better demonstration of the Freudian genetic theory of thinking: what emerges is purely pictorial, a product of condensation and displacement. There is nothing so new or startling about this legerdemain. As I said, it has been done by some of the best contemporary poets and painters. What makes it so original here is the purpose for which it is carried out: namely for the establishment of a philosophy. "The essen-

---

5 Ibid.

tial thing is contingency." "If you existed, you had to *exist all the way,* as far as mouldiness, bloatedness, obscenity were concerned. In another world, circles, bars of music keep their pure and rigid lines. But existence is a deflection."

We have mentioned that during psychotic experiences elements and qualities are observed which correspond to the primary process. Jaspers[6] in his studies on the irreducible phenomena in the mode of experience which can be observed in the beginning of a schizophrenic process gives a description of thinking which is very similar to, if not identical with, Freud's *primary process.* "The environment is different (*anders*), not at all in sensory perception (*grob sinnlich*)—as far as sense perceptions go there is no change. There occurs rather a subtle (*feine*) change which permeates everything with an uncertain, eerie light. . . . The patient has a feeling of unsteadiness (*Haltlosigkeit*) and insecurity which drives him instinctively to look for a fixed point which he could grasp to get a firm hold. This wholeness (*Ergänzung*), this strength and consolation he can find *only in an idea,*[7] just as the healthy person does under similar circumstances. In all situations of life in which we find ourselves oppressed, anxious and perplexed, the sudden consciousness of a clear insight regardless whether true or false, has a reassuring effect. . . ."

Roquentin's exclamation of insight ("And suddenly, suddenly, the veil is torn away. I have understood, I have *seen*") is an illustration of this. Without the liberating idea the preceding experience would mean nothing but a perpetual night of anguish.

---

[6] Jaspers, Karl, *Allgemeine Psychopathologie.* Springer, Berlin, 1923.
[7] Italics in the original.

It is only on the basis of Freud's description of the "primary process" that we understand the leitmotif of nausea in Sartre's story, indeed the reason why somatic sensations such as vertigo, malaise, anxiety are interwoven with the metaphysical adventures of Roquentin. For the world of the primary process, the universe in which stark imagery, not adulterated by conceptualization, is man's habitat—this is normally the world of early childhood. Psychoanalysis has shown that during that phase the child reacts to the immediate experience associated with nutrition and protection, emotionally and somatically, at all times, either with bliss and a sense of well-being, or with sadness and a sense of discomfort. The infant is still *open to the world* in the most literal, carnal sense of the word. The child's first relationship to another occurs through the mouth. The mother and the world *en large*, and the mother and food still form an ill-defined whole. Hunger and anger and joy and satiety and nausea and sadness make up the psychic elements of that which one takes in or rejects. This kind of acceptance or rejection is the only mode of relationship with an *other*.

To translate this into philosophical language, it is as if Roquentin told Descartes: there is no use trying to hold the *res extensa* at a distance. You are inextricably involved with matter (mother), and moreover it is a sticky, messy, oozing business which makes you vomit.

The fact in itself that the philosopher goes unknowingly into this primeval world cannot be used as an argument against him. On the contrary. In our world of abstraction it is only the phenomenology of irreducible data which leads to the bottom of things. Indeed, the very fact that our first encounter with matter is one of *tasting* it and *taking it in* could be used as a refutation of all dualistic philosophies. Pierre Albert-Birot makes Adam say: "I feel that the world enters into me like the fruits I eat, indeed I feed on the world."[8] This is beautifully expressed by Rilke:

> Voller Apfel, Birne und Banane,
> Stachelbeere . . . Alles dieses spricht
> Tod und Leben in den Mund . . . Ich ahne . . .
> Lest es einem Kind vom Angesicht,
>
> wenn es sie erschmeckt. Dies kommt von weit.
> Wird euch langsam namenlos im Munde?
> Wo sonst Worte waren, fliessen Funde,
> Aus dem Fruchtfleisch überrascht befreit.
>
> Wagt zu sagen, was ihr Apfel nennt.
> Diese Süsse, die sich erst verdichtet
> um, im Schmecken leise aufgerichtet,
>
> Klar zu werden, wach und transparent,
> doppeldeutig, sonnig, erdig, hiesig—
> O Erfahrung, Fühlung, Freude—, riesig!

> Full round apple, pear and banana,
> gooseberry . . . all this speaks
> death and life into the mouth . . . I sense . . .
> Read it from the face of a child
>
> tasting them. This comes from far. Is something
> indescribable slowly happening in your mouth?

8 Pierre Albert-Birot. *Mémoires d'Adam.* Quoted by G. Bachelard in "Poétique de la rêverie," P.U.F., Paris, 1960.

Where otherwise words were, flow discoveries,
freed all surprised out of the fruit's flesh.

Dare to say what you call apple. This
sweetness, first concentrating, that it may
in the tasting delicately raised,

grow clear, awake, transparent, double-meaning'd,
sunny, earthy, of the here and now—
O experience, sensing joy—, immense![9]

This poem, better than any philosophical treatise, shows how the primary sensory experience, such as taste,[10] taste perhaps even more because it is the mode of our primary encounter with the other, the *thou* and the world—leads directly to the *urgrund* of being. In other words, the fact that Roquentin-Sartre describes his reaction to the world in terms of a primary oral experience corresponds to a deep intuition. It is only the *content* which is clearly pathological. According to psychoanalysis the first relationship with the mother is always blissful, no matter what happens later. And Rilke's poem expresses that whenever we feed on nature we only extend the primary maternal relationship and we affirm, by an irreducible experience, the

---

[9] R. M. Rilke, *Sonnets to Orpheus,* I, 13. Translation by M. D. Herter Norton. W. W. Norton Co., N.Y. 1942.

[10] The "tastes" referred to in Rilke's poem are in reality smells. There are only four categories of taste, and myriads of smells. When we say of something that it tastes like an apple we are actually referring to smell. Although taste and smell are physiologically apart, phenomenologically they go usually together. It is noteworthy that in French *sentir,* to feel, means also "to smell"—another indication that the oral relationship belongs to the rockbottom layer of our contact with the world. This is also apparent in the symbolism of language. Expressions such as "sweet" or "disgusting" have a global significance, pertaining to relationships far removed from the primary world of taste.

ontological mystery which brackets man and matter. *Das kommt von weit,* this comes from far.

One might argue that Sartre's book is a mere exercise in fiction, were it not for the fact that in *Nausea* most of the elements are touched upon which reoccur in his other works, including the purely philosophical ones.

There occurs in *Nausea* a profusion of words connoting some kind of *urmaterie* of oral and tactile experience (viscous, sticky, oozing, swarming, wriggling, burgeoning, and so on), a kind of array of primeval qualities —which we find again like old acquaintances, more thinly scattered, in Sartre's philosophical work. In his essay on Baudelaire[11] he presents a variation on the themes of *Nausea.* In fact, if one did not know the subject one would think that the entire essay is a paraphrase on Roquentin-Sartre. "He has a deep intuition of that amorphous, stubborn contingence called Life—exactly the opposite of Work—and he is in horror of it because it reflects that gratuitousness of his own consciousness which he wants to cover up at any cost." Or: "If man is terrified at the bosom of Nature, it is because he feels trapped in a huge amorphous and gratuitous existence which penetrates him completely with its gratuitousness: he has no place anywhere, he is just put on earth, aimless, without any reason to be there, like a briarbush or a clump of grass." The last image gives us a clue to the Sartrian universe. As we go from the vegetable kingdom through the animal kingdom to Man we can say, *mutatis mutandis,* that the motherly becomes increasingly personalized. A plant needs only Nature as a collective, a constellation of climate, soil and ecological circumstances, to be "right," to do well. If we conjure the

11 Sartre, Jean-Paul, *Baudelaire,* Gallimard, Paris, 1947.

feminine maternal as a personal principle away from the world of Man he would indeed be *geworfen* (thrown) like a tuft of grass, in an existence of mere contingency.

Here the subjectivism that in Kierkegaard was held together by the central theme, Man's relationship to God, is literally driven to the point of absurdity. In Schopenhauer the *Idea* overcomes *Nature* as one would slay a dragon in an eschatological victory. In Sartre's world the *pour-soi* (a rough equivalent of the Idea) negates the *en-soi* (a rough equivalent of Nature) as one gets rid of a sticky mess. That harmony and order of the spheres which still inspired Descartes and Newton and Kant with a faith in God, has by now become a system of coercion.[12] In *The Flies,* a play which Sartre used as a philosophical mouthpiece, the God (Zeus) addresses the rebel (Orestes) by pointing out to him the harmony of the universe and the beauty of nature, and goes on exhorting him: " . . . Know your sin, abhor it, and tear it from you as one tears out a rotten, noisome tooth. Or else—beware lest the very seas shrink back at your approach, springs dry up when you pass by, stones and rocks roll from your path and the earth crumbles under your feet."

To this Orestes replies: "Let it crumble! Let the rocks revile me, and the flowers wilt at my coming. Your whole universe is not enough to prove me wrong. You are the king of gods, king of stones and stars, king of the waves of the sea. But you are not the king of man."[13]

This play contains, among other possible hidden meanings, a thinly disguised parable of Christianity. Zeus

---

[12] Compare footnote on page 124.

[13] Sartre, Jean-Paul, *The Flies,* translated by Stuart Gilbert, Hamish Hamilton, London, 1946.

has involved the entire City of Argos in which Agamemnon at one time was slain in an unceasing life of atonement. The chief function of this god is to make the entire population perpetually sin-conscious. When Zeus speaks of the death of Agamemnon, he remarks gleefully: "Yet what a profit I have made on it! For one dead man, twenty thousand living men wallowing in penitence. Yes, it was a good bargain I struck that day!" What we have seen earlier, namely that the estrangement from and abhorrence of nature makes for a dour, legalistic concept of religion, is also evident here. Zeus, a wily merchant of souls, engaged in some crafty tit-for-tat, is the Jansenist-Calvinist god against whom Orestes revolts. So would we all revolt if this were God. Love is banished from this theological warehouse. And so it is from the entire Sartrian universe.

Whenever the sexual occurs in the work of Sartre, it is either indifferently physiological or repulsive. There is not a single woman figure of beauty. The role of the woman (Electra) in *The Flies* is remarkable. First she appears as the rebel's (Orestes') helpmate and addresses God (Zeus) in no uncertain terms—simply calling him dirty names. But later she submits to him, and Orestes feels betrayed by her. The way the sexual invariably has the connotation of a visit-to-a-certain-house, together with the devaluation of the womanly, reminds one of that pubescent Manichaeism which pervades so much of the nineteenth century, all the way from Nietzsche to Lenin. It is interesting in this connection that the only scene in the entire work of Sartre which suggests love is the death of a man in the arms of his comrade.[14] The two friends are Marxists (one is a Com-

---

14 In a fragment, *"Drôle d'Amitié"* (*A Peculiar Friendship*).

munist Party member) who escape together from a prison camp but are betrayed. One, Vicarios, is shot by the German guards. As Brunet, the other, cries out in agony over his dying friend, his hand in the other's hair—there we come closest to a feeling of fusion of two beings.

The fundamental mode of all human relationship is conflict. In *L'Etre et le néant,* Sartre plots out the possible relationships between human beings in all commutations within the framework of a quaint Teutonic schema (being-for-itself, being-in-itself, being-for-others), and what finally emerges is a sophisticated form of who-eats-whom. That which is conscious, a person, is a being-for-itself. A non-conscious object constitutes a being-in-itself. In the latter there exists an intrinsic oneness between appearance and being. An object is all outwardness. Its existence is complete in itself. In contrast to this, the subject, being-for-itself, is all inwardness, and completes its existence only through the experience of another. It is only in being-for-others that I receive a nature. "I need from the other person an acknowledgement of my being." It is in the *gaze* of the other that I assume concreteness. This object-like solidity which complements my inwardness at the same time also impairs my freedom. I in turn, by my gaze upon the other, add objective solidity to *his* being. In this situation there exists the possibility that I submit, as it were, and make myself into the object in the eyes of the other. Or, by objectifying the other, I put a limitation on his being. In the first case we have a relationship of masochism, in the second of sadism. Summarized and stripped of its cumbersome nomenclature, the entire network of references boils down to a system of *ownership.* Love is not realizable. And although Sartre professes to start out from phenomenological premises (he studied the philosophy of Husserl and Heidegger in Germany) he excludes huge sectors from the world of the most fundamental experience, and in the end one has the uncanny sensation that all this is part Cartesian, part Hegelian thought, dressed up in the terminology of twentieth-century German philosophy. Although the facts may be disguised by form (novel or drama) or language (phenomenology), life in the end is reduced to a matter of mechanisms and dialectics. This explains Sartre's tie with Marxism, which seems on the face of things such a strange paradox.

We see then that the dualism of Descartes, despite that fateful crack through the middle, still implies some kind of order. The *res cogitans* is reason itself, the *res extensa* can be found to be following immutable laws. Thus phenomenologically the philosophy of Descartes presents an intrinsic harmony, which unites the two halves, by sheer complementariness as it were. In the philosophy of Schopenhauer the *res extensa,* the material world is irrational and evil but still the *res cogitans,* the idea is conceived as pure and potentially capable of attaining primacy over matter. In other words, although a perceptible downward movement occurred from the dualism of Descartes to that of Schopenhauer, there remains one consoling feature: even the material world of Schopenhauer, with all its features of the irrational and destructive, is a redeemable world, redeemable after a fashion.

It is only today, in the era of Sartre, that the estrangement from matter and the maternal has reached a point of no return. At first sight this seems paradoxical because in

Sartrian philosophy existence itself is equated with the archaic experience. In thousands of metaphors nature is indeed conceived as maternal, with a breast—but with a breast from which one turns in disgust. And while in the world of Saint Francis the very multiplicity of things—the myriads of stars, plants and beasts—evoke a sense of brotherhood and prove the infinite significance of every one of us, here multiplicity induces the narcissism of barrenness. What Sartre said about Baudelaire we may say about Sartre himself:

> [Nature] is something huge, lukewarm which penetrates everything. Of that warm dampness, of that abundance, he was in perfect horror. Prolific Nature, which produces one single model in millions of copies, was bound to hurt his love for the rare. He, too, could say: "I love everything which one can never see twice." By this he praises absolute sterility.

Nature used to inspire believers and poets with a sense of something beyond, of infinite goodness and wisdom. *Brüder, über'm Sternenzelt muss ein guter Vater wohnen* ("Brethren, above the dome of stars there must dwell a good father"), thus Schiller's words in the chorus of the Ninth Symphony. "The heavens show forth the glory of God: and the firmament declareth the work of His hands," sings the psalmist. Nature, which thus inspired the psalmist with the idea of the Heavens, is now symbolized by an oozing slime. And beyond it all there is nothing. Above the dome of stars, in the space of transcendence as it were, dwells nothingness. Thus we see that, phenomenologically, Man's faith in God depends mysteriously on that irreducible knowledge of oneness with a Nature which represents the parental. Indeed, the "subject-object" relationship as it varied in the philosophies of Descartes, Schopenhauer and Sartre can be elucidated, as we have seen, if one examines it in the light of a phenomenology of the maternal.

At the sound of it, the very combination "Descartes-Schopenhauer-Sartre" grates on our ears. And yet we see here, quite clearly, three stations on a downward slope. To me, for one, there even exists a hierarchic ladder. Descartes, though the father of Western rationalism, is still a half-brother of the *philosophia perennis.* With the two others in our series we get increasingly the sense not so much of truth but of mood. Schopenhauer as well as Sartre was superb in expressing the climate of a time. That sense of immutability, however, which is the trait of the classical gets gradually lost, and with Sartre, we have finally (if one may be permitted such judgement) reached a contradiction in terms—namely a philosophical fad. But the mood can already be perceived in Descartes. That philosopher's friend, Princess Elisabeth, quite rightly observed that the Cartesian world, that precision rigging cluttered up with *animaux-machines,* completely extraneous to man's soul, gives one a cold shiver. It is the *wire mother* on a vast scale. No wonder that today man finds himself hopeless and with a sense of nausea. There exists a road which leads from the stove at Ulm at which Descartes had his dream, to the chestnut tree under which Roquentin-Sartre had his vision. To the physician these are phases on a chart of sickness. To the Christian they are hints that the drama of the spirit in history today is mysteriously linked to the figure of Woman.

EIGHT

Hedda and Her Companions

Descartes' maternal deprivation was not the true origin of Cartesianism. Nor can Schopenhauer's mother entirely be blamed for the dualism in her son's philosophic system. To speculate as to what would have happened to René and to Arthur, had their childhood years been under the aegis of mother love, is idle—just as idle as the famous question about the relationship of the shape of Cleopatra's nose to the course of history.

Or is it? The fact that Johanna Schopenhauer entered into the genesis of her son's philosophy on the psychological plane may be accidental. But Mother Schopenhauer belongs *generically* to the century of her son's philosophy. In other words, motherlessness (as in the case of Descartes) and the denial of motherhood (in the case of Schopenhauer) may cease to be haphazard psychogenic factors and become features of a larger picture, if we look at philosophy as an expression of the countenance of history.

The period following the beginning of the scientific revolution is characterized by an ascendancy of woman in society, by significant changes in the structure of marriage and family, and by an enmity between the sexes quite unheard of in previous history.

To go into all this in detail would lead us away from our subject. For instance it has been claimed that after each of the two world wars women, at least in Western Civilization, have become increasingly masculinized in their activities and prerogatives.[1] It is also said that in the North American family, under the influence of urbanization and industrialization, power and authority are shifting towards the mother. These and similar statements need to be verified by sociologists, and do not belong within the framework of this study.

It is pertinent to our thesis to begin with a general consideration. The spirit or emancipation that characterizes the period since the scientific revolution is justified precisely because, as we have seen, a woman's occupation has so precious little to do with her womanliness. We all know that she may be housewife and mother and wholly deny her femininity, and she may be doctor and lawyer and be womanly. If things are right, her womanliness helps her to develop her creativeness in whatever work she has chosen. This is the reason why inequality of rights has never added a grain to the "total amount" of femininity in this world (if one could quantify such a thing). Whatever one's definition of "male" and "female" may be, nothing justifies an inequality of rights.

---

1 Zilboorg, G., *Male and Female,* loc. cit.

However, since the emancipation coincided with and was initiated by the scientific revolution, the idea of equality was tinged with a rationalist colour. As we have already remarked, equality was in danger of becoming sameness. George Sand's remark quoted above, namely that one should not overestimate the difference between the sexes just on account of anatomical differences, is clearly the product of Cartesian thinking. Whether the writer was conscious of this does not matter. In this case, human beings can be conceived as Meccano sets, with interchangeable parts. The physical, or better the somatic, is severed not only from the psychological but from the ontological. This also holds true of the work of Simone de Beauvoir, despite her elaborate effort to find an "existentialist" thesis. When she states that the "body is not enough" and "biology is not enough" to define woman as a woman she is, of course, right, but at the same time one gets the impression that she devaluates biology and isolates it from the psychological and social context.

When *equality* becomes *sameness,* an immanent principle of order is lost:

> Take but degree away, untune that string,
> And hark, what discord follows. Each thing meets
> In mere oppugnancy.[2]

Oppugnancy is a good word for it. The first thing that strikes us is that since the emancipation, the phallic woman ceases to be a mythical projection and becomes a figure in the everyday fabric of life. This is so remarkable a phenomenon that we must go into it in detail. The dread

[2] Shakespeare, *Troilus and Cressida.*

emanating from the deeply buried, archaic image of the threatening mother had until then been contained, as it were, by *Mythologisierung.* The witches and the sirens, the harpies and the gorgons, and Scylla and the Sphinx were bad enough. But they were not half as bad as Hedda Gabler, the General's daughter, who kept her set of pistols in perfect firing condition in that middle-class drawing room in which, up to that point, good old aunt Tesman had been embroidering slippers for her nephew. Unlike those mythic ladies, Hedda was "the real thing." A new era had begun. And if we use a lot of space in this chapter to analyze the character of Ibsen's heroine in *Hedda Gabler* it is only because she stands for all the other Heddas with whom the stage of life is teeming. Hedda is a *type,* and since her first appearance she has achieved classical validity. Ibsen, like all great pychologists, is a moralist. And although the dramatist refrains, out of artistic integrity from an explicit moral, to us, the spectators, the moral is implicit.

Only complementariness can make us self-less. The self can be lost only in an *other,* in something which is not-self. It is complementariness which mobilizes our generosity. Hence the phallic woman who denies otherness cannot love. All she can do is compete, and even this often only in an illusionary way. If the male partner is weaker, things don't work out *because* he is weaker. If he is stronger, they don't work out because he is stronger. He cannot win, neither can she. In the first case it is disdain which prevents her from loving, in the second case it is envy.

When perverse rebellious love
Masters the feminine heart, then destroyed is the union
Of mated lives for beast or man.[3]

She cannot be helpmate. After having read a lot of feminist literature, I hasten to add that the word "helpmate" has no connotation of slavishness. It is not meant to be androcentric. It is a beautiful expression, and it pertains equally to man and woman. For just as woman for her greatest creative act needs to conceive from the male, man, for his creative activity, is in need of a mysterious "conception" from the female. "Mysterious" because the process is not cellular. Otherwise the parallel is correct. The function is similarly catalytic. One is surprised to learn how fleeting the encounter of Dante with Beatrice was, but it seems that for that "fathering" of the man's child by woman the mere *presence* is enough, a catalytic presence with no quantitative specification. She has to be around somehow for something to happen: the ancients were right with their idea of the Muse.[4]

This strangely inverted form of conception one can, it seems, trace in the case of every creative act, if one is lucky. I do not know how far one may carry the analogy. But that generosity which we call paternity, of giving oneself to that which the mate has brought forth, of accepting it as one's own although one has been so little involved in the creative process of caring for it—that same generosity is manifested by a normal woman towards her husband's work. Therefore the word "helpmate" has neither a derogatory

---

[3] Aeschylus, *Oresteia.* Tr. by R. C. Trevelyan. University Press, 1922.

[4] Cf. Etienne Gilson, *Choir of Muses.* Tr. by Maisie Ward. Sheed & Ward, N.Y., 1953.

nor an androcentric meaning. The father is "inspirer" and helpmate to motherhood as the woman is "inspirer" and helpmate to male forms of creativeness.

Now the woman who does not accept her womanliness rejects this role. When Hedda burns Lövborg's manuscript she says: "Now I'm burning your child, Thea. You with your curly hair . . . Your child and Ejlert Lövborg's . . . I'm burning it, burning your child." This illustrates what I have just been saying. It is Lövborg who has given birth, and Thea Elvsted, Hedda's rival, has fostered his creature. To anyone who studies Ibsen's play carefully, Hedda's rivalry with Thea is only an accidental feature. She is not so much a rival to another woman as a rival to Lövborg himself. Hedda Gabler would have had to kill Lövborg's "child" in some way or other. At one time, long before the play begins, she made an attempt to be Lövborg's Muse, but she has been unable to give herself to him as a woman, either in this way or sexually. From clinical experience with similar situations, I would say: because he was too strong. To her this kind of "giving" would have meant her annihilation. In order to understand the situation better, let us recount the story. As we have seen, at a time before the action of the play Hedda Gabler had entertained a friendship with a gifted and rather "wild" writer, Ejlert Lövborg. His wildness had proved too much for her, and she had broken off in order to marry, on the rebound, Jörgen Tesman. Tesman is bourgeois and conventional, a crashing bore. He is a scholar "engaged in research in the history of civilization," and in his career in competition with Lövborg. Hedda is not only bored by her husband but irritated by his mannerisms ("Eh?"), his conventionality, the bourgeois coziness with the good aunt and the faithful servant. Tesman is striving for a professional appointment (for which Lövborg seems better qualified), and to please Hedda, he has committed himself to living conditions beyond his means. As the play opens, the two, Tesman and Hedda, are coming back from a six months' honeymoon. Mrs. Elvsted, an old school friend of Hedda's, arrives. She is more womanly than Hedda, the victim of a broken marriage, and she reveals that Lövborg has "reformed," that she has done everything to help him, and in fact it is due to her that Lövborg's manuscript has been completed. Judge Brack then enters the picture, an aggressive man with more of Hedda's own elevated social background. Suspecting the state of her marriage, Brack makes a bid for her, or at least hints that he is ready to be the third partner in a triangle, just in case. In the evening Tesman and Brack go out to a stag party. Lövborg, true to his status as a "reformed" character, stays behind with the ladies but Hedda taunts him for this, and he finally goes to join the men. It turns out to be a wild party in the course of which Lövborg loses his manuscript. Actually, Tesman finds it and unknown to Lövborg brings it home. Lövborg goes straight from the party to Diana, a lady of doubtful reputation, and there, after he discovers his loss and complains of having been robbed, he gets involved in a drunken brawl. On coming back Lövborg tells Hedda that he has "killed" his and Mrs. Elvsted's "child," not realizing that the manuscript is actually safe in the Tesmans' house. Unknown to anybody Hedda burns the manuscript in the fireplace, and hands Lövborg one of her pistols. Shortly after, news arrives that Lövborg has once more gone to

Diana, and in some way (it is not quite clear whether accidentally or with suicidal intent) been shot with Hedda's pistol. The play ends as Hedda shoots herself.

Thus outlined the plot may tell us very little, but when one experiences the drama in its entirety, either on the stage or by reading, one can only marvel at the intuitiveness of genius. Ibsen's biographers claim that he had never encountered a woman like Hedda Gabler, and that only a few of the externals of the story were suggested by real events. Of course he had never encountered anyone like Hedda, just as Shakespeare has probably never met multiple murderers like Macbeth or Richard III. But he knew her with the fullness and immediacy of poetic insight. For anyone engaged in psychiatry this is a composite picture of all the Hedda Gablers of clinical experience. Nothing is missing.

To understand the genesis of such a character, a few words about the psychoanalytic theory of female sexuality. Here we must limit ourselves to certain aspects. According to Freud, the evolution by which the girl reaches femininity is more involved and tortuous than that by which the boy reaches manhood. That deep bond of union with the mother in infancy is the same for boys and girls. After certain primeval nongenital forms of libidinal gratification the child, about one third along the road between birth and puberty (around the age of four), for the first time experiences genital desires and gratifications. Generally this phase passes long before puberty, but the fact that Man, of all animals, undergoes two puberties, as it were, an abortive one in childhood and a "real" one (i.e., associated with development of gonadal function) is of far-reaching psychological significance. It is during that infantile "abortive puberty" that the Oedipus conflict occurs: the child feels a strong attraction to the parent of the opposite sex and a sense of rivalry for the parent of the same sex. It can easily be seen that then the little boy's tie to the mother is different from that early infantile maternal identification of which we spoke. It can also easily be seen that the way in which the Oedipus conflict is solved must be decisive for the individual's later destiny. The child's Oedipus drama is an archaic rehearsal, as it were, for his relationships later, particularly in love and in marriage. Under normal circumstances the tie to the parent of the opposite sex is solved during the process of "secondary identification." The child begins to admire or, at least, model himself after the parent of his own sex. The boy patterns himself after a paternal figure in his environment, the girl after a maternal figure—usually the actual father or mother. It is only in this way that the boy can accept his male role (or the girl her female role) with the advent of puberty. This means that in the human species we see a psychic development of maleness or of femininity *before* the development of physiological sexual function. Evidently, numerous things may go wrong with all this. There are many reasons for which the girl may never enter into a healthy maternal identification. We do not need to go into all this here. Suffice it to say that in such case the woman will never live her womanliness to the full. To her, femininity means merely a *minus,* a deprivation, the fact that one is not a man. What actually happened to Hedda to force her into this development we do not know, and for the understanding of her character it is not necessary.[5] In the original manuscript there exists a mysterious passage in which Hedda remarks that her father was already an old man when she was born. Ibsen deleted this remark, and at any rate it is hard to guess what it means in terms of the "dynamics of the case." To conjure up all the possibilities makes an intriguing game. Was the old general so overjoyed at the arrival of a latecomer (an only child?) that he fostered all the boyish qualities in her? Was his wife much younger and did he keep her (the wife) as a precious child, a pet in the home, as Helmer kept Nora? For more than one reason it has occurred to me that *Hedda Gabler* and *The Doll's House* are complementary plays. Whatever it may be—as a case of paternal identification, of spurious masculinity, as the general's daughter with her target practice—Hedda runs true to form, and any psychiatrist would recognize her the moment she appears on the stage, just as a pediatrician knows a child with measles when he sees one.

The closest Hedda has ever come to love was in that relationship with Lövborg which precedes the action of the play. It is quite obvious that all she had been able to do with this highly gifted fellow, so fascinating to her, was an attempt at ownership, at taking him away so that no other woman would get at him. She had played at picking him up, as it were, but without that commitment of wom-

---

[5] There exists at least one psychoanalytic paper on "Hedda Gabler." *J. O. Wisdom, The Lust for Power in "Hedda Gabler," Psychoan. Rev. 31, 419, 1944.* Here the author reconstructs matters referring directly to the "primary process," and the procedure in the case of a fictitious person is highly speculative.

anly love—because alas, there, lurked the dread of mutilation.

LÖVBORG. It was you who broke it off.

HEDDA. Yes, when there was imminent danger of our relationship becoming serious. You ought to be ashamed of yourself, Ejlert Lövborg. How could you take advantage of—your unsuspecting comrade!

LÖVBORG (*clenching his hands*). Oh, why didn't you make a job of it! Why didn't you shoot me down when you threatened to!

HEDDA. Yes . . . I'm as terrified of scandal as all that.

LÖVBORG. Yes, Hedda; you are a coward at bottom.

HEDDA. An awful coward. (*Changing her tone.*) But it was lucky enough for you. And now you have consoled yourself so delightfully up at the Elvsteds'.

LÖVBORG. I know what Thea has told you.

HEDDA. And you have told her something about us two?

LÖVBORG. Not a word. She's too stupid to understand a thing like that.

HEDDA. Stupid?

LÖVBORG. She is stupid about that sort of thing.

HEDDA. And I'm a coward. (*She leans nearer to him, without meeting his eyes, and says more softly.*) But now *I* will confess something to *you*.

LÖVBORG (*eagerly*). Well?

HEDDA. That, my not daring to shoot you down—

LÖVBORG. Yes?

HEDDA. That wasn't my worst piece of cowardice . . . that night.

LÖVBORG (*looks at her a moment, understands and whispers passionately*). Ah, Hedda! Hedda Gabler! Now I see a glimpse of the hidden foundation of our comradeship. You and I! Then it *was* your passion for life—

HEDDA (*quietly, with a sharp, angry glance*). Take care! Don't assume anything like that.[6]

Behind her commanding appearance and the shooting practice lies a hidden fear. It is the terror of annihilation—for to women like her self-abandonment means death. Yet when others (Mrs. Elvsted as helpmate and Diana as erotic companion) succeed in that which she only spuriously attempted—Hedda cannot endure it. It is a case of dog-in-the-manger. She burns their "child." This burning of a manuscript, the man's creation, is no poetic invention. I have seen this same thing, literally, done by a woman patient who found herself in a similar conflict.

Though it may not have been consciously planned by the poet, the other women in the play, Mrs. Elvsted and Aunt Julle, appear quite feminine. This has to be, and even if it were only by comparison. It is always like this in life. Now towards women like these Hedda can have only a feeling of contempt and condescension, mixed with secret envy of which she is not aware. In her relationship with Mrs. Elvsted there is also a faint undertone of homosexuality so characteristic of the entire constellation.

Women like Hedda seem not to be created for the polarity of love. They waver between either pole. They are often attracted to sensitive men such as Lövborg. Most of George Sand's lovers were Ejlert Lövborgs. The artist's soul is a lock to which this woman wants to be key—and to be key, not lock, is the leading phantasy of her life. But whether she plays at key or at lock, she can never fit because she lacks complementariness. The only form of

---

6 Ibsen, H., *Three Plays*. Penguin, 1950.

union of which her feelings are capable is not the union of love but the union of "power over," of ownership.

This is the outcome of a mysterious inner logic. In an archaic childhood phantasy, the union of love means weakening and destruction. Hence she can think of the encounter of two souls only in terms of power and of defence. Note how the word "power" turns up at the most crucial points of the play. Read, from this point of view, the dialogue between Lövborg and Hedda, quoted above. Or the following:

LÖVBORG. Yes, Hedda; and when I used to confess to you! Told you things about myself that no one else knew in those days. Sat there and owned up to going about whole days and nights blind drunk. Days and nights on end. Oh, Hedda, what sort of power in you was it—that forced me to confess things like that?

HEDDA. Do you think it was some power in me?

The element of taking the man away in order to have him for oneself with the air of exclusive possessiveness, with an unconscious desire to weaken him, and with an ambivalence which precludes true love—all this is obvious in the love life of George Sand, although George Sand was much more feminine than Ibsen's heroine. This comes out, for instance, in the relationship with Pagello, with Alfred de Musset and with Chopin.[7] One cannot help feeling trepidation for these poor fellows whenever she whisks one of them away from their familiar and protective environment into isolation, preferably an unhealthy place. The entire Majorca episode with Chopin

7 Maurois, André. *Lélia,* Harper, 1953.

where, under the most appalling conditions, his tuberculosis worsened instead of getting better, gives one a haunting sensation. It was not only a wish for possession but an unconscious desire to destroy. And it was not so unconscious either. There seems to occur a glimmer of retrospective insight, ever so faint and flickering, in a letter which George Sand wrote to Grzymala (May 12th, 1847):[8]

> For seven years now I have lived the life of a virgin, both with him and with others. I have grown old before my time, and it has cost me neither effort nor sacrifice, so weary had I become of passions, so disillusioned and beyond all remedy. If any woman in the world could inspire him with absolute confidence it was I, and yet he has never understood . . . *I know that many people blame me, some of having exhausted him as a result of my sensual exigencies, some of having driven him to despair by my indiscretions. But you, I do believe, have understanding. He complains that I have killed something in him by deprivation: but I know that I should have killed him altogether had I acted differently* . . .

De Musset and Chopin were men of rich endowment, indeed of true genius, and obviously much more creative than Sand. But they were delicate and vulnerable and exceedingly sensitive, and they lacked maleness—that is to say, in the popular sense of the word. So probably did the fictitious Lövborg. The man of sheer maleness in the popular, biological sense may be accepted as a marital partner by the phallic woman, under circumstances which we shall discuss presently. But he, too, may be experienced as a threat. There are hints in the play that Hedda was, when she married, not only on the rebound from Lövborg

---

[8] Italics are mine.

but trying to avoid an involvement with Brack. And she marries Tesman because there is no emotional risk, and because she looks at him as a provider for her extravagant tastes.

HEDDA (*looking straight in front of her*). And I don't know why I should be—happy. Perhaps you can tell me, can you?

BRACK. Well, among other things, because you've got the very home you wished for.

HEDDA (*looking up at him and laughing*). Do you believe that fantasy too?

BRACK. Isn't there something in it, though?

HEDDA. Oh yes . . . *Some*thing.

BRACK. Very well?

HEDDA. There's this much in it. Last summer I used Jörgen Tesman to see me home from evening parties.

BRACK. Unfortunately I was going quite another way.

HEDDA. True enough. You certainly were going another way last summer.

BRACK (*laughing*). You ought to be ashamed of yourself, Madam Hedda! Well, but you and Tesman, then?

HEDDA. Why, we came past here one evening. And he, poor creature, was tying himself in knots because he didn't know how to find anything to talk about. And so I felt sorry for the poor, learned man.

BRACK (*smiling doubtfully*). You did, did you? H'm.

HEDDA. Yes. I really did. And so, to help him out of his misery, I just said—quite casually—that I should like to live here, in this villa.

BRACK. No more than that?

HEDDA. Not that evening.

BRACK. But . . . afterwards?

HEDDA. Yes; my thoughtlessness had its consequences, my dear sir.

BRACK. Unfortunately, our thoughtlessness all too often has, Madam Hedda.

HEDDA. Thank you. But, you see, it was through this passion for the villa of the late Mrs. Falk that Jörgen Tesman and I found our way to an understanding. *That* led to our engagement and wedding trip and everything. Well, well. As one makes one's bed one must lie on it, I was just going to say.

For the understanding of a great number of neurotic marriages in our day it is important to realize that the material over-demand on the bread-winner is an unconscious device in a neurotic struggle for ascendancy. It stands for the phallic desire, as it were. One of the most uncanny passages in Ibsen's play is the one in which Tesman dares for the first time to resist Hedda's unrealistic wishes (a man-servant, a saddle-horse), and her immediate reaction is to fall back on that great pastime, the gun—that supreme masculine symbol and the symbol of her father's profession.

HEDDA. Naturally, now I shan't get a man-servant just at first.

TESMAN. No, I'm afraid you can't. There can be no question of keeping a man-servant, you know.

HEDDA. And the saddle-horse that I was going to—

TESMAN (*horrified*). Saddle-horse!

HEDDA. I suppose it's no use even thinking of that now.

TESMAN. Good heavens, no! That goes without saying.

HEDDA (*crossing the room towards the back*). Well, anyhow, I still have one thing to kill time with.

TESMAN (*beaming with pleasure*). Thank heaven for that! But what is it, Hedda? Eh?

HEDDA (*at the centre doorway, looking at him with lurking contempt*). My pistols, Jörgen.

TESMAN (*anxiously*). Your pistols!

HEDDA (*with cold eyes*). General Gabler's pistols. (*She goes through the inner room and out to the left.*)

TESMAN (*running to the centre doorway and calling after her*). For goodness' sake! Hedda, darling! Don't touch those dangerous things! For my sake, Hedda! Eh?

In general the reader (or viewer) will do well to watch for the role of the gun throughout the play. It is one way to understand the meaning of the story. Equally significant as the scene just quoted is the fact that the only time we watch her at shooting practice is in the beginning of the second act when Brack appears and she nearly manages to shoot him accidentally.

BRACK (*calling from below*). No, no, no! Don't stand there aiming straight at me.

HEDDA. That comes of using the back way in. (*She shoots.*)

BRACK (*nearer*). Are you quite crazy?

HEDDA. Dear me! I didn't hit you, did I?

And then later, of course, the role of Hedda's gun in Lövborg's and her own death. All this was, like in all great works of fiction and drama, done without the least knowledge of psychological theories. In fact, the play was finished four years before Freud published his first psychoanalytic paper.

Instead of *Hedda Gabler* we could have chosen a case history. However, as we have seen, the poet succeeds in bringing things out in focus, much better than one ever could do on the basis of clinical "material." The most obvious objection is that there must have been similar women at all times, and that, on the other hand, at Ibsen's time there must have existed thousands of normal homes.

Why single the pathological out as a *type?* First of all, we wanted to direct our interest only at the problem confronting Western society. If there have been societies of amazons in ancient civilizations, it would not help the purpose of our study to go into the matter. With regard to the second objection one must realize that the dramatist of social conflicts like Ibsen is never interested in the pathological as such. He does not want to describe oddities for their own sake. Here the freak occurrence points up something typical in the social fabric. The phallic woman in *The Taming of the Shrew* presented, in the huge Shakespearean universe, a little sideshow. She was good for a laugh. By the end of the nineteenth century, the thing had become deadly serious. At the beginning of the seventeenth century (1617) the first mention is made of the "woman of masculine gender."[9] King James was scandalized at the "insolencie of our women, and their wearing of brode brimed hats, pointed dublets, their hayre cut short or shorne, or some of them stilettoes or poniards, and such trinckets of like moment." The clergy was summoned by the Bishop of London and commanded to inveigh against all this from the pulpits.

Shortly afterwards, a delightful book was published on "Hic-Mulier" (the he-woman), "being a medicine to cure the coltish Disease of the Staggers in the Masculine-Feminines of our Times. Exprest in Brief Declamation. Non possumus omnes." The author berates "Hic-Mulier" for wearing manly attire, among other things "a *Leaden-Hall* dagger, a High-Way Pistoll" and for "a mind and

---

9 Camden, Carroll. *The Elizabethan Woman.* A Panorama of English Womanhood, 1540 to 1640. Cleaver Humphreys Press, London, 1954.

behaviour sutable or exceeding every repeated deformitie."[10] The He-Woman replies by pointing out the law of change in nature, meaning that "Male" and "Female" are relative concepts which are bound to change through the ages. Here the argument of Simone de Beauvoir and some of our contemporary anthropologists is naively anticipated, and Camden is probably right in observing that this is the earliest instance of the argument of social evolution applied to the role of the sexes. At any rate, the "High-Way Pistoll" which began harmlessly enough as a fancy "trincket" at the time of King James went off with a bang in the middle-class drawing rooms of the *fin du siècle.* It had taken just over two hundred years.

When we consider a woman such as Hedda Gabler, or the numerous women of whom she is the prototype, we must add a few observations. The first thing we remark is that what comes out in her is no true maleness. A Madame Curie may develop what one commonly considers as male gifts, i.e. talents in the field of the analytical-scientific; and preserve the womanly core of her nature. Women in holy orders, such as Saint Teresa of Avila or Mother Cabrini, have often displayed a physical tenacity, a fighting spirit, a sense of practical affairs worthy of a male "executive type" —and yet that certain sense of the womanly is invariably there, in between the lines as it were. Under pioneer conditions women clear forests, dig wells and build houses—and their femininity persists underneath it like a permanent foundation. Saint Catherine of Siena exhorted, prophetically, the Pope; Saint Joan of Arc rode at the head of

10 loc. cit.

an army. I, for one, in reading their life histories never lose the sense of womanliness. I never have the experience of *perversion* which we get from Ibsen's heroine.

The second observation is the obvious one, of everyday commonsense psychology, that the phallic woman needs, as her counterpart, a passive and weak man. For every Hedda Gabler there is one Jörgen Tesman. He needs her as she is, pistols and all. We hasten to add that the same holds true for Jörgen's passivity as for Hedda's aggressiveness. A man may be doing things which are commonly associated with the feminine, and his "maleness" is not the worse for it. He may devote his life to the care of the chronically sick or the aged, in a situation which demands tenderness and patience—yet he is not emasculated. I am always moved when I learn, in reading about the life of Charles de Foucauld, how he came to perform menial tasks in a household of religious women. It would never occur to me, nor to any unbiased reader, that he, the one-time dashing officer of the French Army, the man-about-town, had changed into a sissy. Jörgen Tesman, whose activity (as "research scholar") is in itself not "effeminate," lacks maleness to the same degree to which Hedda lacks femininity. The two have found a perverse meeting ground.

Neither Hedda nor Jörgen (and none of the men and women for whom their marriage is the prototype) follow their *calling*. In order to do this as a man or woman one must implicitly (not necessarily on the basis of a formulated religious belief) acknowledge someone or something that *calls*. Vocation is derived from *vox*. The idea of equality, not the equality of justice but the equality of levelling, is incompatible with the idea of vocation. Marital union and the family serve the function of a task which transcends each single individual. Once this sense is lost—as it is increasingly in an age in which social unions can be conceived as arbitrary—the idea of vocation is lost. We are no longer called to exploit our gifts to the full, as the Apostle exhorts us; instead of becoming personalities we remain individuals, and instead of growing we regress.

The concept of *call* applies also to human love. In contemplating the scene on the Ponte Vecchio we know that Dante, in his encounter with Beatrice, is being *called.* There is no such call from Hedda to Jörgen or vice versa. Speaking of Dante and Beatrice, this is no poetic idealization. I believe that in a social organism imbedded in and growing out of a tradition in which the primacy of the spirit is silently accepted, these features are typical. In the humblest family, let us say of peasant stock, in which marriage seems to be based merely on the purpose of procreation, with all the appearances of the crude and primitive, the sense of polarity and the sense of calling may be present. It may be hidden and deprived of self-consciousness, as metaphysical movements often are when the structures of tradition are full grown, old and abundant—but it is there just the same.

I have already mentioned the fact that a poet who is interested in the drama of social conflict, as Ibsen was, would never present the marriages of Hedda or Nora as items in a collection of curiosities. We know, of course, that in Ibsen's time, just as in ours, there existed thousands of wholesome families. However, in the study of an epidemic it would be useless to give the description of the healthy part of the population (which is usually the majority). Leslie Fiedler, in a study of the American novel[11] has drawn attention to the fact that in American literature of the nineteenth and twentieth centuries a confusion of the sexual roles can be observed. Male passivity and female aggressiveness are not always as blatant as in our examples, but the hidden element of homosexuality, emerging in Fiedler's work in thousands of varied disguises, is the most remarkable feature. The author traces this back to historical and sociological roots, and for details we must refer the reader to the original. Whatever the validity of Mr. Fiedler's argument may be, he is wrong in limiting his statement to America. A similar study would, no doubt, demonstrate similar features in Northern Europe, particularly Scandinavia, but also in English, Irish, and (in certain aspects) German literature—apparently much less in the literature of Latin countries. Why this should be so, it is again for sociologists to determine. If we may hazard a guess, it is quite possible that Calvinism, Jansenism (the Irish variety) and the fact that the non-Mediterranean countries were earlier industrialized, may have something to do with it.

Freud made the well-known statement that "generally speaking Man oscillates throughout life between heterosexual and homosexual feelings,[12] and failure and disappointment on one side tend to push him over to the other." It is quite conceivable that such oscillations occur not only in the individual in one lifetime but in society

[11] Fiedler, Leslie A. *Love and Death in the American Novel.* Criterion Books, New York, 1960.

[12] He obviously did not mean to imply with this word (*Gefühle*) only *conscious* sexual impulses but, in a much broader sense, all those attitudes and allegiances which enter into human relationships.

throughout history. And it is, furthermore, conceivable that the sociological explanation is not the whole answer—that we enter here into unknown realms of metaphysics of history, precisely the thing we set out, very tentatively, to do in the present study.

To come back to the subject, there were further signs of the uncertainty in the role of the sexes and of regression. In the encounter of Beatrice there is an element of *reverence.* We hesitate to use this word because it often has a mawkish connotation. But it is difficult to find another expression for a tender experience of awe, for that immediate sense of recognition with which one beholds in the *other* one's destiny. In the encounter with the *threat* in woman, however, the feeling of reverence is replaced by fascination. And with the passive, un-manned man this fascination is just as imperious as love would be. This is why Jörgen Tesman seeks his own perdition in Hedda.

There is a beautiful novella by Turgeniev, *The Torrents of Spring,*[13] in which the hero Sanin (the story is known to contain autobiographical elements) sees his love for a young girl destroyed by an aggressive masterly married woman who has made a bid for him. Certain details are important. Sanin finds himself, on transit between Italy and Russia, in Frankfurt for a day. He enters a small Italian confectioner's store to have a glass of lemonade. There a beautiful young girl of nineteen rushes out from the back of the store, with all the signs of acute distress and bewilderment, and implores him to help her; her younger brother, a boy of fourteen, has just lost consciousness in a way she fears is fatal. Sanin goes ahead with rescue opera-

[13] *The Torrents of Spring,* translated by David Magarshack, Farrar, Straus, 1959.

tions and succeeds in reviving the boy who evidently had had a deep fainting spell. A tender and moving love story ensues which leads to Sanin's engagement to Gemma, the young girl. But after the engagement Sanin unexpectedly meets an old friend and makes the acquaintance of his wife. This woman is the classical *femme dominatrice et possessive* of clinical experience, and she immediately sets to work as though on a premeditated strategy. Finally, as the climax of a wild ride on horseback, in the middle of the forest, Sanin succumbs. And this is the end of his relationship with Gemma.

Here, in the initial encounter with the young Italian girl, we have the Beatrice experience pure and simple—that sense of recognition, as though with some mysterious foreknowledge which is characteristic of all love. It also contains a movement which one might best describe as *immediate assent.* But this is superseded, as it were, by that other experience. In the end the man succumbs to *fascination.* He allows himself to be the subject of a conquest. The only difference between this and the conquest in love is that this kind of conquest is always experienced as destruction, as being *sucked into* something perilous. This is typical of the Lorelei phantasy which plays such a great role in nineteenth century romanticism. Just as Beatrice is associated with an eternal upward movement, here a chasm gapes open, which draws one irresistibly down. And just as Beatrice is the woman of Dante's destiny—here, in Gemma's rival, we encounter *la femme fatale.*[14]

[14] The reader who is interested in details about the literary image of the *femme fatale* in the romantic movement, is referred to that brilliant study, *The Romantic Agony,* by Mario Praz. Oxford University Press, 1951.

Turgeniev himself, incidentally, was the child of an extraordinary marriage. His mother, who is generally described as a shrew, was older than his father. It is assumed that the latter married her for money's sake. She ruled dictatorially over children and serfs. When Turgeniev became infatuated with the famous singer Madame Viardot, his mother cut him off from all support, moral and financial. Madame Viardot, who was herself a married woman, never requited his love and merely tolerated his presence. Yet he was never able to extricate himself from that situation. The experience of Sanin with Gemma in Frankfurt is almost literally autobiographical. (In real life the young girl was a Jewess). But the fascination with the aggressive woman proved too strong. Here, as in previous instances, the autobiographical, the poet's own agony, is nothing but the crystallization point for something of more universal significance: the nineteenth century Beatrice was blotted out by the centaur-woman.

The Torrents of Spring, like any work of art, is full of unintended symbolisms. I suppose one could write a study of it alone. I cannot refrain from quoting two passages, before leaving the subject, two passages which highlight the contrast. First, the encounter with Gemma, which has that Beatrician touch. (In fact Dante is mentioned a few times, during the conversations with the Italian family.) There is that element of the *eternalized moment:* "He could now see her delicate, pure profile and it seemed to him that he had never seen anything like it and—had never experienced anything like he was feeling at that moment. His soul was ablaze."

Thus for Gemma. And now the final scene with Maria Nikolayevna:

> The same day, two hours later, Sanin was standing in his room before her like one beside himself and utterly ruined. "Where are you going, darling?" she asked him. "To Paris or to Frankfurt?"
>
> "I'm going where you will be," he replied in despair, "and I'll be with you until you drive me away," and he pressed his lips to the hands of his mistress. She freed them and laid them on his head. Grasping his hair with all her ten fingers, she slowly fingered and twisted his unresisting hair, drew herself up to her full height, her lips curled with triumph and her eyes, wide and bright, almost white, merely expressed the ruthless insensitivity and the satiety of conquest. A hawk, holding a captured bird in his claws, has eyes like that.

The nineteenth century is characterized by a fascination with the shadow of life, the unformed, pre-rational chthonic forces, the primeval humus, hidden from consciousness, in which life begins—all that which Freud was to call "the primary process." For what else is the meaning of decadence, the world of the Baudelaires and the Swinburnes, but the lure of the archaic-instinctual?

> Je suis la plaie et le couteau!
> Je suis le soufflet et la joue!
> Je suis les membres et la roue,
> Et la victime et le bourreau!

Of course, on the substratum of an unredeemed world of blind instinctual groping, all human relationships are those of wound and knife. In that world we are wound and knife at the same time. But to uncover this with an air of symbolic oneness, with the sense of lure—this is the same perilous fascination which makes Sanin leave Beatrice and follow the centaur-woman.

The decadent poet pretends that this plane of the primeval, of "destroy-and-be-destroyed," is man's natural habitat. Freud has pointed out that the sense of the weird, of the *unheimliche,* is derived from *heimlich.* A thing, he says, is *uncanny* precisely because deep down, on the level of subterranean currents, we *know* it. The *uncanny* is the *canny.* The syllable of negation masks frightened acknowledgement. The sado-masochistic polarity is to the poet of the era and the movement of which we speak *heimlich.* But this is *home* only in a most perverted sense of the word, namely the sense in which the caterpillar is the "home" of the butterfly, namely of all that which we ought to have overcome.

However, before we go further into all this, we have to make one more observation. It concerns the *masculinization of feminine libido,* at least in the eyes of the male beholder. When Sanin sees Maria Nikolayevna's lips "curled with triumph" and her eyes expressing "ruthless insensitivity and the satiety of conquest," like those of a "hawk, holding a captured bird in his hands," we are made witnesses of a strange inversion. This could be, but for the switch of roles, the story of one of those poor girl victims of male sexual voraciousness. In fact the "insensitivity" of the conqueror for conquest's sake is one of the pet grievances of all feminists. What makes Turgenev's story remarkable is the reversal of roles and the fact that the man who had encountered his Beatrice is now made to say, like the seduced maiden under the phallic spell: "I'm going where you will be and I will be with you until you drive me away."

The point we want to make is that Maria Nikolayevna and all her successors in a cavalcade from Strindberg to Tennessee Williams are *male projections.* Sanin, the hero of our novel, *wants* his woman like that. This is why he foregoes Gemma. He wants her rapaciously desirous, seeking an object of conquest in him, the hypnotized victim. But this is not the entire story. For very often woman, in this kind of libidinous craving, is frustrated or humiliated. This is the fate, all the way from Miss Julie and her butler to those aging lonely women of Tennessee Williams, who end up mortified and disgraced by lover or gigolo. It is, in the case of the phallic woman, not only a question of male projection. There is also the element of subtle revenge. It is as though, after centuries of Manichaeism, man turned around and made woman experience what it feels like to be frustrated.

Whether such literature is ephemeral or not; whether some of it is contrived for "morbid interest"; whether its author (as in the case of Strindberg) is sick; whether it will stand the test of aesthetic value—all this is irrelevant here. The fact of its popular appeal is significant. The very fact that around the time of Strindberg psychiatry began to leave the confines of the asylum and enter into the area of marriage and family is symptomatic. To understand a Miss Julie, men like Freud appeared on the scene. It is irrelevant that some of the poets of decadence were sick. The genius, sick or not, is moved to creativeness by the things which are "in the air."

Now while the elements of conquest and passivity are

present in all love relationships, the sado-masochistic comes out in the raw. This is perhaps the most characteristic feature of the situations we are talking about. Man and woman are interlocked in a mortal struggle for ascendancy. One of Strindberg's most characteristic plays is called *The Dance of Death.* Compare all this with Dante's statement about Beatrice:

> I tell you, when she appeared from any direction, the hope of her admirable greeting abolished in me all enmity, and I was possessed by the flame of charity which compelled me to forgive anyone who had done me any offence; and if anyone had asked me a question about anything, I should have said only *Love!* with a countenance full of humility.

The poet speaks out of the tradition of a Christian metaphysics of the Person. He also speaks un-self-consciously, naively, as a poet. The same words could have been used by Pierre Besukhov about Natasha, or by Levin about Kitty. In fact they were—*mutatis mutandis*—so used. And as Charles Williams has pointed out, the cheapest novel, play, film may tell the same story. Dante, with the gift of poetic genius, looked right through to the ground: "Love lies asleep in the heart until the beauty of a wise woman (*saggia donna*) causes it, by desire, to awaken, and so in a woman's heart, does the worthiness of a man." That love between the sexes is an epiphenomenon of divine love is based on the Jewish tradition and on the gospel. "In the light of love, Beatrice is seen in her true celestial state," Charles Williams remarks, "in which state she is by Christian doctrine to be precisely as what Dante sees her as being."

The counterpart to all this is the fact that the poets of decadence convey to us in all the perversions of love the sense of the demoniacal.

We acknowledge the reality of the Heddas and the Maria Nikolayevnas from experience, and they are made real to us by the technique of realism. We meet these ladies in drawing rooms, in parks and on *Kurpromenaden.* But Swinburne's phallic woman appears as "Dolores, Our Lady of Sensual Pain."

O garment not golden but gilded,
O garden where all men may dwell,
O tower not of ivory but builded
By hands that reach heaven from hell;
  O mystical rose of the mire,
  O house not of gold but of gain,
  O house of unquenchable fire,
    Our Lady of Pain!

This is one verse from a litany which was apparently intended as profanation. Apart from bring unintentionally comical, the poet does succeed in conveying the fact that all perversion of human love—the rapacious woman, the man who desires woman to be rapacious—contains an eschatological dread. Several poets around that time were strangely preoccupied with the figure of Salome. Our century was ushered in, as it were, by that image. And Salome is, as Ortega y Gasset pointed out, the perfect antagonist of the Blessed Virgin. Just as Woman was promised, in Genesis, to give birth to Him who will crush the head of the serpent, Salome demands the head of the precursor of Christ.

NINE

Tolstoy

Nikolay put the book down and looked at his wife. The luminous eyes looked at him doubtfully, to see whether he approved or not. There could be no doubt of Nikolay's approval, of his enthusiastic admiration of his wife.

* * * * *

Perhaps there was no need to do it so pedantically; perhaps there was no need of it at all, thought Nikolay; but this untiring, perpetual spiritual effort, directed only at the children's moral welfare, enchanted him. If Nikolay could have analysed his feelings, he would have found that the very groundwork of his steady and tender love and pride in his wife was always this feeling of awe at her spirituality, at that elevated moral world that he could hardly enter, in which his wife always lived.

* * * * *

He was proud that she was so clever and so good, recognizing his own insignificance beside her in the spiritual world, and he rejoiced the more that she, with her soul, not only belonged to him, but was a part of his very self.[1]

These are quotations from *War and Peace*. Compare them with the following sentences from *The Kreutzer Sonata:* "What I find more contemptible than anything else is the theory that love is something ideal and lofty; in practice, love is vulgar and swinish." "The word of the Gospel, that anyone who looks at woman with desire has already committed adultery in his heart, does not only apply to strange women but even more so to one's own wife." "A moment ago you mentioned the children. All those lies about children! Children are God's blessing, children are a joy! It is all a big lie . . . The joy which the baby gives to his mother, by his charm, by his tiny hands, his tiny feet, by his entire little body, means much less than the suffering caused, not only by sickness or loss of the baby but by mere apprehension at the possibility of sickness or death."

It is difficult to believe that the quotations from *War and Peace* and from *The Kreutzer Sonata* stem from the same pen. If they reflect the author's view of the world—and they do—then there must have occurred, somewhere in between, a break. The guess is correct. There *is* a break, and strange as it may seem this is usually referred to as Tolstoy's religious conversion.

What happened? Before we answer this question, we must first do away with some fallacies. First, one should not think that the author just happened to describe a happy marriage in *War and Peace,* and an unhappy one in *The Kreutzer Sonata.* There are also unhappy marriages

1 *War and Peace,* translated by Constance Garnett.

in *War and Peace*—Pierre's marriage with Helene, and Andrew's with Lisa. *War and Peace* is a story of human life and, just as in human life, all sorts of things occur. No, *The Kreutzer Sonata* is not *a* story of a tragic marriage; the unhappy railway passenger who narrates the tale expresses the author's own philosophy, the philosophy of Tolstoy after his conversion. *The Kreutzer Sonata* presents a diatribe against sexual love in all forms, with the conclusion that the sacrament of marriage is a big lie and nothing but a licensed form of prostitution. If one founded a Museum of Manicheism, one could add this to the collection of nineteenth century oddities. At one point of the story the narrator even quotes Schopenhauer; we should have expected it.

The second error would be to assume that the quotations from *War and Peace* are examples of poetic embellishment, and that *The Kreutzer Sonata* represents a plunge into reality where it hurts most—the kind of thing people call "a fearless exposure." This touches on the problem of literary veracity. The first quotation, taken out of context, may sound "romantic." Actually, the universal appeal of *War and Peace* lies precisely in its truthfulness, in that naive certainty with which only the greatest poets have evoked the experience of evidence—Dante through the poetic-allegorical and Shakespeare through the poetic-dramatic. In *The Kreutzer Sonata* the technique is more naturalistic, in a photographic sense, and part of its popular success at the time was precisely due to that. People must have felt that, with the setting (a chance acquaintance in a railway compartment telling his life story—the kind of situation anybody can get into), the fact that sexual matters are called by their real names, and the fact that the authorities of State and Church clamped down on the book—here must be truth! This would be an appeal to nineteenth century religious liberalism. In reality, the entire *Kreutzer Sonata* is pathological material presented by a wily craftsman. The writer has used, consciously and not naively, story technique as a means of getting a sermon across. It is a pamphlet dressed up in narrative form.

The third error would be to assume that this change, from the creator of Marya, Natasha, Kitty and Anna to the disillusioned and cynical fellow who utilizes the span of a Russian train ride to justify the murder of his wife—that this extraordinary turnabout is due to Tolstoy's own experience in marriage. It may have seemed so to him, but if it did he was a victim of delusions. Such a view of his own marriage would have been insane. There exists a great amount of research on the subject, and the fascination is not always that of objective curiosity. (One of de Montherlant's misogynous heroes remarks that he cannot get Tolstoy's marriage out of his head. No wonder!) It is difficult to present the truth of the matter convincingly, and to present the source material in all its details would make this into a post-graduate thesis. There is no doubt whatsoever that Tolstoy's wife originally, before her reaction to his conversion, was the good wife of Scripture. This is no exaggeration.[2] Her wealth of moral resources makes one gasp.

---

[2] The latest work on the subject, *Married to Tolstoy,* by Lady Cynthia Asquith (Houghton, Mifflin, 1961) is a scholarly book, and as unbiased as any book of this kind can be. It is, incidentally, also well written. To recommend one out of a great number of studies may render one suspect of bias, but this cannot be helped. I have been able to trace the views which blame Tolstoy's marital tragedy on Countess Tolstoy to two sources. One is Alexandra, one of Tolstoy's children. The other source is that of "Tolsto-

Sonya bore Tolstoy thirteen children, ran the vast household in Yasnaya Polyana and Moscow, looked after the education of the nine children who survived, acted as her husband's publishing agent and secretary (according to one of the sons she copied the draft of *War and Peace* alone seven times!), and one senses that this super-human achievement was accompanied by that indefinable glow of womanly presence. After the arrival in rapid succession of five children, she begged Tolstoy for a pause—and he was scandalized!

The fact that Natasha and, particularly, Kitty are modeled after her is well known. From the engagement scene in which Levin writes his proposal on a mirror in the form of initials of words that make an elaborate sentence, and Kitty guesses each word, to the scenes of motherhood and family life—all this is known to be autobiographical. Whatever changes may have come over her in later years were prompted by the change in *him,* and not the other way around.

The main point of her detractors is that, after his conversion, when he wanted to give his property and his publishing rights away, in order to embrace a life of poverty, she fought this decision tooth and nail. But we must remember that she was a practical housewife, the education of the children was expensive, and she felt that the ones who would benefit from giving up his royalties would not be poor people but wealthy publishers. Moreover, if there really had been a solution to his wish to live in poverty, he would have found it without her and without

---

yans," i.e., people who approached their hero as one approaches the founder of a faith (he himself regarded them with ironic reservation, he was no "Tolstoyan"), and who shared the views of Pozdnyshev, that ferocious travel-companion in *The Kreutzer Sonata.*

breaking the bond of love. Berdiaev has pointed out that the converted Tolstoy, who preached Christianity with such maximal demands on the masses (vegetarianism, conscientious objection, abandonment of all, even innocent worldly pleasures), did not do so from a platform of moral superiority, since he had not been able to solve his marital conflict in the light of the Gospel. Thus we see that there is no marital disappointment to justify the philosophy of the gynocidal hero of *The Kreutzer Sonata.* What then had really happened?

I think we can better understand the meaning of Tolstoy's conversion, and his significance as the religious and moral reformer, if we begin by looking at the place of religion in his *entire* work, including his writing *before* his conversion. We see immediately how utterly nonsensical it is to regard the later Tolstoy, the preacher, as Christian, and the earlier one, the author of *War and Peace,* as pagan (as he himself wanted us to think). All "naive" art, as long as it is good art, is spiritual. What Charles Williams said of Shakespeare, namely that he "expressed supernatural values in natural forms," can be said about all great nontendentious art. When we bracket Tolstoy's novels with the works of Shakespeare, we do not merely state a whim of personal taste. The great novelists agree on this. *War and Peace* has often been considered the paradigm of all novels. Even Flaubert who was after all contemporary, and did not have the vantage point of distance, immediately compared Tolstoy to Shakespeare. Tolstoy's work evokes that irreducible experience of immediate evidence which only the summits of art create in the reader or the beholder or the listener: that well-known "this is so—it cannot be different!" Mario Praz, in a remarkable study of the nineteenth century novel, makes a comparison of the novel as an art form with Dutch genre painting of the seventeenth century. Without going into the historical and aesthetic sides of his argument, we can say about *War and Peace* and *Anna Karenina* precisely this—that, as in the paintings of Vermeer that depict members of the comfortable class of burghers in everyday situations in their homes there is that glow of the eternal which preceding generations got only from religious or heroic subject-matter, so it is in the great novels of Tolstoy. There are meetings of general staffs, soirées and battle scenes, gambling sessions, duels and débutante balls; people fall in and out of love, get married, have children and grandchildren, and die—and lo and behold: the "realistic" technique succeeds in evoking a reality which reflects an entirely different light. Underneath the surface of realistic veracity, we look right through to the bottom of eternity, at poetic truth. This is the difference between *War and Peace* and any other historical novel based on conscientious research, or *Anna Karenina* and any other realistic novel on a marital theme. Now the core of this truth, in spite of all the reflection and research that went into the work, was found naively and un-consciously. One must not be misled by those ramblings on the philosophy of history with which *War and Peace* is interspersed. All that is essential to the novel, all that has given it and *Anna Karenina* their unique positions in the history of art, has been created with the same non-reflective sureness which characterizes Shakespeare or Vermeer or Mozart. *War and Peace* is a *Welt Theater,* in the sense of Shakespeare's and Mozart's work. Somebody once remarked that everything human occurs in this novel, and therefore we encounter the spirit not only as a supernatural glow which enlivens reality but also overtly. In other words, we encounter religion as it affects the everyday lives of some people. This appears particularly in the person of Marie Bolkonska. To me Marie, with her hidden life of prayer, the anonymous radiance of love with which she affects the lives around her, has always been the image of the Mystical Body. And this impression is so strong precisely because it is neither explicit nor was intended by the author. On one occasion, Andrew and Pierre surprise Marie as she entertains "God's People," pilgrims, in the kitchen (the clandestine contact with these people was the only instance in which she went against the wishes of her tyrannical father). This occurs immediately after Pierre had tried to explain his newly found creed of Freemasonry, and Andrew replies with his ideas on religion—certain notions of German humanism of the time of enlightenment. The encounter, immediately following this, with Marie and her foolish pilgrims is quite similar to the dialogue on religion which takes place between Faust and Margarete. Andrew rejects Marie's world of childlike faith with benevolent irony. He will find that faith much later, in a scene of discovery to which we shall come presently. In other words "religion" appears in the work of Tolstoy, before his conversion, as the *central theme*—but in a way essentially different from the way it came into it after his conversion.

With Tolstoy the poet, as he appears before his conversion, faith was a matter of the immediate, non-reflective insight of genius. With Tolstoy the preacher, after his conversion, religion became a matter of conscious, intellectual rumination. This began at the age of fifty. It was then that his famous crisis occurred—a sudden attack of inner paralysis, with horrible feelings of guilt about his past life and temptations to despair and suicide. From all the sources available, it was a perfect textbook case of involutional melancholia. Clinical labels do not mean much when it comes to the riddle of a man's fate, but they serve their purpose as a practical shorthand. The "mode of onset," the "symptoms"—to use textbook language—everything is there. There were individual variations, and in his case they were due to the plasticity of genius. (That genius itself is not always a saving grace is shown in the case of the Austrian novelist Stifter, a victim of precisely the same thing whose life ended in suicide.) Alongside Tolstoy's truly abominable sense of guilt arose the haunting question of the meaning of life: what is it all about? Tolstoy became convinced that the only answer to the mystery of life was to be found in religion. This sounds like a platitude and if one wants to appreciate the sense of the drama behind it, one must go to the biographical sources. A summary, albeit inadequate, of Tolstoy's faith, the final outcome of his struggle, can be stated as follows: The pivotal point of the Gospel is the "Do not resist evil" of the Sermon on the Mount. This means that no matter how evil the adversary, how cruel the injustices of oppressors, the only permissible means of defence are non-violence and passive resistance. Only voluntary poverty can overcome social injustice. Established institutions, the State, and the sacramental and ritual aspects of Christianity serve to keep the poor in ignorance and submission. The Gospel must be stripped of all this and of the miraculous, down to the core of moral teaching. Jesus was the noblest of men and the wisest of teachers but no God.

Such a summary seems unjust, and gives no idea of the convoluted and painful road which led to this position. For example, Tolstoy was always convinced that the humble people were the only ones to hold the solution to life's riddle, and they held it in their faith. And it seems that he never lost that conviction, even when he had arrived at the views just outlined. Moreover, during the initial phase of his crisis, he made an attempt to go back to the practice of the Orthodox religion. However strange it may seem in such a poetic genius, the approach to faith had by now become strongly intellectual. The "break" meant many things—it also meant a mysterious divergence between intellect and heart. Prince Andrew's Western rationalism, which looks on the Orthodox faith of his sister Marie with brotherly tolerance, represents undoubtedly a facet in Tolstoy's own personality. Andrew-Tolstoy has a proud mind. "Proud" is a cliché but the right word. After the conversion, that same proud rationalism was channelled into the religious bed, as it were. Tolstoy's attitude towards Christianity, as it manifested itself socially and politically, became fiercely censorious. Mind you, there *was* a lot to censor. The visible Church in Russia *was* an accomplice of power. It *was* corrupt in many members, and it maintained official silence in some of the most dreadful outrages against justice and charity. Let us not be mistaken: there is in the later Tolstoy, with all the air of the sectarian and the crank and all the neurotic under-pinnings, a tone of fury and warning which is truly prophetic.

But let us first go back to the crisis of depression in the middle of Tolstoy's life. I have used the clinical label, fatuous as it may seem in such a case, of involutional melancholia. To savour the strange experience of clinical recognition (still stranger in psychiatric "entities" than in the case of typhoid fever or lobar pneumonia), the reader would do well to study the episode in any one of the well-documented biographies,[3] and then "look it up" in a basic textbook of psychiatry. Now the psychoanalytic theory of these depressions is as follows. The child receives, even before any formal moral training, a kind of "natural" premoral formation. Its first encounter with a world of regulations is predominantly negative. The world of the forbidden precedes the world of the ideal. The very first regulatory education, such as training for order and cleanliness, warning against the handling of breakable objects and so on, may signify to the child an initiation into dread. Even under the most favourable circumstances the child gets to know the "Don't" associated with the first notion of punishment and reward, of retaliation and pardon, before a positive ideal, a "Do!", can develop. Here, as so often in psychology, the evolution of the individual parallels the evolution of the race. The earliest, primitive forms of morality in peoples are those of warnings and prohibitions, and the morality of a positive ideal comes later. It is the same in the child's life as in the history of human society. Something analogous also exists on the level of the historical drama of salvation. Under normal circumstances, that deep geological stratum of dread remains subdued and

---

3 Among the more recent ones the description of the crisis is more clearly presented in *By Deeds of Truth* by M. Hofmann and A. Pierre (Orion Press, New York, 1958) than in the otherwise scholarly *Leo Tolstoy* by Ernest J. Simmons, Knopf, New York, 1959.

inactive. But under abnormal conditions it erupts and threatens to destroy us. When this happens, we feel ourselves as though accused by a cruel master who comes to mete out the maximal punishment. Hence the monstrous aspect of guilt in these cases. The archaic form of "conscience," which puts in an appearance during depressions, is in reality a person or persons whom we have internalized; some ancient external threat we have gobbled up, as it were, and which speaks to us now through our own thoughts. During pathological depressions we become ventriloquists in reverse—the voice of guilt in us is, in its origin, the voice of another, of another who is long forgotten. That primitive juridical authority within is excessively harsh. This is not justice as we know it. It is too closely associated with a primary drive of cruelty. And the cruelty is not as self-punitive as it seems at first sight; the sense of self-punishment is compromised, so-to-speak, by its kinship with true cruelty, outward-directed. Thus the guilt of the melancholy patient has nothing to do with healthy guilt feelings, for in all true morality justice is wed to charity. To change our geological metaphor, the appearance of the threatening accuser is rather like a surfacing of deep-sea monsters who ought better remain banished to the bottom.

Many of our melancholy patients, even after the acute illness has passed, remain settled in a world thus distorted. In studying some of the work of the later Tolstoy, particularly some of the posthumous stories, such as "Father Sergei" or "Thirty Years", one has an unpleasant feeling one cannot immediately place until one realizes: this is a sense of glee, the glee of cruelty. For example, in "Thirty Years" a man is murdered in the depth of a forest and there are no witnesses. The victim prophesies to his murderer with the clairvoyance of the dying that, in thirty years to the day, his death will be avenged. You follow the murderer through thirty years—first of scepticism, then of puzzlement, of apprehension and finally of fear. And on the thirtieth anniversary of the crime, he dies in panic of a heart attack. This story of thirty years of refined torture has just enough of the undertone of sadism to distinguish it clearly from divine justice. Some people call this kind of thing old-testamentary, in a misunderstanding of the Old Testament. Puritanism, once the mask is off, has clearly sadistic features. Newman once remarked that there is no true mysticism without asceticism. In the same vein one may say that there is no true asceticism without charity. The intransigent nature of the puritanical (or Jansenistic) ideal is derived from the deep currents of our instinctual life rather than from the spirit. The sectarian Tolstoy once remarked that, of all the worldly pleasures, the most difficult one for him to give up was hunting. In a sense, he never renounced it, because the relentlessness with which he pursued Beauty—in music, in the fine arts, in Shakespeare, in Dante, in his own great works, in women, in his wife—was the relentelessness of bloodsport. He stalked Beauty as one stalks the fleeing deer.

This brings us to another point. In studying the biographical material, it is evident that more than once the Countess was scandalized by her husband's newly acquired views on sex and marriage, and on the harmless pleasures of life, such as soirées and balls and concerts. But what is more subtle and perhaps evident only to the eye of the psychologist is the fact that the shock was intended. The sadistic component of puritanical morality, that strange glee which goes with the prosecution of "sin," was meant to hurt *her*. It would go beyond the scope of this chapter to adduce the evidence. Now we know from psychoanalytical experience that such destructive hate is, at bottom, aimed at the mother. The wife in such a case is an innocent victim; she serves, without realizing it, as a stand-in. Nor does the husband realize that, in reality, his hate is aimed at the archaic prototype.

The fact that this once beautiful marriage, this Levin-Kitty or Pierre-Natasha story, was turned into a nightmare, a scene of bitter warfare, a story of the wife-killer Pozdnyshev—this tragic outcome can be explained only on the basis of an original drama far back in the dim zones of the archaic. So clinical experience tells us. Here we can only guess at the origins. Tolstoy lost his mother at the age of two. According to all sources available, Marie Bolkonska in *War and Peace* is his mother's portrait. The awkward appearance, those beautiful eyes, the intense spiritual life, bashfully hidden, the love for the poor and the pilgrims, the devotion to her husband (Tolstoy's father seems really to be portrayed in Nikolay Rostov), her submission to the tyrannical father—the entirely lovable and unforgettable Marie, all this is said to be historical and on this all biographers agree. How he who never knew his mother could have painted her so vividly is another question; like his biographers, he can have known her only from hearsay.

Psychoanalytic studies have shown that the two-year-old child does experience grief at the loss of the mother. Moreover, the child looks at the death of the mother frequently as though it were a case of leaving, of wilful abandonment, and this is associated with resentment. In other words, the original ambivalence (love-hate) which the child harbours towards the mother may be deepened to a degree which allows no resolution, in the case of the mother's death. I have loved you, you have abandoned me, and therefore I hate you.

Whether all this is really the explanation in Tolstoy's case is not essential to our argument. There exists, even without more detailed knowledge, enough material to account for such marked maternal ambivalence, and for the fact that the big breaking point in Tolstoy's life—the time of his depression and conversion—is also the breaking point in his relationship with his wife. Consider the hate-provoking trivialities: "In me there often raged a terrible hatred of her. Sometimes I watched her pouring out tea, swinging her leg, lifting a spoon to her mouth, and hated her for those things as though they were the worst possible crimes," and then compare this with an earlier passage (from a letter to a cousin): "While I write, I hear the voice of my wife, whom I love more than all the world. I have lived thirty-four years without knowing that it was possible to love and be so happy. Why does such a being as she love me?" Nothing could prove more clearly what psychoanalytic observation shows—namely that the voice of hate has nothing to do with objective reality (he says that much himself), and that it erupts out of the strata of pre-objective experience.

Thus we discover in the intransigent morality of the puritan, with its thinly disguised cruelty, two components: mobilization of primitive destructive forces (a pathological primitive superego) and hate of the mother.[4] These two things belong mysteriously together. We say "mysteriously" because there comes a point when all psychological schemas must stop. Does the child hate the mother because the mother represents the punitive element? or is the mother who suddenly withdraws her love (by disappearing) associated with the dread which is, after all, a dread of loss of love? What matters here is this. The spirit thrives only in a climate of belonging, of rootedness and of trust. The component of confidence within the phenomenon of faith is, on the natural plane, derived from the relationship to the mother. According to psychoanalytical observations the polarity "trust-distrust" makes its appearance right after birth. It is the *leitmotif* of the first movement, as it were. Erikson who has described the phases of life in terms of principal themes makes this one the first theme. Hence faith, blind abandon, is on the natural plane, man's primeval act—if one may here use the word "act." In a previous chapter we have pointed out the paradox of the human condition—that man, the summit of the mammalian scale, should enter into this life to pass first through an eternity of utter helplessness and dependence. From a

4 Tolstoy's hostility to his wife was fostered by Chertkov ("the king of the Tolstoyans"). There was in this friendship undoubtedly an element of latent homosexuality. Sonya suspected this; at any rate, she saw the sinister role of Chertkov and felt as powerless as Gretchen felt towards Mephisto. With it all she still maintained, even to Chertkov, an attitude of charity, or at least she made a good try.

theological point of view, on the level of grace, it is an extraordinary fact that the antithesis of utter abandon and distrust should lie at the deepest layer of human life. In natural terms, faith grows out of the relation of child and mother. Distrust appears as the foil, as it were. When one reads the story of Tolstoy's conversion in all its phases, with the eventual doubt of the incarnation and of the sacramental in the life of the church, of the destruction of the faith of his childhood, that entire *denial of the sensory*—there is no doubt about it: what he was converted to was a position of *dis*trust.

Loving abandon is not only a constituent of Christian faith but also a constituent of Christian morals, for morals cannot be separated from faith. If morality is divorced from faith, it regresses and becomes a juggernaut driven by explosive fuel. When, after Tolstoy's conversion, his marriage had developed into a focus of hate, the poor Countess confided to her diary that *before* his conversion they had had more Christianity. And she was right, of course. Indeed, even in his doctrine of non-violence, noble as it is objectively, one cannot help but feel, at every step, an element of "reaction formation"—that is to say, an unconscious defence against boundless aggressiveness.

As we have seen, not long after his conversion Tolstoy began to reject the Church as a corruption of the Gospel and as evil. This can be explained on the basis of the social and political abuses of the Church in Russia, but not entirely so. After all, other Russians of the nineteenth century, such as Gogol and Soloviev and Dostoievsky saw what Tolstoy saw, and did not lose faith in the Mystical Body.

Indeed, Tolstoy's pure morality (Dostoievsky called it a "religion without sky"), which rejected miracles and sacraments as deceptions, had little to do with his abhorrence of the scandals of the visible church. However, at the bottom of this there was a grandiose paradox. The ethos of the Gospel would never have taken root in his soul, had it not been for the Church. We know that those pious aunts of his childhood, those nannies and peasant women were the only ones responsible for his faith. Throughout Tolstoy's work, before and after his conversion, there moves an endless army of little and hidden people—all those Marie Bolkonskas and Platon Karataievs, those pilgrims and cobblers and coachmen and bee-keepers—who love and suffer silently in a spirit of trust. They are the Mystical Body. From them the poet received of the wine of the living Church, out of which he was later to make his own distillate. *He* lived on their wine, but on his distillate *they* could not have stayed alive for a day.

This, I feel, is the paradox of all moral systems which are derived from Christianity and set up in opposition to it. Tolstoy was a foe of Marxism. The reason is evident, even if it were for nothing but the doctrine of non-violence.[5] And yet, when we separate (as Tolstoy did) the bone of morality from the flesh of faith, we create a support of sorts—a skeleton, dry and cold and with a frightening rattle. This, I believe, all rationalist and "scientific" *systems* of morality have in common. We see the same in Marxist puritanism as it seems to manifest itself for ex-

[5] After he had become an enemy of the Czarist regime and had been excommunicated by the Church, the Bolsheviks courted his favour, but he predicted that the dictatorship of the proletariat would develop into a tyranny worse than any Czarist regime had ever been.

ample in present-day China. The difference between a morality imbedded in the life of the sacraments and the Gospel on one hand, and a moral system on the other (as it is presented under pragmatic or positivist or Utopian or "scientific" forms) is the same as the difference between things *grown* and things *made*. Love can neither be planned nor managed, it can only be sown and nurtured. Here, too, the mystery of the womanly is bound up with the mystery of the supernatural life.

Thus we understand why Soloviev, the greatest religious thinker of Russia in the nineteenth century, attacked Tolstoy in violent terms, linking him with the Antichrist. On the surface this seems not only outrageous but paradoxical: Soloviev had himself been in opposition to the traditionalist forces in Russia as represented by Crown and Church. He himself had come out with public statements about the hypocrisy which tainted the social fabric of Christianity (such as antisemitism, or the sanction of capital punishment, and so on). In doing so he had lost his job, his source of livelihood. Moreover, in his own private life he practiced many of the things which Tolstoy preached. He lived in voluntary poverty, abstained from meat, made one day of complete fast every week, and gave whatever little he saved in doing so to the poor. However, most of this became known only after his death, and he attacked Tolstoy precisely because of the latter's moral maximalism. It seems paradoxical to the point of comedy that Soloviev, who in his personal life was a sweet and truly Franciscan soul (he served, as is well known, as model for Dostoievsky's Alyosha), condemned Tolstoy for his doctrine of non-violence!

Soloviev held that Tolstoy's individualistic morality, which rejects any idea of the incarnation of Christianity in a social organism, is logically bound to reject the divinity of Christ. He regarded Tolstoy's position as fundamentally destructive and, in its own way, on the same level as Nietzsche's pagan individualism and Marx' materialist collectivism. Now this apparent paradox is resolved in the light of Soloviev's idea of God-Man and of *Sophia*—a principle of feminine wisdom in the world, immanent in womanhood and transcendental at the same time, a kind of cosmic *She*—an idea which is bound up with his concept of the Church.

Thus we see from a study of Tolstoy's personal evolution how a de-carnated "religion" is linked with the negation of woman; and we seem to see the threads by which the tragedy of one man's life is connected with an ontological mystery.

Here we must cautiously insert a hypothesis: namely that the naive unreflectiveness of the poet is, in Tolstoy's case at least, associated with the unreflective and naive in *eros*. In other words when Tolstoy, after his conversion, rejected art as immoral—except when it is used as a vehicle for moral teaching—it was not only an ugly Puritan who spoke but also a genius who had become estranged from the Muse. Maxim Gorki once remarked: "Certain features in the characters of the women in *War and Peace* could have been known only to a woman, and it must have been Sonya who prompted Tolstoy. I think too that there would have been even more theorizing and less harmony in Tolstoy's great novel had the feminine influence upon it not been so strong. And it was most likely at Sonya's request that the moralizing part was postponed to the end where it interfered with nothing and nobody." This is, of course, a simplification. It is impossible to think that Sonya "prompted Tolstoy," that she helped him *technically* to get a better idea of what's going on inside women or men, or of any other matter intrinsic to his work—and if she did, this part of her rôle was not essential to the artistic success. And yet Gorki touched on a truth. When Tolstoy writes only for the sake of poetry, completely devoid of the tendentious, one page on the most trivial everyday scene reveals more of the eternal spirit than all his pamphlets on religion put together; and this form of creativeness, out of the soil of creation, is linked with the fate of sexual love. It seems that Sonya was somehow aware of this, although she could not have conceptualized it. While he had already become the preacher and pamphleteer, estranged from his own origins by an entire cordon of Tolstoyans and reformers, she kept faith in the poet as one maintains a religious belief under the impact of scepticism. Once he announced to her in a letter from Moscow that a purely narrative idea had come to him, and she answered: "What joy I felt, when I read that you again feel an impulse to write in a poetical vein. That is what I have so long hoped and waited for. In that lies your salvation and happiness . . . This is the kind of work for which you were created. Without it there can never be any real peace for your soul." From this remark alone we see that, with all the immense throng of "followers," she still remained wed to him by *interior knowledge.*

And this remained so to the end, notwithstanding his famous final flight from her. We must not forget that, with all the open conflict, there are many signs that an inner bond between man and wife remained intact. In order to present our thesis we had to present the facts diagrammatically. In reality, things are never quite so simple. For one thing, the artist was never vanquished by the pamphleteer. The conversion in 1878 is not a demarcation line which really divides preaching from poetry. *Hadji Murat,* which contains no religious message, was written quite late. In such works as *Master and Man, The Death of Ivan Ilytch,* in many of the legends and folk tales, the power of naive creativeness emerges intact. Although Tolstoy came to regard *Uncle Tom's Cabin* (because of its moral message) as greater than *Hamlet* or *War and Peace,* he never succeeded in becoming an artistic Mrs. Beecher Stowe. And the Christ who roams his calendar stories is still the Christ of the ikon corner, and not the chairman of the Society for Moral Reform. Genius is not killed so easily.

Marie Bolkonska, that type of the eternal Church, remained in the background to the very end, and I believe that he never ceased groping for her. There is that famous passage in *War and Peace* about Andrew who, mortally wounded at Borodino, for the first time recognizes his sister for what she really is:

> Prince Andrew could restrain himself no more and wept tears of love and tenderness over his fellow-men, over himself, and over their errors and his own. "Sympathy, love for our brothers, for those who love us, love for those who hate us, love for our enemies; yes, the love that God preached upon

earth, that Marie sought to teach me, and I did not understand, that is why I am sorry to part with life, that is what was left me if I had lived. But now it is too late. I know that!"

We have reason to believe that the dying Tolstoy, like Andrew, came back to the faith of Marie. During the course of his famous flight from home, some remarkable events occurred which are either minimized or entirely omitted by most biographers. After the old man left his home under the cover of darkness (on the night of October 26th), only accompanied by his servant Duchan Petrovich, the first goal of his secret trip was the Optina monastery. This in itself—considering the excommunicated, the sectarian—is strange. In his younger years Tolstoy had made pilgrimages there. This time he went with the explicit purpose of talking to the Prior, Father Joseph. It seems that the porter did not answer quickly enough, and the aged poet, with the restlessness and impatience which characterized that entire episode of the flight, turned away to spend the night at the monastery's guest house. However, even there he left precipitously at three o'clock in the morning on the 29th (not without having properly signed his name in the guest book). In view of the idea we have of Tolstoy's later years it is equally remarkable that the next stop of his trip should have been a convent—the convent of Shamardino. There Tolstoy's sister Marya lived as a nun. He intended to stay in Shamardino for about two weeks. Tolstoy had always maintained a particular affection for this sister, an affection which was mutual. Although it is held that Marie Bolkonska is modeled after Tolstoy's mother, it is possibly no coincidence that he gave her the name of his own sister.

However, Tolstoy could not stay at the convent because Alexandra, his daughter, came and warned him that his wife was about to track him down. (It is quite conceivable that Alexandra made him leave out of jealousy towards Marya.) At any rate, a few days later, when he was lying on his deathbed in the station-master's house in Astapovo, the Metropolitan of Moscow wired a paternal greeting which was withheld from the dying man. Moreover, the Holy Synod wanted to send Starets Joseph to Tolstoy's bedside but the monk happened to be sick. Thus, in his place, a Father Varsonofy arrived from the monastery with the sacraments. In vain did he plead to be allowed to see the dying man. Tolstoy's entourage, particularly Alexandra is seems, felt that the sight of the priest would be too much of a shock. For the same reasons Sonya was not admitted to the side of her dying husband, and it is moving to read how she pleaded, nearly crazy with grief and frustration, to be allowed at least to enter the room. With what we have said, it is ironical and symbolic that the Church and the wife should have been the ones forcibly kept away from the dying man.

The fact that Tolstoy, under the premonition of approaching death, headed for the monastery to see the Prior, and then to the convent to see his sister, is most remarkable. Unfortunately, no record seems to exist of his last conversations with Marya. But a strong inference may be drawn from a note which Father Varsonofy wrote to Countess Alexandra Tolstoy, when he asked for permission to be admitted to the dying man's side: "You know that the Count had expressed in front of his own sister, your aunt who is a nun, the desire to see us and talk with us in order to obtain peace for his soul, and that he deeply regretted that he had not been able to fulfill this desire." The plea was received on November 5th and was refused. On the morning of November 8th, 1910, Tolstoy died.

TEN

Kierkegaard

One of the results of the triumph of rationalism has been to bring out even more blatantly the foolishness of the Christian faith. Faith has always been the great paradox: a synthesis of sublime intellect and perfect madness. That element of madness becomes increasingly more evident. As "enlightenment" advances, as the world is being mapped out by the geographers of objectivity, it becomes more foolish to hold on to the certainty of things we do not see. Don Quixote is, as Unamuno has pointed out, the prototype of the Christian in our time.

The intelligence in faith has little to do with cleverness. It is not the quotient of mental dexterity. It is rather intelligence as Saint Thomas or Dante understood the word: the capacity to enter into a union of being. In a society of enlightenment this intelligence, the Sun of Reason, loses its central place. Faith becomes literally *ec-centric*. The exemplar of this kind of eccentricity, of that Don

Quixoterie of faith in modern times, is Kierkegaard. Since his time, frightening victories have been won in that objectification of human existence of which he had been so singularly aware. In that respect he would not see much difference between the two sides of the Iron Curtain if he were alive today. He would see Christianity as being in a state of siege, cut-off from all sides; Kierkegaard was the prophet of loneliness.

His life and work were dominated by that ominous fission of which we spoke on several occasions in earlier chapters—the break between idea and life. As a young man he wrote briefly on Descartes. Later his interest turned to Hegel, whose philosophy had then begun to dominate the European scene. As we have seen, one can still conceive of Descartes' philosophy, at least theoretically, as limited to the methodological basis of science. This is its permanent merit. Experimental objectivity is possible if the subject is clearly severed from that which he observes. However, Kierkegaard was one of those who saw clearly that "scientific objectivity" would not stop there but would engulf the subject himself and thus in the end threaten the destruction of man. Let us repeat his words: "The scientific method becomes especially dangerous and pernicious when it encroaches upon the realm of the spirit. Let science deal with plants, and animals and stars; but to deal in that way with the human spirit is blasphemy."[1]

Hegel had gone one step further than Descartes. In his philosophy the thinker himself, the *res cogitans,* was

---

[1] S. Kierkegaard, *Concluding Unscientific Postscript,* trans. David F. Swenson, introduction and notes Walter Lowrie, Princeton University Press, 1944, p. 15.

gobbled up, as it were, by the system. Man, the beholder, became part of what he beheld, and God, the Idea, and Nature all entered into an objective "system" with its own dialectical machinery. Thus God ceased to be transcendent, and became immanent. In an intricate process of self-realization of the Idea, religion was an "also-ran." With the objectification of everything, including religion, faith became meaningless. It ceased to be faith. Against this huge precision-tooled Hegelian system, indeed against the entire juggernaut of rationalism, Kierkegaard rose up single-handed. It was a true case of foolishness in the eyes of the Greek: a Quixotic battle, like fighting tanks with bows and arrows.

We have pointed out that in the realm of the aesthetic the "subjective" is not necessarily synonymous with "untrue," as it is in the language of science. It is precisely in the same meaning that Kierkegaard insists on the "subjective" in Christianity. No Hegelian system of God and the Idea, of the historical process with its dialectics and of natural history can, he says, ever direct me to my destiny: this I find only in the *personal encounter*. Pascal (a spiritual ancestor of Kierkegaard) had opposed the God of Abraham, Isaac and Jacob, the God of the devouring fire—to the God of the philosophers. Since Pascal, however, rationalism had made great inroads. It was, as Kierkegaard saw it, reflected in the structure of bourgeois society of the nineteenth century. We have seen that in Descartes' philosophy Christianity had become a knick-knack which was not thrown out only because of its antique value. In the same sense the weakening of "religion," its absorption as one among many bricks in the building of society is the corollary of Hegel's philosophy. Now just as in the Hegelian system religion was allotted its proper place by the philosophy professor, in the bourgeois society of Kierkegaard's time "religion had its definite place." It was fine for the purpose of keeping things under control, and for weddings and funerals. About the fact that "religion had its definite place" the tolerant men of enlightenment were in agreement with a benevolent clergy. The Denmark of Kierkegaard's time, with its state religion, was quite typical of this. Faith had ceased to be the devouring flame for which we should be prepared in immolation; instead "religion" was kept at a proper temperature to provide coziness for well-disposed folk.

Against all this Kierkegaard affirmed his formidable *Either/Or*. Either you are for me or against me, says the Lord. God spits the lukewarm out of His mouth. Abraham, whom Scripture calls "the father of faith," was to Kierkegaard the prototype of all believers. By being ready to sacrifice his own child, he passes the only true test of faith, namely to go beyond reason, to the very point of madness. Kierkegaard's pages on Abraham belong to the most beautiful writing in the history of Christianity.

Kierkegaard recognized that the smooth absorption of Christianity as one departmental number in the social edifice was intrinsically related to the triumph of rationalism in Europe. He made a distinction between *Christendom* and *Christianity*, and he could no longer see any link between these two. On the one hand there was "religion" which had become one of the sectors of varying usefulness for the "functioning" of "social groups," and on the other hand there was the mad surrender of the soul to God, the struggle towards self-immolation which is a mysterious and unique act in the depth of each person. Needless to say the conflict is not confined to Protestant Denmark of the 1840's. We encounter it in Newman, in French Catholics such as Léon Bloy, and in some of the religious thinkers of Orthodox Russia of the nineteenth century.

What makes the case of Kierkegaard unique is something else. There is a strange complexity about his person: a touching, angelic purity of intention, an imperishable childlikeness which makes him a brother of Novalis and of Hölderlin,—and then there is the other, the shadowy, perpetually restless, Ahasveric element about him as if he had been born old and *tainted* by knowledge. He was the first to introduce the concept of anguish into philosophy, and in this too, he is preeminently modern. Human anguish is never entirely explained biologically or psychologically. There remains an ontological sediment: the tension of Man stretched eternally between being and non-being. Yet, while with some of the most austere mystics who live in the solitude of Gethsemane, there is always in the background an awareness of Easter to come, like the tonic following a dominant—with Kierkegaard we get a feeling of loneliness in perpetuity, the contradiction of a Christian soul in irredeemable anguish. As Kurt Reinhardt put it: "His integral supranaturalism thwarted his comprehension of the fulness of life, reality and human nature: it cut short his vision of a world redeemed and transfigured by Divine Love Incarnate."[2] Why should it have been so? In order to

---

[2] Kurt F. Reinhardt, *The Existentialist Revolt,* Frederick Ungar, 1960.

find an answer to this question we must look at Kierkegaard's life.

Soren Kierkegaard was born on May 5, 1813, the seventh and youngest child of Michel Kierkegaard. He was a latecomer; his father was fifty-seven and his mother forty-five at the time of his birth. Michel Kierkegaard was a prosperous merchant in Copenhagen at the time. Michel's own childhood had been spent in dire poverty in a small, scattered rural community on the island of Jutland. At the age of twelve he had been taken by a well-meaning relative to Copenhagen, and it did not take long before he was on the road to success. At thirty he was a wealthy man. He married late but after two years of marriage his first wife died childless. The year of mourning had not yet passed when he married again, this time his maid and householder, Ane Sorendatter Lund, who in fact was a remote relative. Four months after the wedding the first child, a daughter, was born.

Kierkegaard's philosophy cannot be divested from autobiographical facts and observations. Even in this sense he is the true founder of Existentialism: here philosophy cannot be pursued as objective *calcul* or detached speculation. We have seen that he set out on his Quixotic adventure by fighting the big "system"—Descartes and Hegel. Thus the matter of truth as a personal drama is even more evident here than in the case of his spiritual ancestors, Saint Augustine and Pascal. Now in this drama the relationship with his father is the pivotal experience. However, while in the lives of other great men we have to ferret out the facts and surmise, speculate and tediously reconstruct in order to solve the riddle—in Kierkegaard's case no such search is needed. It is all there, for everybody to see. Nowhere in all literature are there such self-revealing pages on the Father-Son story. It is the leit-motif which provides theme and counterpoint from the beginning to the end of Kierkegaard's work.

In view of all this, it is the more striking that in all his work not a single word may be found on his mother. "He wrote so much about woman, and so beautifully, though at the end so spitefully, was able to think of her only as the counterpart of man, and except when he wrote about 'Mary the Mother of God' he rarely dwelt upon the noblest and tenderest aspect of woman as a mother."[3] It was as though the mother had held no definable place in this family. Michel Kierkegaard looked after everything, even the purchase of food. There are indications that he looked upon the "forced" marriage as an accident to the end of his life, and never allotted to Ane the moral place of wife and mother of the family, and that Soren was in this, as in so many other respects, deeply linked to the father. Michel Kierkegaard thought only of his *first* wife as his "wife." He did so not entirely without remorse. One day he rushed to see his close friend, Bishop Mynster, and said: "Good God, I have been thinking so much today of my blessed wife. . . . I thought of her so long . . . here are two hundred dollars. Will you give them to the poor?"[4]

Kierkegaard describes his father as "the most melancholy man I have ever known." There was a mystery to all this, which the father was later to reveal to the son in an

---

[3] Walter Lowrie, *A Short Life of Kierkegaard,* Anchor Books (Doubleday, 1961).

[4] Walter Lowrie, op. cit.

extraordinary scene of confession. Until then, however, the father's melancholia was like some dark vapor which pervaded the family's and Soren's life. Not that the father was without warmth or affection. The entire story is a strange mixture of dread and tenderness. When little Soren once upset the salt on the table the father flew into a violent rage and called him a "prodigal son"! At school Soren was compelled to be dressed in sombre, old-fashioned clothes which set him off from the rest of his class, and got him the nickname of Choir Boy. It is well known how children suffer when they are marked among their classmates by such superficialities. During his student years, when Soren revolted against father and religion, he became a fashion blade, and ran up formidable tailor bills which the father paid, apparently without protest. In fact, with all the father's rigidity, there was that air of tenderness so characteristic of an aging father and his youngest child.

How deeply the father's spirit of puritanical discipline had already affected the child at the age of five can be seen from a description of Soren's first schooldays. The following passage is from *Either/Or,* hence the fictitious name Eremita. But the account is strictly autobiographical:

When I was five years old I was sent to school. Such an event always makes an impression upon a child, but the question is, what impression. Childish curiosity is engrossed by the various confusing conceptions as to what significance this may properly have. That such was the case with me too is quite likely; however, the chief impression I got was an entirely different one. I made my appearance at the school, was introduced to the teacher, and then was given as my lesson for the following day the first ten lines of Balle's *Lesson-Book,* which

I was to learn by heart. Every other impression was then obliterated from my soul, only my task stood out vividly before it. As a child I had a very good memory, so I soon learned my lesson. My sister heard me recite it several times and affirmed that I knew it. I went to bed, and before I fell asleep I catechized myself once more; I fell asleep with the firm purpose of reading my lesson over the following morning. I awoke at five o'clock, got dressed, got hold of my lesson-book and read it again. At this moment everything stands out before my eyes as vividly as if it had occurred yesterday. To me it was as if heaven and earth were to collapse, this would not exempt me from doing the task assigned to me, from learning my lesson. At that age I knew so little about duties; I had not yet, as you see, learned to know them from Balle's *Lesson-Book* (which was a primer of morals), I had only one duty, that of learning my lesson, and yet I can trace my whole ethical view of life to this impression. . . . When I was two years older I was sent to the Latin School. Here began a new life, but here again the principal impression was the ethical, although I enjoyed the greatest freedom. . . . I knew only one duty, that of attending to my school, and in this respect I was left entirely to my own responsibility. When I was sent to this school and the prescribed school books had been bought, my father handed them to me with the words, 'William, when the month is up you are the third in your class.' I was exempted from all parental twaddle; he never asked me about my lessons, never heard me recite them, never looked at my exercise book, never reminded me that now it was time to read, now time to leave off. . . . I got a thoroughly deep impression of the fact that there was something called duty and that it had eternal validity. In my time we studied grammar with a thoroughness which in this age is unknown. Through this instruction I received an impression which had a singular influence upon my soul. The unconditional respect with which I regarded the rule, the reverence I cherished for it, the contempt with which I looked down upon the miserable life the exception led, the righteous way, so it seemed to me, in which it was tracked down in my exercise book and always stigmatized—what else is this but the distinction which lies at the bottom of every philosophical way of thinking? When under this influence I regarded my father, he appeared to me an incarnation of the rule; what came from any other source was the exception, in so far as it was not in agreement with his commandment.[5]

He could easily be "exempted from all parental twaddle"; because by that mysterious process of identification the father led already a perfectly autonomous existence inside little Soren. And this should remain to the very end. There is one detail which to me has always been particularly significant and moving: the father bequeathed a sum of money to Soren, to be paid to him in regular installments. After drawing the last installment, on the way home from the bank, Soren collapsed unconscious in the street, and was dead within a few weeks.

It seems that only once, in his early student days, Kierkegaard rebelled after his own fashion against the father. He passed through a phase of libertinism—the young lion of Copenhagen society, a kind of Nordic variant of some Stendhal or Balzac hero of the age.

However, to keep within the proportions of our study, we have to make straight for the scene of the father's confession. From all we know, it seems to have occured on Soren's twenty-second birthday. It was then that the father "came clean." He told Soren that when he, Michel, had

[5] Walter Lowrie, op. cit., pp. 34–35.

been twelve years old he found himself on a desolate hill on Jutland, tending his father's sheep. He was then so oppressed by the perpetual dearth and misery of his people that in a sudden attack of despair he raised his fist towards heaven and cursed God—a God who was presented as Infinite Love and who in reality allowed such abysmal suffering! Shortly afterwards his fortune turned, and for the rest of his life he became blessed with earthly riches and a big family. One should think that to any man of faith this would be a counterproof—the hint from a loving God that things were not as bad as all that. Not so to Michel Kierkegaard. He considered the heavenly blessings which occured after the blasphemous outburst as a sign of damnation—a kind of mocking hint from an unforgiving Deity. This perversion of thought is, incidentally, not as extraordinary as it seems. We see among our patients not infrequently a kind of "Polycrates complex"—a superstitious dread which comes with material success, a feeling that luck means guilt. It seems remarkable that Kierkegaard never, in his entire work, makes a single allusion to Calvinism. For the entire story might properly be understood in a Calvinist atmosphere; the father's "curse" represents some kind of twisted, divine nemesis. What is even more important to realize is that the father's pre-occupation with his "blasphemous act" and the ensuing damnation was only a screen, conscious or unconscious, to cover up the true curse. The "true" curse derived from his "lustful" relation to the maid during the year of mourning for his first wife, which led to the precipitate marriage. It is true that Michel regarded such an act of verbal aggression as he had once committed in childhood as an example of one of "the sins against the Holy Ghost which cannot be forgiven." However, after studying this story in all its dismal details one cannot help reaching the conclusion that the idea of *perpetuation* (the father succeeded in conveying to the children the awareness of some divine vendetta on the entire family!) could never have taken root, even in the old man's consciousness, if the "original sin" had not been a sexual one.

And here are two passages from Soren's *Journal:*

> It made a most horrible impression upon me the first time I heard that indulgences contained the statement that they compensate for all sins, *etiam si matrem virginem violasset.* I still remember the impression it made on me when several years ago in youthful enthusiasm for a master thief I let fall the remark that it was after all only a misuse of powers, that such a man might well be able to reform, and Father then said with great seriousness, "There are crimes which one can contend against only by God's constant help." I hastened down to my room and looked at myself in the mirror. Or when Father often remarked that it would be a good thing if one had such a venerable old man as a confessor to whom one could open oneself.[6]

* * * * *

> If something is to become thoroughly depressing, there must first develop in the midst of the most favorable circumstances a suspicion whether things are all right, one is not clearly conscious of anything so very wrong, it must lie in family relations, there the consuming power of original sin shows itself, which may rise to the point of despair and affect one

---

6 Walter Lowrie, op. cit., p. 60.

more terribly than does the fact which confirms the truth of the presentiment.[7]

Professor Lowrie's comment is quite apposite:

> This man who was his father had violated his mother when she was a virgin! His mother! Horrible! His father had seduced a servant-maid who was entirely dependent upon him. S.K., who boasted in later years of his prowess as a police detective, likely enough began to exercise this talent in his youth, and this was surely the first fact he would ferret out. But doubtless he learned more than this. This was likely not the first transgression of the sort his father was guilty of, for he married rather late in life, and the extreme moral severity of his later years may well have been a reaction from the dissoluteness and sensuality of an earlier period.[8]

From what we have learned so far, it is understandable that Kierkegaard's imagination should have been fascinated by two biblical pairs of "father and son." We have mentioned one pair already, namely Abraham and Isaac. The other one was that of David and Solomon. What intrigued Kierkegaard particularly in that story was Solomon's reaction when he discovered his father's sin of concupiscence. There is no doubt whatsoever that in Kierkegaard's own life these two pairs of "father-son" are linked by an inner bond. And he himself represented both sons, as it were—Solomon as well as Isaac. He remarked on several occasions that there exist in each generation three or four men who are unknown victims, who must suffer in hiddenness, as though this was a law in the economy of

---

[7] Op. cit., p. 59.
[8] Walter Lowrie, op. cit., p. 61.

salvation. The idea is similar to that of "victim souls" of Catholic mysticism. And Kierkegaard considered himself as one of those. The path of solitude and agony was self-chosen. Between the shepherd father cursing on the hill of Jutland and Abraham offering the sacrifice on Mount Moriah exists a logical link—"logical" in the sense of interior necessity. If you prefer psychoanalytic terms Kierkegaard was an inverted Oedipus who offered himself for the killing.

It is at this point that we have to introduce the story of Kierkegaard's great love, Regina Olsen, and the story of the "seducer." As we shall see, the two belong together. In 1835 Kierkegaard became preoccupied with the figures of Don Juan and Faust. This was, incidentally, around the time of the father's confession, and five years before Kierkegaard's first encounter with the great love of his life. It was only in 1849, a long time after the story with Regina was over (actually it was never "over," at least not for Soren) that Kierkegaard wrote the *Diary of the Seducer.*

Kierkegaard is not easy to read on account of his oscillating, protean style, if for no other reason. His pen was by turns acid, poetic, reflective (even along the lines of traditional philosophy and theology) and witty. Understanding is not made easier by the use of numerous pseudonyms and fictitious characters. The latter were made up of composite pictures of people he knew, and facets of his own personality. This way of presenting things was not only prompted by the romantic taste of the time. Firstly, it seems that he used these devices to *appear* "un-systematic," in contrast to the great philosophers of the eighteenth and nineteenth centuries. Moreover, behind this elaborate masquerade there is a play of hide-and-seek with the reader and, I believe, with himself. He promenaded among his own creations like a man in a mirror labyrinth.

The Diary of the Seducer is a horrid book; there is no other word for it. There is a peculiar air of cold, diabolical cynicism about it. It could easily be, without changing a word, a chapter in Dostoievsky's *The Possessed,* right next to Stavrogin's confession. It belongs to those books that give you the sense of a haunting presence, and you are glad to put it aside once you are through. One finds it hard to believe that it comes, even as a fictitious story, from a soul as sensitive and gentle as Kierkegaard's.

Briefly summarized, the story is that of a young man who sets out to get a young, naive and innocent girl to fall madly in love with him, and once he has her that far, and seduces her—to drop her. All this is planned and carried out with the detachment of a surgeon planning an operation. Johannes, the story's hero (the word jars in this context), manoeuvers, engineers and manipulates the woman's feelings as one masters and runs the functions of some mysterious machinery which, if not mastered, might be dangerous. In the course of this remarkable operation he procures the services of another young man, Edward, whom he gets to fall in love with her so that he, the seducer, may more easily step aside once the ghoulish task is completed. The way I put it here, this may sound too scurrilous and bizarre, but in the original story it all develops with amazing logic. We should remark here that there exists invariably, in all stories of seduction that element of the *Männerbund,* the league of men. For every

Don Juan there is a Leporello, for every Faust a Mephistopheles. For the seducer, the man who approaches woman for conquest's sake only, without the possibility of lasting inner involvement, is always homosexually tied. Thus seduction for seduction's sake, the "Don Juan neurosis" is based on a conniving, a plot of men—whether overtly (as in the legends of Faust and Don Juan) or surreptitiously (as in Kierkegaard's story) or only in phantasy.[9]

Under "June 7th" we find in Johannes' diary the following entry:

> Now Edward (who by now is in love with her) and I have become friends. Yes, this is true friendship, a beautiful relationship; it could not have been better in the best period of ancient Greece.

In Faust's and in Don Juan's case there remains a reconciling element, however mild. For one thing, Faust never seems to feel entirely at ease about Mephistopheles' plot to "get" the girl, and at the end of Part I, long before the final solution, breaks down in terror. In Leporello's case there is the saving grace of humour. Neither terror nor humour enters into Johannes' relationship with Edward. Unlike Mephistopheles, Edward does not even realize for what he is being used, and unlike Leporello there is an air of ghastly seriousness about the entire story. However, what makes this fiendish logbook more

---

[9] I believe that the fact that the first visit to the brothel is so often carried out not alone but in a group of men, is not only due to an easier overcoming of inhibitions. There is probably that same element: namely that the love-less heterosexual encounter is often the manifestation of a homosexual tie.

remarkable than anything else are the entries in which Johannes makes observations on his victim and on womanhood in general:

> A young girl, in many ways, does not develop like a boy; she doesn't grow. She is born. A boy begins right away with his development and needs a long time to complete it; a girl needs a long time to be born but then she is born all at once as a grownup person. This makes her charm and her wealth. The moment she is born she is a finished product; but this moment comes late. Thus, she is born twice, the second time when she is being wed, or rather, at that moment she ceases to be born. Not only does Minerva rise out of Jupiter's head, or Venus in her glory out of the waves of the sea—actually the same thing happens to every young girl provided that she is not spoiled by precocious development. She does not wake up gradually but at once. Nevertheless, she dreams longer (than the young man), provided that she is not prematurely torn from her sleep by the foolishness of people. The enchanting and infinite wealth of woman lies precisely in this state of dream, of unconsciousness.

It is a beautiful passage. The last few lines could be literally taken from Novalis, or from some of the authors we have quoted in an earlier chapter. It is even more succinctly expressed in one sentence in Johannes' diary: "Woman is substance, man is reflexion." Or take the following:

> The Fathers of the Church are divided about the Assumption of the Blessed Virgin; to me it is not at all incomprehensible because she actually did not belong onto this Earth any more. But the lightness of a young girl is quite incomprehensible; it mocks the laws of gravity.

But then the "young girl," duly commented upon, is treated as a target of attack, in the cold language of strategy, as though Clausewitz had edited a manual on seductive technique:

> I would, of course, be able to take her quickly by surprise but she would soon be fed up, because with her such approach can never have a lasting effect. The most useful and obvious approach would be an ordinary, conventional engagement. Perhaps her surprise would be greater, she would not trust her own ears if she got an ordinary proposal from me, if I just asked for her hand instead of making her drunk with passionate declarations of love. . . .

The strategic mastermind cannot refrain from philosophical asides:

> The damned thing about such an engagement is the ethical part. Just as in service, in life, too, the ethical is always the boring. How tremendous the contrast: under the constellation of the aesthetic everything is pleasant, lovely, fleeting; the moment ethics come in, everything is coarse, ugly and incredibly boring. . . .
>
> I don't want to take leave of her, for there is nothing more repulsive than the tears and lament of women. Everything changes, and yet nothing can be changed. I *have* loved her but now my soul can no longer be bothered with her. Were I a god I should do to her what Neptune did to a nymph—I would change her into a man.
>
> One thing I'd like to know: could one work oneself out of a girl in such a way that she'll imagine proudly that *she* was the one who broke off because *she* got tired of it all? This would make an interesting epilogue, would be of psychological interest and would enrich one's erotic observations.

Indeed, it is as though in the person of the seducer cold intellect, pure reflexion were out to trap and slay pure nature, unreflected substance, personified in the girl.

Cordelia hates and fears me. What does a young girl fear? The intellect. Why? Because intellect means the negation of her entire womanly being. Manly beauty, an agreeable character and all that means by which one can make certain conquests but never a complete victory. Why? Because then one fights the young woman on her home ground; and on her home ground she is the superior. With such means one can make her blush, one can make her lower her gaze but one can never provoke that indescribable choking anguish which brings out her true beauty.

After the operation is accomplished, Cordelia reacts with abysmal, unremitting hate, so that even her character seems to have changed. Here is a passage from her letter to Johannes:

I don't call you mine because you have never been mine, and for the fact that I once thought so I have to pay dearly. And yet I call you mine: my seducer, my traitor, my enemy, my murderer, the root of my misery, the grave of my joy, the abyss of my misery. I call you mine and call myself yours, and just as it flattered your senses at one time when they bent over me in proud adoration, now the echo of a curse goes back to you, a curse in all eternity.

This is quite different from Gretchen's language after she had been dropped by Faust. It is more like the attitude of Dona Ana towards Don Juan, if anything only worse.

Thus far fiction. What about real life? Kierkegaard met Regina Olsen for the first time at the house of a widow

Rordam when he was twenty-four and she was only fourteen. The account is in many ways strangely reminiscent of Dante's fleeting encounter with the child Beatrice on the Ponte Vecchio. There was an immediate experience of *recognition,* of that love which seems to be a lightning revelation of something that had been there since eternity. The story unfolded properly only two years later. To grasp it more fully (no one can hope to grasp it entirely) the reader has to study Kierkegaard's biographies and his *Journal.* Briefly told, it was like this. Even during the passing encounter at the Rordam's two years earlier, Regina had been impressed by "the liveliness of his mind" and by his conversation which "welled up and was captivating in the highest degree." Now, when he declared himself to her she responded immediately, with the utter uncompromising abandonment of a loving woman. It seems that the moment he had awakened this feeling in her he became startled and fearful. In fact, her naive abandonment and her spontaneity made him feel only more acutely his true curse—his over-reflectiveness. Like the other gloomy Dane (to whom he has often been compared) he laboured under the 'pale cast of thought.' The moment that the two were engaged, he found out that he could not be *engaged* (*engagé*), that is to say *involved* simply and un-consciously, with his *being.* And the fact that she *was* involved precisely in that sense made him fearful of "having dragged her out with him into a current." The more she "surrendered and was transfigured into the most lovable being" the more he felt beset by dread and melancholia.

All this took nearly a year. He had declared his love in September 1840, and he broke the engagement on August

11, 1841. The story of the break makes agonizing reading. He had rationalized, towards himself, that he could not tie her to his melancholia and to the curse of the Kierkegaards. He probably used similar arguments towards her before he broke the engagement irrevocably. Therefore, when the blow fell, she took the whole thing as a manifestation of illness (which, in a different sense, it was), tried to see him once more, and left a note in his apartment, in which she implored him "in the name of Christ and by the memory of his deceased father" to change his mind. "Her father, who interpreted my behaviour as eccentricity, begged and adjured me not to forsake her, 'She was willing to submit unconditionally to everything.' "

Soren's reaction to all this was to postpone the final break. All he did only prolonged the agony.

> She fought like a lioness. From time to time I said to her bluntly, "Yield now, let me go, you can't stand it." To this she replied passionately that she would rather stand anything than let me go. I tried also to give such a turn to the thing that it was she who broke the engagement, so as to spare her all mortification. This she would not hear of . . .
>
> Then it broke, after about two months. (On October 11, 1841. In the meantime the thesis had been defended on September 16, and the book was ready for the printer on the twenty-ninth.) For the first time in my life I scolded. It was the only thing to do. I went from her immediately to the theatre, for I wanted to see Emily Boesen . . . The act was over. As I went up to the second parquet, the Councillor [Regina's father] came down from the first and said, "May I speak with you?" I followed him to his home. "She is desperate," he said, "this will be the death of her, she is perfectly desperate." I said, "I shall still be able to tranquilize her, but

the matter is settled." He said, "I am a proud man; this is hard, but I beseech you not to break with her." Truly he was proud, he touched me deeply; but I held my own. I took supper with the family that evening. I talked with her, then I left. Next morning I got a letter from him saying that he had not slept all night, that I must come and see her. I went and talked her round. She asked me, "Will you never marry?" I replied, "Well, in about ten years, when I have sowed my wild oats, I must have a pretty young miss to rejuvenate me." She said, "Forgive me for what I have done to you." I replied, "It is rather that I should pray for your forgiveness." She said, "Kiss me." That I did, but without passion. Merciful God!

In order to help her to forget him he played the role of the cynical profligate, and allowed rumors to spread in Copenhagen about his dissipated life. He did succeed in fooling some people, but not her. She looked through it all with the eye of love.

Unlike Don Juan or Faust or Johannes, he would later pray for her every day for the rest of his life, "at times twice." And for all we know, his prayers may have been heard. For, contrary to the victims of his legendary prototypes, she settled down in what seems to have been a happy marriage after all. She married Fritz Schlegel, a high civil servant who became Governor of one of the Danish colonies in the South Seas, and she outlived Soren by half a century. She died in 1904, after having witnessed Soren's posthumous fame.

Stories of broken engagements like this one are nothing extraordinary. We also know that the reasons with which Soren justified his step (his melancholia; his father's story; the "family history"; a need to be free from ties to pursue his spiritual destiny) were attempts to explain something away, something which actually arose out of a depth he himself was unable to fathom. Of this he must have been aware. For, the problem of the seducer had begun to hold his interest *before* he fell in love with Regina. And he elaborated it later so as to hint at an ontological mystery.

Before we go into that, a few words on the psychoanalytical aspect. The neurosis of Don Juan, the man who is fascinated by conquest but unable to love, has been frequently made the subject of psychoanalytic studies. In such men the ambivalence towards the mother is so deep and the homosexual tie is so strong that they cannot commit themselves to woman other than by an ambivalent and sadistic relationship. And they are mysteriously compelled to go through this act of conquest and flight in an eternally repetitive experience. One could call men like these hit-and-run lovers, if such word were not a paradox. Because love is the opposite of hit-and-run: the lasting commitment. Psychological insight cannot compress the drama of life into a formula. Freud when he makes psychoanalytic observations on geniuses restricts himself to answering isolated questions, and the mystery of creativeness is left alone.

Kierkegaard shows himself to us unsparingly; his philosophy is an unending meditation, and the meditation a relentless self-search. His open childlike faith meant also faith in all of us, those who listen to his confession. And because his thought was shaped in the climate created by Goethe and German romantic philosophy—it anticipated Freud to an amazing degree. If we speak today of Kierkegaard's identification with the father—he knew it. He felt both liberated and imprisoned by this.

> Thus, in my peculiar way, I loved Christianity; to me it was venerable; though, humanly speaking, it made me deeply miserable. This was all tied up with my father, the human being I loved more than anybody else. And what shall I say? I must confess that it was he who made me miserable—out of love. His fault was not a lack of love; it was that he treated a child as one treats an old man.[10]
>
> The anxiety with which my father filled my soul, his own terrible melancholia, a lot of things I could not even write down. I was so frightened by Christianity, and yet deeply drawn to it.[11]

It seems most probable that the father had meant to drop Ana, the maid who was to become Soren's mother. And Soren, in his story with Regina Olsen, was compelled to live through the father's conflict and carry out the father's unfulfilled wish. Psychoanalytic observation shows that such interpretation is far from being fantastic. Kierkegaard surmised, at least, that the father entered into his relationship with Regina in some way.

> I who was an old man on the very day on which I got engaged, a thousand years too old to be able to love a girl—which I should have known before and which I know only too well now when the sorrow of it all has aged me another thousand years.[12]

---

10 Kierkegaard, S., *Collected Works,* German edition by Christoph Schrempf, Vol. 10, Jena 1922.

11 Kierkegaard, S., Tagebücher, I, 427, ed. by Theodor Haecker, Munich, 1923.

12 Draft for a letter to Fritz Schlegel. From H. Lund, Soren Kierkegaard's Verhältnis zu seiner Braut; Briefe und Aufzeichnungen aus seinem Nachlass. Leipzig, 1904.

From the father's world he also inherited a Manichean terror of sex. Thus, in spite of his prophetic awareness of that Manichean wound in history, the wound in his own flesh never healed. Does not his continuous preoccupation with the "aesthetic" and the "ethical" mean that he was unable to reconcile beauty with goodness? No wonder that Mozart's *Don Giovanni* so often, in his writings, serves as the paradigm of the "aesthetic!" It is as though beauty were simply the hedonistic—that is pleasure without commitment or responsibility, the pleasure of the *tempter* and the *tempted*. Kierkegaard's "aesthetic" is not the beautiful which is a foretaste of the timeless. It shows the face of Lilith rather than that of Beatrice. The Kierkegaardian dialectics of the aesthetic and the ethical, of the aesthetic which is "dethroned" by the ethical—all this would have been quite alien to, say, Dante. That the morally good remained fleshless and divested of beauty, we can understand from Soren's own dark history. It is not only a matter of Northern Manichaeism. It is the schism between the paternal and the maternal in his own origins. For just as Michel remained, in his own fantasy, unmarried to the mother of his children, so to Soren the carnal never became nuptial and remained lure and bait forever. Hence the "aesthetic" and the "ethical," "substance" and "reflexion" remained forever divorced. "What I lacked was this: to lead a complete human life, and not only one of the intellect."[13] "I have actually not lived except as a spirit; I have not been human. . . ."[14] The spirit here is ghost-like reflexion, roaming, unredeemed by substance.

---

[13] Tagebücher, I, edit. by Theodor Haecker, Munich, 1923.

[14] *Collected Works*, German Edition by Christoph Schrempf, Vol. 10, Jena 1922.

We follow this life as spectators follow a tragedy. We have spoken of the angelic feature of Kierkegaard, the sweet Prince of guileless sincerity. His first encounter with Regina, the child-girl, was the encounter with Beatrice—the perfect antithesis of Johannes' plot. "Thou, Queen of my heart [an allusion to the name Regina], enclosed in the depth of my bosom, there where distances from Heaven and Hell are equal—thou unknown Deity! . . . mightily filling my spirit to make me transfigured. And I feel it is good to be here."[15] This could be a quotation from Dante. And it might have ended just like that, as a poetic union or as terrestrial marriage. For it to get so horribly twisted into the story of the "Seducer," a cleavage was needed. This cleavage existed in him already when he met her—it goes way back to a time when he was not even born yet—to the disunion of his parents. Something had gone wrong with Love itself, in the world into which he was born. This, I believe, is the secret of that other Kierkegaard, the haunted, Ahasveric one, the discoverer of anguish. Nature is the soil of Grace, and the love of the sexes is a prototype of divine Love. This is also the reason why his rationalizations—he could not marry Regina because of his vocation or the family illness—must have seemed untrue even to himself. "Had I had faith I would have remained with Regina. Thank God, this I know now."[16] With how much suffering must such insight have been bought! And with that Dantesque algebra of love he might well have inverted the equation: had he stayed with Re-

15 Tagebücher, I.
16 Tagebücher, I, 195.

gina he would have found faith. Przywara[17] has justly summed up what Soren's faith needed for its perfection: "The pride of sacrifice can only be overcome by a humble willingness to let oneself *be* loved." (*"die Überwindung von Opferstolz in demütigem Sich-lieben-lassen."*)

When we get to know patients who experience the panic which Kierkegaard experienced with Regina we observe, phenomenologically and apart from all psychoanalytical significance, something which is best described as *terror of the irreversible* or *terror of the commitment,* which is closely related to the fear of death.

Kierkegaard was right when he observed that maleness means reflexion and womanhood means substance. Reflexion, unredeemed, is forever restless and insatiable. It searches without finding peace. It is only in union with substance that it finds eternity.

Later generations will find it remarkable that the nineteenth century, the era of the rationalist and the irrational, of technological progress and romanticism, brought forth three of the greatest thinkers in the history of Christianity—Kierkegaard, Newman and Soloviev. It is quite possible that these three will later be shown to prefigure, each in his way, the ecumenical trend of a time to come. There is, in spite of the various roots (Protestant, Anglican and Orthodox) a parallelism of growth. But Kierkegaard whom Karl Barth, quite justifiably suspects of hidden Catholic trends, remained forever roaming a no-man's land of anguish, listening to the echo of his own cry, without ever hearing the voices of the hidden choir. And

17 Erich Przywara, S. J., *Das Geheimnis Kierkegaards.* R. Oldenbourg, Munich and Berlin, 1929.

although the Kierkegaardian conflict between the "religion" of Establishment and a faith in the living Christ is justified within the framework of his thought, there remains an unexplored space. For even in the most conventionalized forms of communal life, the Church is mysteriously alive. Even in seemingly fossilized norms of "religious" life you unite with unknown souls. But this is where Kierkegaard's personal tragedy comes in. For throughout Kierkegaard's work, with all his search for the authenticity of the apostolic line, one has never the impression that the Mystical Body was a live experience; one does not feel that this feverish prayer was ever in unison with the "little ones." Léon Bloy, with whom he has little in common except a hate of the religion of bourgeois convention, was brother to the peasants of La Sallette and to the streetwalkers of Paris. There is none of that in Kierkegaard—for such a sense of communion implies a common motherhood.

ELEVEN

Goethe

The names lined up for the purpose of this essay—Descartes, Schopenhauer, Sartre, Tolstoy, Kierkegaard and Goethe—make an odd combination. The lack of chronological sequence heightens the feeling of the incongruous. To see Kierkegaard ushering in Goethe who was of the generation of his father; the prophet of our present-day anguish followed by a man on whom many look as a late straggler of the Renaissance! Yet, precisely with this sequence we anticipate the solution. Kierkegaard was tormented by a question to which, as we shall see, Goethe found the answer. Goethe, like Kierkegaard, was obsessed throughout his life by the person of the seducer as a mystical key figure. However, while to Kierkegaard the problem of Faust and of Don Juan were two separate issues—"doubt" and "sensuality"—to Goethe they were two aspects of the same thing. Faust, the activist whose story of conquest is tinged with the insatiability of a compelling need unredeemed by love; Don Juan, the conqueror who at the moment of fulfillment is moved on to the next victim by a restlessness akin to doubt—here are twin figures, Nordic and Mediterranean but of the same stem. Goethe knew that the two were closely related. He seized this with the immediacy of poetic grasp. And so the entire First Part of *Faust* is devoted to the story of a seduction. It is, seen from the girl's side, one of the tenderest love stories in world literature; seen from the man's side it is a story of love mixed with crime and horror. The criminal part of it is, in its own particular way, even more terrifying than that of Kierkegaard's Johannes. The difference is that here the daemoniacal is more directly implied, and that, before the final curtain falls on Part One, we perceive in Faust signs of guilt.

Kierkegaard was not the only one who would have dissociated Faust and Don Juan. Charles Lamb wrote, during Goethe's own lifetime, with what seems to us today singular obtuseness: "I thoroughly agree with you as to the German Faust as far (as) I can do justice to it from an English translation. 'Tis a disagreeable canting tale of seduction which has nothing to do with the spirit of Faustus —curiosity. Was the dark secret to be explored to end in seducing of a weak girl, which might have been accomplished by an earthly agency? When Marlowe gives *his* Faustus a mistress, he flies him at Helen, flower of Greece, to be sure, and not at Miss Betsy or Miss Sally Thoughtless."[1]

Goethe did bring his Faust together with Helen—in

---

[1] Letter to W. Harrison Ainsworth, Dec. 9th, 1823. From the *Works of Charles and Mary Lamb,* vol. vi, Methuen, London, 1912.

Part Two, but Charles Lamb could not know this at the time. But this would probably not have changed Lamb's view of the matter. And we cannot even blame him for his obtuseness. For it seems that here Goethe discovered an esoteric truth through personal suffering.

Insatiable seducers and insatiable searchers must always have existed. But the interest in Don Juan and Faust as poetic prototypes is modern and occidental. It is a post-Renaissance and post-Reformation theme.

We are inclined to distrust historians who classify entire civilizations. We suspect, in a science which strives towards objectivity, anything which smacks of the label and of the slogan. This is our first reaction to the term "Faustian" applied to the modern civilization of the West. And yet, if one looks for a common denominator to characterize the civilization which followed the Middle Ages, the figure of Faust is as good as any. The theme is one of unfettered open curiosity towards Nature, of an endless trail of victories over those physical forces which used to dominate us; and the negative side of it is a climate of feverish activism, of a restlessness for which there is no stop.

That picture of eternal restlessness occupied the literary imagination in the figures of Faust, Don Juan and Ahasverus. And from what we have just been saying it is understandable that this should have occurred only after the time of the Renaissance. Ahasverus the Wandering Jew, first mentioned by an English monk, made his first appearance in German literature in the sixteenth century, and in that language alone has been dealt with in over thirty variations. The Don Juan legend found its first literary expression in the seventeenth century. By the early nineteenth century, around and after the time of Byron and Goethe, poets seemed to be obsessed with the theme of Don Juan. Goethe toyed for a long time with the theme of Ahasverus and left a literary fragment. As well as by the figures of Don Juan and Faust, Kierkegaard was occupied by Ahasverus. The Austrian poet Lenau treated all three subjects—Faust, Don Juan and Ahasverus—at one time or another. The German, Christian Grabbe, bracketed "Don Juan and Faust" in one drama. Soon other male figures under the curse of eternal restlessness, such as the Flying Dutchman, were added. The point is that in these disguises appeared the anguish of the "modern": the hunter and the hunted who roam a vastness of space and time, in need of redemption. Just as the Kafkaesque theme—a man who is an anonymous cipher caught in impersonal machinery—expresses the anguish of the twentieth century and has found numerous literary variants in our time, so did the subject of Faust—Don Juan—Ahasverus express the anguish of the early Romantics. The reason seems evident: the Renaissance and the Enlightenment had brought about a spirit of free inquiry. But the dark side of all this was a sense of *loss of roots.* What Faust, Don Juan, Ahasverus, the Flying Dutchman and similar figures have in common is *homelessness,* and an inability to find peace.[2] In two of them—Faust and Don Juan—this takes the form

---

2 It seems remarkable that Wagner himself attempted to explain why the theme of the "Flying Dutchman" was specifically modern. He remarked that the earth-girdling sea is the "new home" for modern man, following the middle ages, and that the true home the Dutchman is looking for is the Eternal Woman. (cp. Richard Wagner, A Communication to My Friends, in "The German Classics of the Nineteenth and Twentieth Centuries." German Publication Society. New York 1914. Vol. XV, 214.)

of *perpetual craving* and *insatiability*. If we deviate for a moment to analyze this phenomenologically we find—quite apart from any psychoanalytical consideration—that it may throw light on the problem of Time and Freedom. In "tradition-bound" societies such as the medieval or the Hindu the danger is stagnation. One may get immobilized by one's roots, as it were. In a future-oriented, unhistorical civilization the danger lies in restlessness. This, too, implies an impairment of freedom, only in a more hidden way—hidden because mobility, the very symbol of freedom, is unlimited. The potentially shackling element of "tradition-bound" civilizations resembles that of a compulsive neurosis of the ritualistic type. What robs the patient of his freedom is the *past*. The phenomenon of the irresistible is *a pull from behind*. The Faustian life resembles the neurosis of *addiction*. The phenomenon of irrestibility is a *lure ahead* and what robs the patient of freedom is the future.[3]

All those figures, in folklore and in literature, are invariably male. The element of damnation is always there, at times in the form of a pact with the Devil. And wherever woman comes into it at all, she is deeply bound up with the protagonist's mystery. Indeed, either by implication or openly—such as in Goethe's *Faust* and in *The Flying Dutchman*—he finds his redemption through her. As may be remembered, the Flying Dutchman is to roam the sea under a perpetual, self-inflicted damnation. He is allowed on shore every seven years, in search of a virgin

[3] This has nothing to do with psychoanalysis. Psychoanalysis is a *genetic* psychology, and therefore everything is referred to the past but on a plane independent from the phenomenology of time.

maiden whose love alone can release him from his curse.[4] With the Romantics the theme, by sheer repetition, lost some of its impact. (Nietzsche spoke of "das ewig erlösende Frauenzimmer"—the forever-redeeming female.) Numerous symbolic disguises enter into the story. The sea, the mother of life who threatens us with open jaws, is the one to whom the captain is tied by his curse. Tolstoy who was equally fascinated by the Faustian theme —in his case in the sense of insatiable acquisition for the sheer sake of acquisiton—left us his famous parable on "How much Earth a Man needs." A rich Russian peasant learns about some tribe in the East on whose land a lot of luscious soil is still to be had. He goes there to buy. But the elders of the tribe tell him that they do not want to sell. He may take freely any amount of land which he can circumscribe by walking within one day. If he returns by sunset to the top of the hill from which he set out at sunrise, he may take possession of that which he was able to stake out by walking. He first calculates his stake quite shrewdly, knowing his limits of a day's good march. But as he walks along, the temptation of more land luring from afar is too great; he cannot refrain from taking in more and more, from running farther and farther—and at sunset he arrives, panting and exhausted at his point of origin— and drops dead. The elders of the tribe laugh, and dig a grave: this is how much earth man needs. This was written at a time when to Tolstoy a story had to end with a moral. But it still has (contrary to the author's aesthetic theories)

[4] It is noteworthy in this connection that in the earliest version of *Don Juan* the hero's first amorous adventure is, after having been shipwrecked, with a fishermaiden who shelters him in her cottage.

the power of great writing. It contains, as a parable, the Faustian theme, the metaphysical problem of the conqueror for conquest's sake who is unable to stop (this had held Tolstoy's interest especially in the person of Napoleon), and the entire moral problem of material possession. However, even here—if we remember the over-determination of symbols in psychoanalysis, and what Dante remarked about the levels of meaning in a story—the symbol of woman comes in: the Earth, with the strong implication of the "nourishing," and the return to death in her womb. The hero, addicted to material possession, "bites off more than he can chew"—and ends up by being swallowed. We have in this story a fusion of two elements: *mobility* (a crazed mobility which cannot find rest except by physical death) and *oral greed.* The fact that the man finds his nemesis with an Eastern tribe may be an unconscious echo of Napoleon, or may even reflect that certain feeling about the West we encounter in Slav thinkers of the nineteenth century. At any rate, when the Elders, with a big laugh, receive the dying man to dig his grave, we are reminded of that "this-is-how-it-all-ends" feeling of the ancient plays of *Faust* and *Don Juan.*

This literary detour was necessary to see Goethe's *Faust* in its proper context. In the framework of this study we want to confine ourselves only to one aspect of *Faust*—the Gretchen tragedy and (as we have done in the case of Kierkegaard) the *mystique* of the seducer. In order to understand this we must begin with Goethe himself.

All human lives are elusive, the lives of geniuses more, and Goethe's most. With the incredible wealth of talent goes, in his case, a glittering multiplicity of appearances. Just when you think you have him in focus, say as the encyclopaedic genius, with his innocent openness to the world, the artist-scientist (quite justly has he been compared, in this respect, to Leonardo)—you lose him again, and there goes the dashing Byronic idol, the Northern Romantic; you have settled for that when there appears the Weimar courtier, the portly Geheimrat, conservative and mildly stuffy; then the lover of the Roman elegies, a Martial *redivivus;* the poet of *Werther* and the man who classified the minerals of the Bohemian Forest. This is not merely a matter of vast gifts. It belongs to the "dynamics of the personality," as a present-day glib terminology would put it; it goes far beyond mere mental dexterity. For one thing, one Goethe always saved the other. If he had been only the poet of *Werther* he would have died Werther's death. There may even have been a flight into multiplicity, not in the primitive sense of becoming scattered out of anguish. He loved masquerade, in the literal sense of the word, at parties for instance. And for all we know he may have, unconsciously, used his *personae* to hide.

Whatever the case may be, it all goes to show that one cannot draw a psychological portrait of Goethe so as to elucidate something which he himself regarded as his own central mystery. It also goes to show that to be selective, to pick here and there what we need for our present study, is no injustice to truth. For no matter how thoroughly we may approach our subject, no matter how detailed we should become—the area we are looking for, that place in the history where the psychological and the ontological meet, remains equidistant from all points of the circle.

Every student of Goethe is sooner or later struck by a tragic paradox. That fortunate Olympian, the favoured child of the gods (Thomas Mann has, quite justly, pointed out that he was "*in* with Nature," that his creativeness, contrary to that of the sickly Schiller, arose out of a sense of well-being) this man of a thousand victories knew all the time anguish, the deadly shadow. As you get to know him you feel like someone who buys a beautiful castle but soon discovers that he has bought a ghost in the bargain, a spectre that cannot be laid.

This sense of puzzlement is the more disturbing since there is about Goethe none of the anonymity to which we have become used in the cases of Dante and Shakespeare. We know too little about the personal lives of those two to find out how specific contents of their work came about. When Middleton Murry draws inferences from certain features of Shakespeare's work to Shakespeare's life his conclusions are to the psychologist quite plausible. But still, it is all guesswork, and that obscure space between personality and creativeness remains mercifully shrouded. Goethe is the first great confessor among artists of that rank. He almost invites us to peep.

Furthermore, if we select, it is also for the sake of economy. To give a detailed biography would go beyond the framework of this study. *Not* to select, would be out of a wrong sense of fairness. And the puzzle of creativeness is such that, no matter how much detail one offers, the result always remains patchy.

The first instance in which Goethe speaks of a relation to a woman with an open sense of guilt is after his experience with Friederike Brion. " . . . here (with Friederike) for the first time, I was guilty. I had wounded the fairest heart in its very depth; hence the epoch of dark regret . . . became painful, yes, unbearable." The two stories of broken engagement of which we are best informed, namely Friederike and Lili (there were other similar experiences) resemble one another so closely and resemble Kierkegaard's story with Regina so, I am tempted to use the word "ridiculously," that we are prompted to end up with a cold clinical term—"typical." One reason for which common feeling shrinks back from psychological autopsies seems to be that an event imbued with that quality of the irretrievable and unique which ennobles all tragedy, is found to have a recognizable pattern, like measles or renal calculus. *"Sie ist die Erste nicht,"* "She's not the first one," says Mephistopheles in one of the most memorable scenes of *Faust,* when Faust finds out that he has, by dropping Gretchen, murdered her, morally and physically. Throughout *Faust,* Mephistopheles is by turns witty, urbane, and humorous. Whenever he becomes cynical, it is usually the cynicism of the stag party. It is therefore the more remarkable that this *"She's not the first one"* is, in the context of that particular scene, the only truly satanical remark in the entire drama. It is as though, for a fleeting moment, the stage lit up in a ghoulish light, and evil had taken its mask off. Faust reacts to the fiendishness of that remark with a terrible outburst of rage. It is the only time that the devil provokes him into fury. By then, alas, he is entirely in the devil's hands.

Friederike Brion was the daughter of the village pastor of Sesenheim near Strassburg when Goethe was a student at the University there. There is a lot of biographical material to enable us to visualize the setting: decent folk, the father a humble good-humoured man of fifty-three, the mother a dignified woman of forty-seven; four daughters of whom the oldest was already married, and one son. Goethe who, as I said, loved masquerade, made his first entry disguised as a poor theology student, and for the next he borrowed special finery from the son of the tavern-keeper in another village and appeared dressed in it, carrying a big baptismal cake. Students' practical jokes have not changed much in two hundred years, but the two masks he used may be of strong, albeit unconscious, significance.

The entire story is one of painful tenderness and beauty. To me, for one, no women in Goethe's biography come out with the same degree of reality as the figures of Friederike and Lili. Should this be so because we are made more sensitive by the plot of the story? It is worthwhile for the reader to resort to Goethe's reminiscences and to the biographies to get the kind of well-rounded picture. Unforgettable, the student's horseback rides to Sesenheim, the moonlight scenes, the promises under the jasmine bower, the parents' obvious happiness at the turn of events—I think our nostalgic response, as in all love stories, is due to the fact that we identify so easily with the couple, and enjoy this identification. It makes a happy story up to a certain point. Then, at this point Goethe discovers that to her this is the great event for which her entire life had been a preparation—while to him it is suddenly only a passing experience. In the first letter (to a friend) which gives an inkling of the break to come he says: "And yet, it would be better if I could say I am happy . . . Who may say, I am the unhappiest? Edgar asks. This, too, is some consolation, my dear man. My head is like a weather vane when a thunderstorm comes up and the winds are changeable."

Thus, within a couple of months after the first doubt he made the final break. Here is his account of the farewell: "In such tension and bewilderment I could not leave without seeing Friederike once more. These were embarrassing days, the memory of which has not stayed with me. When, already in the saddle, I stretched my hand out to her, tears were in her eyes, and I felt awful." Yet, he did not have the courage to *tell* her about the hopelessness of their engagement, and he wrote the final word in a letter from Frankfurt. "I had to leave Friederike at a moment when it nearly cost her life," he confessed later.

The episode with Lili Schönemann, four years later, was quite similar except for superficial circumstances. The Schönemanns were prominent Frankfurt bankers, and therefore Lili's social background resembled Goethe's own. (Goethe's family, particularly on his mother's, the Textors', side was "best society.") Moreover, since Sesenheim there had been the experience with Lotte; *Werther* and *Götz* had been published, and Goethe was now internationally famous. None of this takes away any of the spontaneous, down-to-earth happiness which the reader can share. Indeed, one of the striking features of these stories is that one never has the feeling of the merely adventurous; one is never touched by any sense of foreboding—until the break. If two people ever seemed to be made for one another—these were the two. If one did not know what is going to come, one could not help that "aha," that click which good novelists are able to convey in their love stories. *Mutatis mutandis,* just to give a thumb-nail sketch, one can say that, if Friederike resembles Marie Bolkonska, Lili was a Natasha Rostov. She loved Goethe from the bottom of her heart. And he, who felt equally attracted to her, had a notion that this time it was the real thing. "It looks as though the threads of fate which until now I have been running up and down in rotation, came to a final knot." (Letter to Herder, March 25th, 1775.) The formal engagement came about when a forthright and practical friend of the Schönemann family, a Demoiselle Delf from Heidelberg, happened into the room in which the two had found themselves alone, and firmly suggested: "You two shake hands!"

"I was facing Lili," Goethe says, "and gave her my hand; she put hers into mine, not hesitatingly but slowly. After a deep breath we fell into one another's arms, with profound emotion . . . Just as, until now, the loved one had appeared beautiful, fair, attractive—from now on she appeared dignified and somehow significant. She was like a dual person: her beauty and charm belonged to me, this I felt as strongly as ever; but the nobility of character, the self-assurance, that thorough solidity—all this remained her own. I saw this, I beheld it and I enjoyed it all like some capital from which I would draw interest for the rest of my life." After that, who would possibly guess the outcome? Yet even at that very moment, it seems to us now, his uncertainty must have come back. At any rate, very soon the engagement felt to him as oppressive as a nightmare. When Count Stolberg appeared in Frankfurt and invited Goethe to a trip to Switzerland, he accepted eagerly. He wanted to "try out if he could get along without

Lili." A short trip had been planned, but Goethe ended up by staying away for ten weeks. The Schönemann family who, in the meantime, had somehow gotten wind of the Friederike affair, were utterly perplexed and scandalized.

After it was all over, and when Goethe finally left for Italy (actually, he was interrupted en route and was called to Weimar) he wrote this in his diary: "Lili, adieu . . . The decision is made—we must live our roles to the end, each for himself. At this moment I do not fear either for you or for myself—no matter how bewildering things may look. . . . Am I the only one in the world to wallow in never-ending, innocent guilt (*unschuldiger Schuld*)?"

To enable the reader to understand these episodes better, just a few words about the further destiny of the two women. Friederike never married. She died in 1813 at the age of sixty-one. She must have been a person of exceptional sweetness and warmth; it is particularly in her relationship with nephew and nieces ("my aunt is like an angel") that the shadow of Marie Bolkonska appears—Marie, as she would have been if she had never married. On Friederike's tombstone, in the village churchyard of Meissenheim, we read the lines:

> *"Ein Strahl der Dichtersonne fiel auf sie*
> *So reich, dass er Unsterblichkeit ihr lieh."*
>
> "A ray from the Poet's Sun fell upon her,
> So rich—it lent her immortality!"

Lili was only seventeen at the time of the broken engagement. Within one year of the awful experience she (quite obviously on the rebound) became engaged to a businessman, a Monsieur Bernard, who soon after went bankrupt and called the engagement off! When she was only twenty she finally married Herr von Türckheim, a landed aristocrat, mayor of Strassbourg—twenty years her senior and, from all accounts, a strong and sympathetic person. However, there are many signs that she was unhappy for years following the episode with Goethe. As late as 1784 Lavater wrote to her: "It is an honour to suffer, to desire suffering and to be able to suffer; to suffer in acceptance of that which cannot be changed; to bear silently the bearable; each night to wait for the morning that must come; to work, within the circle of one's life, quietly, seriously and gladly, and to ascend through a *must* towards a *happiness*. It is only in this way, my dear Madame Türckheim, that we prepare in the eyes of Heaven for supernatural joys, for the regal honour." When we meet her during the French Revolution, with a caravan of her children, disguised as a peasant woman about to bring vegetables to the market, one of the smaller girls at her hand, the baby bundled over her back, wading across the Saar river, in hair-breadth escapes from the revoltionary army (her husband had been forced to flee ahead across the German border), we see her as Natasha.

In both cases, Friederike and Lili, we cannot help feeling: "What a wife she would have made for Goethe!" As a matter of fact, so did he himself feel for many years to come. One may think that the episode of a young man breaking off love relationships at the age of twenty-one and twenty-five is nothing so exceptional, and that one should not read things into it. But looking at it in the context of Goethe's entire life, particularly his experience with other women, there is no doubt: here lay his tragedy. It is, incidentally, most remarkable that just at the time of his break with Lili he made his first notes for the idea of *Faust* and *The Wandering Jew*. The first one followed him to his death. The second one he abandoned again, obviously because the Ahasveric idea, the image of the man cursed to a life of eternal wandering, is exhaustively treated in *Faust*.

Incidentally, just as Kierkegaard felt an irresistible need to go back to Regina, as a token of final reconciliation (but was prevented from doing so by Fritz Schlegel), Goethe, too, felt compelled to revisit the victim, once it was all over. He was more fortunate. Eight years after Sesenheim he visited Friederike and her family, and he also visited Lili when she was Madame Türckheim and the mother of children. In both instances the people involved were courteous and affable. Friederike had become dangerously ill after he had dropped her. But eight years later ". . . she led me to that bower, and I had to sit there; and it was good. We had the most gorgeous full moon. I inquired about everything—I stayed for the night (with the family) and said farewell next morning at sunrise, greeted by friendly faces, so that from now on I can think with happiness again of that corner of the world and can live in inner peace with the spirit of the reconciled girl."

"Inner peace!" There are many signs that he was incapable of such self-deception. In 1773, shortly after the catastrophe, he had sent to Friederike through his friend Salzmann, a copy of *Götz von Berlichingen* with the remark, "Poor Friederike will be comforted when the unfaithful man (Weislingen, one of the *dramatis personae*) is poisoned." He never sent her *Faust,* perhaps because the implications of a literal analogy would have been offensive and misleading. But the very fact that he worked his way through more than fifty years' hard labour to end up at those final verses, in which the victim soul of the woman freely restitutes Goethe-Faust to eternal reconciliation, shows that "inner peace" cannot have been the real thing. Ibsen's famous statement that to be a poet means to sit in judgement over oneself has never been better illustrated. In the play *Clavigo* which is based on one of the memoirs of Beaumarchais, the hero has abandoned his loved one, Marie. As he leaves her behind she falls sick with some chest malady. This is literally the story of Friederike. "I cannot get rid of the thought of having abandoned Marie," says Clavigo, "that I have deceived her—call it what you want." In another minor play, *Stella,* the hero Fernando is set in dramatic conflict between two women, Cecilia and Stella, who are quite obviously modelled after Friederike and Lili. Fernando, just as Weislingen in *Götz,* is a weak character, and we have already remarked that Goethe saw himself in the traitor Weislingen who gets his dramatic comeuppance. He must have projected himself into all these portraits because it was around that time that he remarked, in letters: "I am quite unbearable . . . I know I am doomed," and "I should perish if I did not now write plays."

We have picked out the stories of Friederike and Lili. Actually Goethe's entire life, when it comes to women, reads like a psychoanalytic case story. This is also what makes us reluctant, lest we get so carried away by the "typical," by all that which is of the world of "mechanisms"—

that we lose the sense of mystery, the sense of the metaphysics of sexual love. For the mere curiosity of a psychologist, everything is there. The immediate universal appeal of *Werther* was due to the fact that the Oedipus tragedy had been presented in the right terms for the contemporaries of Rousseau, for a generation indulging in nostalgic introspectiveness. The same readers who eagerly followed Robinson Crusoe in his isolation in nature, followed Werther onto his island of self-pity. We have made allusion to the well-known dichotomy between the woman as an object of sexual desire, and the "woman on the pedestal," a division which is normal in the life of the adolescent but should be resolved in spontaneous synthesis in the adult. It is startling to see how men who, in other respects reach such heights, in this respect remain arrested in perpetuity. Certain facets of immaturity may perhaps be even necessary to stimulate creativeness. At any rate, genius in itself is no ferment for ripening. For just as we cannot add, by consciousness, one cubit of our stature, we cannot speed maturity by *intention*. We grow, but even a genius, by mere acquisition of knowledge, cannot hasten his growth:

> *"Uns bleibt ein Erdenrest*
> *Zu tragen peinlich"*
>
> "Bear we in cumbered flight
> Earthly remains"[5]

And it was precisely that adolescent duality of which we spoke which Goethe had to carry with him through life, like a stigma. He was continuously *torn* between women,

---

[5] This and all the following translations from *Faust* are quotations from "Goethe's Faust, Part One and Part Two," 2 vols., translated by Philip Wayne, The Penguin Classics, Penguin Books, 1959 and 1961.

not in indecision—much worse: like a ship whose rudder and sail are set at cross purposes. When his friendship with Friederike was at its height, he had a dream in which he saw himself standing between two women, Lucinde (the dance-master's daughter) and Friederike, who looked pale and sick. One week after the *Werther* episode with Lotte Buff had come to an end, he fell in love with Sophie Laroche, the ex-mistress of Wieland, and at the same time with her daughter who was engaged to be married to a wealthy widower, Brentano. While he was engaged to Lili there was a Lottchen Nagel, "a girl of the lower classes who lived in a poor basement flat."

When Goethe approached forty, at an age when most men get their enjoyment of creativeness by seeing a family grow up, the cleavage became only more evident. This was the time when his friendship with Frau von Stein had come to a height. Most biographers claim that, among all of Goethe's women, Frau von Stein was spiritually the most indispensable, as it were. She was his Muse. We learn of an affinity of hearts and a constantly flowing exchange. Frau von Stein was a married woman, mother of seven children, and wife of a Weimar nobleman whose chief interests seem to have been horses, and the more carnal pleasures of love. She obliged her husband, but only dutifully, and all her frustrated *platonic* needs were fulfilled in her friendship with the poet. She was a kind of Lady Chatterley in reverse. Underneath her silhouette Goethe wrote something which Dante might have written: "What a spectacle to see how the world is mirrored in this chalice. She sees the world as it is, and yet through the medium of love." I believe that here the cleavage was for the first time "neat" because Frau von Stein, with all the poetic depth of soul, was aloof and prudish (even those charming women characters in *Wilhelm Meister* she judged to "behave improperly" and she found that the poet had applied a "bit of dirt" to every single one of them!), and thus allowed the friendship to blossom fully without burdening Goethe with guilt. In *Tasso* (for all I know, the first treatment in world literature of a paranoid character), an over-sensitive poet, forever with a chip on his shoulder, is soothed in his torment by a Princess who is quite obviously modelled after Frau von Stein.

And then came the period of *The Italian Journey.* Here, it seems, Goethe for the first time abandoned himself to physical love fully, unfettered by remorse, in his relationship with "Faustina," the daughter of a Roman innkeeper, a young woman of twenty-four who had been widowed at twenty, the year of her marriage. After his return to Weimar in 1788, it looks as though he wanted to continue where he had left off with "Faustina," this time in his friendship with Christiane Vulpius, a worker in a factory that made artificial flowers. He took her into his house, and Christiane lived with him as his mistress and housekeeper, and bore him five children.

Nobody can remain unmoved by the pagan beauty of the Roman Elegies. But back in Weimar the common-law marriage made for a double life that must have been oppressive. Society judged harshly. Frau von Stein was unbending in her disapproval. On one occasion, when Goethe tried to remove misunderstandings "(Does it hurt anyone? Who can care about the feelings I bestow on this poor creature? Who cares about the hours I spent with you?"), Frau von Stein wrote on top of the letter a laconic: "Oh!! . . . ," and one can just see her recoil. Böttiger, a Weimar professor, is quite representative of the people of good standing: "They (the Roman Elegies) burn with the flame of poetic genius, and theirs is a unique place in our literature. But honourable women are scandalized by the brothel-like nakedness of it all. Herder is quite right in saying that he (Goethe) has put an imperial seal on impudence. From now on the Hores[6] ought to be spelled with an initial W added. Most of these Elegies are written at his return, in the first frenzy over Madame Vulpius. Ergo . . . " As long as the marriage remained common-law (Goethe married Christiane officially only in 1886, after eighteen years of life together!), Christiane stayed in the kitchen and remained more or less hidden when guests appeared. To me it always seemed that nothing brings the man Goethe closer to us than this extraordinary marriage. Christiane never read any of his works. And although he was aware of her limitations ("the realm of the spirit does not exist for her") there are, on both sides, many proofs of love. She was natural, warm, quite unaffected and unpretentious ("Farewell, and think of your Christelchen that loves you tenderly, and don't make eyes at the ladies!" (Feb. 14th, 1798)) and would have given her life for him. As a matter of fact, she nearly did. The very last event which prompted him to look for the sacramental seal was when she protected him physically from a threatening rabble of soldiers. This happened during the Napoleonic campaign of 1806. They got wed on October

[6] Goethe edited a literary magazine, *Die Horen* (The Hours). I am adapting the pun to the English language, with the same meaning.

19th, but Goethe had engraved on the rings the date of the danger, October 14th, 1806! One is touched in this case by the seemingly trivial. To appreciate the human side of the story, one has to look at it against its background. To begin with, there was much curiosity on the part of the intelligentsia, a lot of which has the air of small-town nosiness. Wilhelm von Humboldt wrote in a letter to his wife: "Have I already told you that he addresses her *Du* (Thou) and she addresses him *Sie* (You)? This, my dear child, is what I would call respect!" And Schiller in a letter to a friend: "Goethe's mind is not enough at peace because his miserable homelife, which he is too weak to change, causes him plenty of trouble." And soon after, again Schiller to the same friend: "No one can go against the moral law without invoking punishment on himself. He could have found a loving spouse at the proper time—and how different his life would be now! The opposite sex is destined for something higher than just an implement for sensual gratification, and there is no substitute for a happy home. Goethe himself cannot possibly esteem a creature that gave herself like that; nor can he force others to honour her and her family. Yet he cannot simply stand it when she is not being accepted (by society). Such a situation is apt, in the long run, to sap the strength even of a powerful man. This is not the kind of obstacle one can overcome by struggle; it is rather like a gnawing sensation of which one is dimly aware and which one tries to deaden . . . " Is there a hidden note of Pharisean glee? In those days such judgments were not as priggish as they would appear today.

However, Schiller did touch on an important point. I believe the reason why Goethe never became the National

Poet in the sense of that immediate, ethnic, Kiplingesque appeal, as Schiller did, was precisely this—Goethe knew what he himself called the "daemoniacal," the chiaroscuro, the negative potentiality of life, the persistent dark chord beneath a victorious theme.

August (Augustus) was the only one of Goethe's and Christiane's five children who survived infancy. There are many indications that August's tragedy was not only that of the famous man's son but also that of illegitimacy and the thousand unspoken conflicts which went with it. He turned into a drinker (as his mother apparently had been, only more so) and his own marriage to Ottilie was not only tragic but anticipated some of the dismal and sordid characteristics of late nineteenth-century bourgeois drama.

This is the background against which we have to see the old poet, the creator of the final scenes of *Faust*. It is a dimension often neglected, and yet quite necessary for our understanding. Try to visualize the day of Christiane's death. Goethe, who could not bear to see a dead person—and hence, as so frequently happens, could not see a person dying either—was lying in one room of the house, with what seems to have been not more than a common cold. August had retired to another room, remote from the one in which his mother lay dying, incapable of going to see her, and drinking. Apparently for his own reassurance Goethe summoned the man who, for years, had been his secretary. Here is the diary entry on the day of Christiane's death: "June 6th. Slept well, feeling much better. My wife's end is close. Last terrible struggle of her nature. Towards noon she passed away. Emptiness and deadly silence within me, and outside. Arrival and solemn entry into town of Princess Ida and of Bernhard. Counsellor Meyer. Riemer. In the evening the town brilliantly illuminated. My wife to the morgue at 12. I in bed all day." And the following day: "June 7th, 1816. Did not sleep particularly well. Numerous condolences. Got up. Counsellor Meyer. At noon with August."

Adele Schopenhauer, the philosopher's sister, who had incidentally been the first to accept Christiane in society ("I think, if Goethe has given her his name we can, at least, give her a cup of tea") left us the following description of Christiane's death: "The death of that poor Goethe woman was the most ghastly affair I have ever heard of. Alone, in the hands of heartless attendants, she died practically without anyone caring for her. No friendly hand closed her eyes; nothing could move her son to go to her, and Goethe did not dare . . . "

Ghastly is the word. When I once visited Goethe's house I saw there, among other things, a small scale model of one of the first railways which an Englishman had sent him. And it occurred to me how wide the arc of time stretches in a long life, in this case from a year when Bach was still alive right into the period of the Industrial Revolution. What a span! And what a span when you think of the *praeceptor Germaniae,* the Olympian, with his apparent serenity, his sense of the classical, the measured and the harmonious—and then visualize him in the house on the Frauenplan on the day of his wife's death. A renaissance humanist, a spiritual contemporary of Erasmus, who shared the world of Gogol!

It is not that private lives did not always have multiple planes. What do we know of Dante's marriage? Much less than we know about Beatrice. This is not the point. The point is that in the nineteenth century men began to become preoccupied by those multiple planes. The measured and harmonious *was* at the same time the questionable and doubtful.[7] This, I believe, is the secret of Goethe's life. Even in this sense he was the first modern.

---

[7] I have avoided going into the psychoanalytical aspect of all this more than is necessary for our purpose. Freud's own paper on a childhood reminiscence from *Poetry and Truth,* although dealing with one simple aspect (fraternal rivalry) is strikingly convincing. Otto Rank's thesis (Rank, O., *Das Inzestmotiv in Dichtung und Sage.* Deuticke, Leizig and Vienna 1912), about the central significance of Goethe's love for his sister Cornelia, appears well supported by certain leit motifs. It is quite extraordinary to watch the "brother-sister" constellation in Goethe's work. In *Faust,* Valentin comes to revenge his sister's shame; Clavigo is killed by Marie's brother (the Valentin story in reverse!)—and then we have the relationship of Orest and Iphigenie in *Iphigenie auf Tauris.* Goethe's father was not unlike Kierkegaard's: a serious, duty-bound man, apparently somewhat devoid of humour, of upright Lutheran piety. The mother, Frau Rath Goethe, has become an over-life size, semi-legendary figure to all those who have received their literary education in a German-speaking country. And as long as there are German letters one will probably keep hearing her putter around somewhere in the background of the German literary parlour ("Frau Aja") as a member of the family—with her wisdom and commonsense, her loquacity, and her sense of humour. For more detailed psychoanalytical observations on Goethe, his lines of identification with father and with mother, the ambivalence of his relationship to both, the reader is referred to the psychoanalytical papers by Rank, Th. Reik (Reik, T., *Warum verliess Goethe Frederike? Eine psychoanalytische Monographic.* Imago *15,* 400, 1929), Hitschmann (Hitschmann, E., *Psychoanalytisches zur Persönlichkeit Goethes.* Imago *18,* 42, 1932), and others. Eissler's study came too late to my attention to be considered for the present essay (Eissler, K. R., *Goethe. A Psychoanalytic Study. 1775–1786.* 2 vols. Wayne State University Press. Detroit 1963). There is only one tentative suggestion I should like to add. Like so many mothers in her situation, Frau Rath in her maternal attachment seems to have unconsciously favoured the tragic fission between Goethe's literary woman friendships on one hand and his sexual gratifications on the other. When she talks of his needs of a "Bettschatz" ("something good for the bed") there is behind that an unconscious wish to see her female rival devaluated. Consequently, Goethe's own unconscious resentment of this and his ambivalencc towards the mother comes out in the character of Martha Schwertlein, the woman who, in connivance with Mephisto, "procures" Gretchen for Faust.

The Goethe who ran off to Jena every time his housekeeper-mistress gave birth, and the man whom we have just been picturing in that Gogolian death scene, is the same who wrote: "Whoever attacks the state of matrimony, whoever by word or deed tries to undermine this very basis of a moral society, has to pick a bone with me. And if I cannot persuade him, I refuse to have anything further to do with him. Marriage is the beginning and summit of civilization. It tames the brute, and even the most civilized one has no better opportunity to prove that he is civilized. Marriage must be indissoluble; for it brings so much happiness that any unhappiness here or there is completely outweighed by that. . . . It may at times be inconvenient, this I can well believe—and this should be so. Aren't we also married to our conscience which we often would gladly get rid of, because it is much more inconvenient than any husband or wife could ever be?"[8] This is a beautiful passage. Hypocritical? On the contrary. Later in the nineteenth century, realists saw what was sordid behind the façade of civilization and went on a huge romp of "exposing." As a matter of fact, this is not over yet. With Goethe it was the other way around. He possessed that immediate sense for the inner reality of things which is perhaps the most typical feature of what we call the "classical," and all his work has to be understood out of a paradox—the dialectic antithesis between *"alles Vergängliche"* *(all things corruptible)* and *"das Unzulängliche"* (the ineffable, better perhaps the unattainable).

And this is, strange as it may seem, where Gretchen,

[8] *Die Wahlverwandtschaften.* Part one, Chapter 9.

the victim girl, comes in. For that famous last strophe of *Faust,* in its entirety, reads as follows:

"Alles Vergängliche
Ist nur ein Gleichnis;
Das Unzulängliche
Hier wird's Ereignis;
Das Unbeschreibliche
Hier ist's getan;
Das Ewig-Weibliche
Zieht uns hinan."

"All things corruptible
Are but a parable;
Earth's insufficiency
Here finds fulfillment;
Here the ineffable
Wins life through love;
Eternal womanhood
Leads us above."

At first glance the celebrated last two lines look like the most magnificent non-sequitur in world literature. Yet, these are the words with which the poet concluded his life's work. What is it all about? What is it that gives meaning to these last lines? If I may come back to the concepts of Gabriel Marcel, Faust, the frenzied activist, foregoes *being* in favour of *having*. But *having* divested of *being* is illusory. It is impregnated with a limitless and eternal insatiability which leads to destruction. The man of "free inquiry," untied to the anchor of faith, is hell-bound. In the same scene in which Faust pronounces a solemn curse on Love, Faith and Hope, he signs a contract with the salesman of Nothingness. It is significant that he adds "Patience" to his triple curse.

> "Und Fluch, vor allem, der Geduld!"
> "And cursed, above all, be patience!"

To the modern temper of activism, patience—literally the virtue of "suffering"—is inacceptable. And yet, it is only in this that we can find redemption. Let us suppose that Goethe had allowed Faust to earn his eternal salvation *only* by the great humanitarian works he achieves at the end of Part Two. The solution would have been pat and "modern." But it would have been untrue. Nothing shows more the character of Goethe as one of the mystic and prophetic *illuminati*—that he was not content with that solution. The spirit of unbridled activism, of insatiable curiosity and conquest, needs womanhood, the holy passivity of the *"be it done unto me,"* as its complement. This is the nuptial union of being. And it is only through this that Faust finally finds his redemption.

But we are anticipating. It is quite logical that the man of "free inquiry"—"free" in the sense of being cut off from faith—must forego the union of love and of contemplation. There is, literally, not a minute's rest. Faust knows this, and in singular defiance makes it the basis of his pact, when he and Mephisto first negotiate the deal.

> "Werd ich zum Augenblicke sagen:
> Verweile doch! du bist so schön!
> Dann will ich gern zu Grunde gehn!
> Dann mag die Totenglocke schallen,
> Dann bist du Deines Dienstes frei,

Die Uhr mag stehn, der Zeiger fallen,
Es sei die Zeit für mich borbei!"

"If to the fleeting hour I say
'Remain, so fair thou art, remain!'
Then bind me with your fatal chain,
For I shall perish in that day.
'Tis I for whom the bell shall toll,
Then you are free, your service done.
For me the clock shall fail, to ruin run,
And timeless night descend upon my soul."

The Devil, always the sport and gentleman, asks him to think it over.

"Bedenket wohl, wir werden's nicht vergessen."
"This shall be held in memory, beware!"

But Faust, by now already bitten by the fever, impatiently persists:

"Dazu hast du ein volles Recht,
Ich habe mich nicht freventlich vermessen.
Wie ich beharre bin ich Knecht,
Ob dein, was frag ich, oder wessen."

"And rightly is my offer thus construed!
What I propose I do not lightly dare:
While I abide, I live in servitude,
And whether yours or whose, why should I care?"

Like the true addict who's got his first taste he does not care any more with whom he is signing up. It's got to be fast.

And fast it is. Unlike the greatest of all medieval

poems, which tells the story of a well-measured walk, the poem of modern man is that of an erratic chase.

> "Stürzen wir uns in das Rauschen der Zeit,
> Ins Rollen der Begebenheit!
> Da mag denn Schmerz und Genuss,
> Gelingen und Verdruss,
> Mit einander wechseln wie es kann;
> Nur rastlos betätigt sich der Mann."

> "Now plunge we headlong in time's racing surge,
> Swung on the sliding wave of circumstance.
> Bring now the fruits of pain and pleasure forth,
> Sweet triumph's lure, or disappointment's wrath,
> A man's dynamic needs this restless urge."

"Rastlos." Restless. An air of restlessness permeates the entire drama until the final scene when it all comes to a halt—and then we find ourselves suddenly back in the world of Dante, as it were. However, throughout that running sequence of adventures, encounters, and enterprises, you have that strange sensation you often get with our present-day Fausts in business, in industry, in "organization"—namely not knowing whether our man is being chased or chasing, whether he is fleeing *from* or running *after* something. (On one occasion, in the throng of the Walpurgisnacht, Faust remarks: "You think you push, and you're *being* pushed.")

Now it is most extraordinary that when the signatures of the pact are scarcely dry, the very first adventure for which Faust enlists Mephistopheles' help is one of love. In this way the poet achieves a remarkable result: throughout the baroque and scurrilous meanderings of Part Two, no matter whether Faust is betrothed to Helen or descending into the Realm of the Mothers, whether he is occupied in making a laboratory robot or in wrestling fertile land from the ocean, he is already tainted. He is a man with a past. Actually the Gretchen episode seems an everyday trivial one, but this makes it only the more dreadful. Faust is the fellow who has got a girl "into trouble" and then left her in the lurch. He has driven her to insanity, to infanticide. In his remorse he tries to free her from the dungeon but then *she* wants to be left alone. And while, in Part Two, he is engaged with emperors and gods and wrestling with esoteric mysteries, you have that unpleasant sense in the back of your mind—the feeling of unfinished business. What has happened to that little girl? Hasn't he her life on his conscience and, by the way, her brother's and her baby's? No orphic wisdom seems to get us away from that. Only at the very end does the dénouement come. There is no reason why the drama of *Faust* should not have been like that of *Don Giovanni,* and following the crime at the beginning the reader could sit back and await the comeuppance at the end. Indeed, this had been Goethe's idea at one time. The only reason why it is not so, why Mephistopheles does not go home with a juridical victory (this is what a neat fulfillment of the written pact would have been) and why, instead, freely given Grace triumphs at the end—the only reason rests, mysteriously, in the soul of woman. The first hint comes in what the *Doctor Marianus* says about the Blessed Virgin:

"Höchste Herrscherin der Welt!
Lasse mich im blauen,

Ausgespannten Himmelszelt,
Dein Geheimnis schauen."

"Pavilioned in the heaven's blue,
Queen on high of all the world,
For the holy sight I sue,
Of the mystery unfurled."

Following the chorus of the women penitents (Saint Mary Magdalen, the Samaritan woman, and the Egyptian Maria) it is Gretchen's turn, with a variant of the moving prayer which at one time at the height of her earthly trouble, she had prayed in front of the statue of the Blessed Virgin.

Now we understand better those final lines which, at first, were so startling:

"Alles Vergängliche
Ist nur ein Gleichnis;
Das Unzulängliche
Hier wird's Ereignis;
Das Unbeschreibliche
Hier ist's getan;
Das Ewig-Weibliche
Zieht uns hinan."

"All things corruptible
Are but a parable;
Earth's insufficiency
Here finds fulfillment;
Here the ineffable
Wins life through love;
Eternal Womanhood
Leads us above."

Works of poetry, like dreams, are multiply determined. We have already, in a previous chapter, quoted Dante on this matter. To apply this to *Faust* we can say that the First Part is, above all, superb theatre which can be enjoyed, like any great play, for its sheer dramatic power, quite independent of any analytical reflexion. The Second Part can be enjoyed for its poetic and allegorical imagery. You can leave it at that. But if you go further, then you open up an intricate set of Chinese boxes.

There is, of course, the autobiographical level. From what we have said about Goethe's life, the Gretchen tragedy is not difficult to understand. However, it is not limited to that; on the contrary, the reality of the poem begins where the personal stops. *Faust* is neither an autobiographical statement nor a case study. To begin with, Goethe always knew that sexual love is bound up with mystery. Love was a dying-in-one-another in order to be born into a new life. The seducer's flight from Woman was a flight from life-giving death. The *West-Eastern Divan* contains a love poem which is remarkable among the myriads of love poems of world literature:

"Sagt es niemand, nur den Weisen,
Weil die Menge gleich verhöhnet . . ."

"Tell no man, tell wise men only,
For the world might count it madness . . ."

We are warned that we are about to enter an esoteric region:

Selige Sehnsucht
Sagt es niemand, nur den Weisen,

Wiel die Menge gleich verhöhnet:
Das Lebend'ge will ich preisen,
Das nach Flammentod sich sehnet.

In der Liebesnächte Kühlung,
Die dich zeugte, wo Du zeugtest,
Uberfällt Dich fremde Fühlung,
Wenn die stille Kerze leuchtet.

Nicht mehr bleibest Du umfangen
In der Finsternis Beschattung
Und dich reisset neu Verlangen
Auf zu höherer Begattung.

Keine Ferne macht dich schwierig,
Kommst geflogen und gebannt,
Und zuletzt des Lichts begierig,
Bist du Schmetterling verbrannt.

Und solang du das nicht hast,
Dieses: stirb und werde!
Bist du nur ein trüber Gast
Auf der dunklen Erde.

Holy Yearning
Tell no man, tell wise men only,
For the world might count it madness,
Him I praise who thirsts for fire,
Thirsts for death, and dies in gladness.

Thou wast got, and thou begattest
In dewy love-nights long ago;

Now a stranger love shall seize thee
When the quiet lamp burns low.

Thou art freed and lifted, taken
From the shadow of our night,
Thou art drawn by some new passion
Towards a nobler marriage-rite.

Distance cannot weight thee, soaring
Where the far enchantment calls,
Till the moth, the starfire's lover,
Drinks the light, and burns, and falls.

Die and grow! Until thou hearest
What the word can say,
The world is dark and thou a wanderer
Who has lost his way.[9]

The poem begins with an allusion to the moth which seeks the flame and finds death in what it seeks; and it ends with allusion to the gospel. "Stirb und werde!" "Unless the seed falleth into the ground and dieth . . ." Intertwined with these two thoughts we find the poem of sexual union. To seek sexual love but refuse self-abandonment is the same as the refusal of the divine call. How daring, to tie up the allusion to the gospel with the image of sexual love! Hence the esoteric signpost and warning in the first two lines.

Tell no man, tell wise men only,
For the world might count it madness.

---

9 Translation by F. Melian Stawell.

For the commitment in love, whether between Man and Woman, or between the human being and God—death must occur. It is as though both kinds of union were part of the same mystery. This is the reason why in the language of Saint Paul and in the language of the mystics the union of Christ and the Church, of God and mankind are interchangeable with the marital union.

The ". . . bist du nur ein trüber Gast auf der dunklen Erde" evokes the mood of ". . . I am quite unbearable . . . I know I am doomed" after the flight from Friederike. It evokes the Ahasveric image, the man damned to eternal restlessness.

> The world is dark and thou a wanderer
> Who has lost his way.

In the uncommitted there is, instead of immolation, a terrible endless return. It is the vicious circle of Sisyphus. Don Juan-Faust's refusal arises out of anxiety, and, in turn, leads to the restlessness of the unredeemed. That which appears to Don Juan-Faust as freedom is actually the opposite—a compulsion, something akin to physical necessity. The resemblance to physical necessity comes out clearly in a simile which Faust himself uses. He compares his own stormy movement through life to a tumbling stream. In other words, what *appears* as a course of liberation, of the unfettered and the free—is in reality something like the force of gravity, blindly compelling.

> Bin ich der Flüchtling nicht? Der Unbehaus'te?
> Der Unmensch ohne Zweck und Ruh,
> Der wie ein Wassersturz von Fels zu Felsen brauste
> Begierig wütend nach dem Abgrund zu?

Und seitwarts sie, mit kindlich dumpfen Sinnen,
Im Hüttchen auf dem kleinen Alpenfeld,
Und all ihr häusliches Beginnen
Umfangen in der kleinen Welt.

I the uprooted, I the homeless jade,
The monster I, whose only aim is this:
To scour the rocks like any blind cascade
Racing and eager for the dark abyss.
While she from passion sweetly lived aloof,
With senses of a scarcely wakened child,
The alpine paddock and the cottage roof
Her busy tender world and undefiled.

The two contrasting metaphors—the cascade tumbling wildly towards the abyss, and the self-contained world of the little cottage—are the most appropriate symbols of Faust and of Margarete. This is their true polarity. Out of this polarity we may understand the story on all levels of meaning. Keep it in mind when you hear the famous dialogue on faith. This dialogue takes place after the seduction, and it is actually prompted by Margarete's wish to talk to Faust about Mephistopheles. In our context it is so important that we reproduce it in its entirely.

MARGARETA. Promise me, Heinrich!

FAUST. Dear, I promise true.

MARGARETA. Please tell me what religion means to you.
Although I think you very good and kind,
I doubt if worship weighs much in your mind.

FAUST. Let be, dear child! You feel my love is sure:

For those I love, death's pangs I would endure,
Nor any man of church or faith bereave.

MARGARETA. But that's not right: we must believe.

FAUST. We must?

MARGARETA. Why yes—forgive that I persist:
You don't regard the Holy Eucharist.

FAUST. Regard it, yes.

MARGARETA. But not with faith or need:
You never go to mass, or say your creed.
Do you believe in God?

FAUST. Sweet, who can dare
To say that he believes?
Ask anywhere—
A sage or priest—and you will see
The answer seems like mockery
Upon the asking.

MARGARETA. Then you don't believe?

FAUST. Nay, darling girl, no need to misconceive.
For who can say that name
and claim
A very certain faith?
Or where is here with feeling
Of some revealing
Who dares to say it is a wraith?
He that's upholding

All and enfolding,
Holds he not,
Folds he not
You, me, himself?
Towers not the vault of heaven above us?
Does not earth's fabric bear us bravely up?
Do not the friendly eyes of timeless stars
Still gleam upon our sight?
Gaze we for nought in one another's eyes?
Is not life teeming
Around the head and heart of you,
Weaving eternal mysteries
Seen and unseen, even at your side?
Oh, let them fill your heart, your generous heart,
And, when you lose your being in that bliss,
Give it what name you will—
Your joy, love, heart, your God.
For me, I have no name
To give it: feeling's surely all.
Names are but noise and smoke,
Obscuring heavenly light.

MARGARETA. All that is very good and right:
Our pastor nearly says the same,
Only his words are somewhat different.

FAUST. Beneath the sun
From many hearts the self-same cry is sent:
Each has his way and speech. Then will you blame
My offering as irreverent?

MARGARETA. What now I hear

Were well enough, if I were reconciled;
But something fails, and terribly I fear
You have not Christ within.

FAUST. My child!

MARGARETA. Alas, alas, it troubles me
To see you in such company.

FAUST. How so?

MARGARETA. The person who accompanies you
Fills me with horror through and through.
Nothing has chilled me since my life began,
As does the dreadful visage of this man.

Faust expresses Goethe's own religious outlook—the ill-defined Spinozistic pantheism so familiar to us from many of his utterances and the modern intellectual's refusal to be bound by teaching.

Gefühl ist alles;
Name ist Schall und Rauch,
Umnebelnd Himmelsglut.

Feeling's surely all.
Names are but noise and smoke,
Obscuring heavenly light.

If we had nothing but this scene to prove Goethe's poetic genius, it would be sufficient. For if that dialogue between the proud scholar and the illiterate girl implies a debate—we are not at all sure that Faust is the winner. In fact, the dialogue does imply a debate, and most of us, even those who do not share Margarete's faith, feel that she has the upper hand. In order to understand this read this scene over, and then turn immediately to the final scene of Part Two. Then it becomes clear to everybody that Margarete is the winner.[10]

We have mentioned that the theme of the Ahasveric man who can be redeemed only by the love of a simple girl echoes throughout the romantic era. But it would be quite wrong to link this up with the aesthetic climate of the time, and think of it as merely a subject for a romantic ballad. Dostoievsky, whom one cannot very well classify as a Romantic, had, without being aware of it, found the Faustian theme and the Goethean solution in *Crime and Punishment.*

The themes of "seducer" and "innocent girl," of the "haunted criminal" and the "good prostitute" belong even to the recurrent types of *kitsch.* They surely must have occurred in hundreds of melodramas. We must not be misled by this. The appeal to bad taste often hides a truth. And it is one of the earmarks of the greatest in art that we

---

10 All this is even more remarkable since Goethe, in his personal life, was anti-Catholic. Offhand one should expect someone of the *largesse* of Goethe's humanism and of his Spinozistic view of the world, to be above the Protestant-Catholic controversy. Quite the contrary. For example, when, with the generation of Novalis, the first trend towards Catholicism occurred among German intellectuals, Goethe reacted with extraordinary bitterness. With actual converts (Friedrich Schlegel, Zacharias Werner) he broke off all contact. He felt that the latter should no longer be granted access to the University of Jena! To be sure, there are many indications to show that his anti-Catholicism was merely a psychological and sociological phenomenon, something to be understood on the political and parochial level of the early nineteenth century, and out of the Lutheranism of his childhood. But it is rather suggestive that the violence, so incommensurate with his Olympian detachment in other things, was a "reaction formation," meaning that here lay a conflict.

find that the theme a genius chooses might, but for a small difference, be *kitsch*. It was due to such confusion of values that Charles Lamb was dismayed to meet Sally Thoughtless in *Faust*. Stendhal put it more cynically when he observed, "Faust compacts with the devil to do what every one of us has done in his youth—to seduce a milliner."

Raskolnikov, in the truly Russian manner, does a lot of philosophizing about his murder. He has come to believe that the value of a human life can be rationally determined. It can be statistically evaluated, as it were. A superior intellect like his may, if the necessity arises, dispose of the life of a worthless old pawnbroker who is, in addition to everything else, a loathsome character. Life seen in terms of logistics—this is sheer *maleness*, unfettered and crazed. This idea could easily have been sold by Mephisto to his contract partner, but it so happens that the plot of *Faust* does not ask for it. Raskolnikov, like Faust, makes his discovery in the nick of time, and through a woman. It is only through the intermediation of Sonya that he finds the road to redemption.

Faust's and Margarete's and Raskolnikov's and Sonya's respective dialogues on faith are no arguments in the sense of intellectual debate. They go deeper. Man and woman represent precisely those poles of an ontological antithesis of which we are speaking in this book. Goethe, who himself was insatiably hungry for knowledge throughout his life, was at the same time fully aware of the danger of scientism. Faustian hunger for knowledge, science autonomous, torn from the motherbed of simple wisdom, implies an activist principle which is infinitely expansible. But this hunger will end in self-devouring. Science must be contained. Unless it is tempered by the values which transcend it, it will destroy us all. If Man's relationship to Nature is nothing but that of technological victory, it amounts to a love-less union of Man and Nature, a rape, and this will end in perdition. The poet entered the realm of Christian gnosis[11] precisely at the point where he saw this drama linked with the drama of love between the sexes.

There are several kinds of wisdom.[12] There is worldly wisdom, the kind which one commonly associates with men like Montaigne or Emerson or Lichtenberg. Goethe himself is one of the most eminent examples of this. But Goethe the poet knew more than Goethe the thinker, and he knew that the mystery of wisdom is by no means exhausted on this level. There exists another wisdom in the order of Grace, infused from above, given to the little ones. And in a world, top-heavy with distension, it is littleness which maintains, in God's paradoxical physics, the precarious balance. Here we must draw attention to a remarkable parallel. The saints of the nineteenth century place great emphasis on hiddenness, littleness and childlikeness. This comes out most clearly in the life and teaching of Ste. Thérèse of the Infant Jesus but by no means only in her. It comes out equally in the life of Ste. Bernadette Soubirous. Needless to say, this is not confined to women—we meet it in St. Seraphin of Sarov, in the Eastern Church, and St. Konrad of Parzham and Charles de Foucauld in the Catholic Church. Hiddenness and littleness

11 The word is here not used to connote a historical group or movement, but simply to indicate an act of "sight."

12 Cp. Jacques Maritain, *Science and Wisdom,* loc. cit.

are the traits most naturally associated with the Annunciation, with childlike compliance, the open and expectant attitude towards the Spirit. With the last scenes of *Faust* we have also entered an era of the Blessed Virgin. It is as though all this were the only possible answer to autonomous reason maddened with pride. Now the poet expressed that very insight, and the parallel is the more remarkable since it has so precious little to do with whatever convictions Goethe consciously held. In his twenties, when Goethe was already beset by the conflicts which led to the conception of *Faust,* he wrote the famous Prometheus poem. Prometheus, who surges upward with the gesture of usurping power, was, incidentally, not only a symbol of the young poet. The image of Prometheus forms a recurrent preoccupation of the last century. It plays a great role in the language of revolution—the prototype of Man who despises all aid *from* above, who strives upward himself to get his due.[13] This is precisely the opposite of the *orans* of the Annunciation. Thus, we see that Goethe's work spans the polarity of our existence. For the Promethean fever will be healed only by the attitude of childlike expectancy—Man's readiness for Grace.

> Here the ineffable
> Wins life through love;
> Eternal Womanhood
> Leads us above.

Faust is a Christian mystery-play written by a pagan. As we have said, Faust ends where Dante ends. But his peregrina-

---

13 The young Karl Marx wrote a poem on Prometheus, and later made allusion to him in his doctoral thesis!

tions have led him through regions which Dante did not know; and he is made richer by new errors and new insights. Unlike the pilgrim of *The Divine Comedy* who was led by the child-virgin Beatrice, Faust and Raskolnikov are redeemed by women who have been broken by the world—the mad child-murderess and the prostitute. This emphasizes the tattered and the bedraggled that are characteristic of our time. And yet, with all the devastation we may have wrought—the heart open to infused wisdom remains the heart of immutable virginity.

TWELVE

Marginal Notes

The Precious Equilibrium.

In the beginning of this study we remarked among the many approaches to the subject of womanhood two basic trends. On one hand there exists a tradition as old as mankind: that sexual polarity is the expression of an *ur-prinzip* which pervades all levels of being; on the other hand, there exists a new approach which considers that tradition as a naive cliché and relegates it to the museum of prescientific oddities.

If the second approach were assured, that museum, vast as it seems already, would be in for an enormous enlargement. I doubt whether the Judaeo-Christian tradition would survive. The unspeakable mystery of the *and*—of God *and* His Creation, of God *and* His People, of Christ *and* the Church—would be conjured away. For Jewish esoteric tradition and Pauline theology teach that Man and

Woman share that "and." The sexual "and" is a reflection of the other—all being is nuptial.

To the Christian, the entire sense of history is tinged with this. The earliest prophetic message of eschatological significance refers to Woman (Gen. 3:15). Hence it is no surprise that she appears at the end of history, bigger than life, clothed in the Sun, the moon at her feet. Everything, the entire tortuous plot of Salvation, has to fit in between these two tableaux, and it does. At the central moment of the drama, equidistant from the two points, occurs the *fiat,* the second *fiat,* the creaturely one which complements the *fiat* of creation. The "Thy Will be done," that unconditional Yes which we pronounce everyday in prayer and which leads to a thousand little incarnations, at one central moment of history, as a unique manifestation of freedom, led to the Incarnation. To modern ears the word "freedom" jars in this context. To us freedom, the unshackled, means action. And yet, the stillness in the nod of *assent* was equalled in freedom only by the original freedom of the creative *act.*

This is, in short, the Christian belief. In the present study we confronted this belief with natural anthropology, presented by psychoanalysis and phenomenology in our time. The astounding result is that the Christian image of Man and of History, far from becoming relegated to the realms of superstitition, seems confirmed.

Let us first look at our six test cases. To begin with, there is one thing they all have in common—a definite Manichaean streak. If we regard, for the moment, the spirit as opposed, irreconcilably opposed to nature, to the flesh, then we have the common point of conflict of all these men. The six are an ill-assorted lot, no doubt, but they are like a chain gang, chafing against the same iron. At first sight there appears nothing remarkable about this. The Manichaean wound, as a focus of pain, is an old story. For example, a theory has been put forward that the apparent dualism between married life and the love of passion, between *agape* as life-giver and *eros* as a harbinger of death, is specifically European and goes back to the Middle-Ages and to the Manichaean movement.[1] One would have to know an awful lot of history to be able to prove or to contend this. At any rate, there is nothing new about the Manichaean conflict. On the contrary, one is inclined to feel that it is just one aspect of a bane which belongs to the human condition. What then makes our six men illustrative of the "modern" version? To say that there is the common contagion of Manichaeaism seems to say very little. The variations are as vast as the differences in character which separate our six. The only Manichaean pure and simple among them is Schopenhauer, and he differs from the ancient version merely by the fact that there is implied in his work a reaction against rationalism, enlightenment, and at the same time a revolt against the glad tidings of Christianity. On the other hand, Tolstoy Number One, the Tolstoy before the conversion, shows to me no trace of the malady. Kierkegaard and Goethe convey a sense of continuous struggle, in life and in thought. To Roquentin-Sartre Nature is the disgusting milk, and in Descartes' philosophy Nature is altogether un-mothered. Here is a set of variations in which the theme always comes

---

1 Denis de Rougemont, *Love in the Western World,* Pantheon, 1956.

through—at times clear, at times disguised. In what then lies the importance for us?

To answer this question it is best to continue where we left off—with Goethe. Of all the subjects treated he seems to be getting closest to a *mysterium*. The key to "Faust" is provided by the Prologue together with the final apotheosis. In the former the hero becomes the object of the Devil's bet with God, in the latter he encounters, as a central figure, the Blessed Virgin. His fate is first expected to be the result of a bargain between God and Satan. But at the last moment the devil is cheated of his deposit. That initial atmosphere of the Prologue—of the sport-like give-and-take, the reckoning of odds—is broken by an unexpected mood of freedom at the very end. And this entirely unexpected *dénouement* is tied in with that Feminine Presence, the *mater gloriosa* of the final scene. She provides the *termino fisso d'eterno consiglio,* the fixed end-point of eternal counsel.

It is most remarkable that Goethe, an unabashed self-commentator, was exceedingly diffident on this point. There is no trace of interpretation in any of the journals, letters or recorded conversations.[2] The poet's shyness resembles that of Scripture. The Gospel is exceedingly sparse when it comes to this theme. The announcement about the seed of Eve, tremendous as it is in its implication, is tucked away in one little phrase in the account of Genesis. And speaking of Mariology, one of the main points of theologians outside the stream of Catholicism and Orthodoxy,

[2] This is, incidentally, true about everything surrounding the subject. Eckermann, the keen recorder, baited Goethe about the idea of *Das Reich der Mütter* (The Realm of Mothers) in "Faust," but for once the poet declined comment.

has been precisely the fact that there is so little reference to Mary in Scripture.

The *fiat* of creation is infinitely manifest. All you have to do is to look around. The *fiat* of assent is infinitely hidden. Their complementariness is, as we said, the foundation of freedom. Man is invited to borrow, as it were, the *fiat* of creation in his activity but the *fiat* of assent is the gesture which keeps human creativeness from the abyss of the demoniacal.

Love and Power.

Now if one took the trouble, one could demonstrate that every single conflict we touched upon in the preceding essays can be reduced to one fundamental pair—Love and Power. Love and Power as a moral antithesis are at work inside every human being, regardless of sex. Love and power is the polarity of all human relationships. All relationships between human beings can be reduced to one of these two, and all moral conflicts arise out of a tension between the two. All true love for another means a renunciation—painful or effortless, conscious or unconscious, intentional or unintentional—of power. (Inversely, all power over another is an impairment of love.) The reader may distrust such an axiom. At times the antithesis is disguised beyond recognition: there are clinging forms of love which mask possessiveness; there is a form of authority, in fact all true authority, which resembles power but is based on love. And so on. One could go on interminably making one's point. Suffice it to say that the antithesis is not only one of psychology. It cannot be fully understood except ontologically. It begins with the mystery of the

Godhead. God started, one might say, His relationship with man by renouncing power over him. As Creator, He could have made men marionettes, without the gift of freedom. As Saviour, He could have brought salvation, without the question of cooperation. In either case it would have made for a much more ordered state of affairs than that which we see—except that this would be the orderliness of machinery.

To come back to our subject, with the present scientific-technological burst of human creativeness goes a phantastic increase in power over matter. Our ability to "master" nature is unheard-of, in comparison with the beginning of the scientific era three hundred years ago—even with fifty years ago. And this seems to be only the beginning. One might argue that here we are talking of power over matter, and to drag a hypothetical antithesis "power versus love" into it seems to mix things up. Obviously the antithesis of "power versus love" applies to human affairs and cannot be applied to the relationship between Man and Nature. But things are not as simple as all that. As we shall see our relationship to nature colours our relationship to our fellow-men. This is puzzling and disquieting. You cannot topple a hierarchic picture of the world in one sphere without causing upheaval in another.

We shall presently come back to the subject of "Man and Nature." In the immediate context we cannot avoid touching on the moral problems posed by technology. For it is technological progress which, by its absurd speed, drives home to everyone the moral problem of power. When it comes to that, people stop at the problem of the Bomb. But there are other problems—concerning the power of man over man—for example the problem of managerial power and of the vast technical power to create appetites and to satisfy appetites. If the phrase were not too hackneyed one would have to say that these powers are "godlike." In this context we frequently encounter a fallacy quite similar to the one of Goethe in his attitude to the exact sciences. When one reads certain Christian writers of the twentieth century one gets an impression that technical progress in itself is evil.[3] Such an attitude, too, implies a subtle form of Manichaean thinking. As a matter of fact, the technological burst of creativeness has all the earmarks of the greatest phases of civilization—and of all that which is morally and aesthetically good. There is something about technology which is related to the classical and objective in the history of art. There is about this kind of "making," say of a jet plane, some of the same creative anonymity which went with the making of medieval architecture. "In the case of a dynamic shape like an aeroplane there is neither any reason nor any need for the collaboration of engineer and artist. All such machines, except for their colouring, or some surface design, to modify their shape, develop in accordance with a law of efficient evolution as absolute as that determining the shape of the tiger, the wasp, or the swallow."[4] We are making creatures. It is as if we were called upon to populate the world with objects which relieve us of muscular exertion and of brain exertion. Bergson foresaw that, once automa-

---

[3] This is implied in some of the work of Eric Gill, Father McNabb, O. P., and others. At times, the work of Aldous Huxley and of Max Picard conveys a similar impression.

[4] Wyndham Lewis, "The Artist," Encounter, Sept. 1963, p. 65.

tion is generally organized, an enormous amount of human energy will be available for creativeness. Needless to add, if this should not come about the resulting vacuum will be filled by some kind of instinctual "flooding." It is obvious that such a dilemma cannot be considered outside the moral sphere. Hence the two faces of technical progress: on the one hand a sense of aesthetic joy and moral goodness; on the other the image of the Sorcerer's Apprentice, with that vertiginous feeling of an un-ending crescendo.

In order to understand better that sense of vortex and frenzy we must come back to the phenomenology of power. All power, for power's sake, is habit-forming. The phenomenology of power and the phenomenology of addiction show remarkable parallels. An addict gets to know an experience of euphoria, an extraordinary sense of well-being, at his first acquaintance with the drug. As he wants to renew the experience he will soon have to take a greater quantity. But the pattern changes; the addict without the drug is not just a normal being without a sense of happiness: he is in distress. And soon it is this distress which dominates his life. The drug is no longer needed to produce bliss: it has to be taken for a merely negative purpose—namely to escape misery. The amount of drug necessary to ward off misery increases with an inexorable law. Our man is by now a vessel with a leaking bottom; no matter how much he takes, he needs still more. Then a shuffling occurs in the hierarchy of appetites; the need for the drug is more imperious than the vital instincts, hunger, thirst or sexual desire. And there is a shuffling in the moral sphere. The need is such that any degree of deceit, any form of crime has to be committed to obtain the drug. In the end, taking the drug is no longer just a matter of avoiding distress and misery—the days of bliss being long past—but a mere avoidance of collapse and, in many cases, of death.

In order to compare this with the phenomenology of power it is best to take extreme examples—Napoleon, Hitler, Stalin and the like. In scrutinizing such lives we see that there occurs invariably an initial experience, quite comparable to that first encounter with the drug. There is the initial sense of heightened well-being through the first taste. But following a mysterious law, the "dose" must be increased to achieve the same result. Soon the initial bliss wanes, and more power has to be felt to stave off a sense of distress. Power addicts are miserable people. We say of a man like Hitler that at a certain phase he was at the "height" of his power. In reality there is no zenith, just as there is no zenith of addiction. The vessel keeps leaking and demands more. Such insatiability is a demoniacal mirage of infinity. In all cases of addiction there exists an initial sense of *increased freedom,* while in reality the subject becomes increasingly *fettered by necessity.* In the end all freedom is gone, and the subject is encased in a system of forces which are as compelling as the laws which govern inert matter. The drug addict as well as the power addict makes an initial choice to obtain some thing, and before he realizes it that thing has obtained him.

Gabriel Marcel once remarked that *all* temptation may be a temptation towards power. The inversion of this statement is more obvious: all power contains a temptation. And although it is less evident, this is also true about technological progress, the power over matter. It has been said, unjustly, that Goethe had a blind spot for the then beginning industrial revolution. On the contrary: he skipped a century—and saw the moral problem before anyone else. This is, as we have seen, one of the many facets of *Faust* and it is even more clearly expressed in *The Sorcerer's Apprentice.* Either intentionally or with the un-consciousness of the poet, the absent Master is meant to be God. The apprentice, once he has imitated the creative act, does not know how to make the thing stop. Here again, we have that sense of the bottomless. *Die Geister, die ich rief, die werd ich nicht mehr los,* "the spirits I invoked, I can't banish anymore,"—could also be said by an addict or by a Macbeth. The thing the apprentice first tried, has finally gotten *him.*

The Person and Society.

That law of insatiable expansion, that "unstoppable," makes the power over matter imperceptibly extend into the sphere of human relationships. I suspect that this is one of the reasons why technological progress makes some people apprehensive. When you travel for the first time in a trans-atlantic jet you cannot help being seized by the enthusiasm which all human creativeness evokes. Such achievements can only be good, if you insist on moral criteria. This is the reason why I have no patience with the romanticism of the spinning wheel. But when I listen, in the course of my work, to accounts of experiments on "group dynamics"; when I have a glance into the work of human riggings, with the wired glass cage and the observation booth; that dummy life of the set-up "situation" in which love and hate, acceptance and rejection are analyzed as vectors—then I suddenly share the horror of Blake and of Goethe, and of Kierkegaard. Without knowing it concretely, this is what they, with prophetic genius, dimly surmised. This is what Kierkegaard really had in mind when he regarded the human sciences as "blasphemous." In other words, the danger is that technical conquest does not stop at matter and leads to the reification of the person. This is the world of slow and noiseless violence in which we live already.

Before we go on from here, one more word about a subject which we have briefly touched upon in previous chapters, the antithesis between organism and organization. In one case the grouping and order among human beings follows an intrinsic law of *growth;* in the other case it follows an extrinsic law of *making*. All human collectives contain these two elements in varying proportions. The human family is an organism more than an organization. A business company is an organization rather than an organism. The Mystical Body is, as the name implies, first an organism and only secondarily an organization. I believe that scandals in the history of the church occurred whenever the sense of organization prevailed over the sense of organism. Although the organizational everywhere implies a temptation of power, it is needed as a complement, as it were, to the organismic. It seems that the fallacy that the political is evil in itself stems from the same apprehension which makes people feel that the technological is evil in itself. The "organismic" in societies, such as the medieval or Hindu, without objective self-consciousness, brings with it the danger of being imprisoned in the magic, the miasma of the soil, of being victimized by superstition, famine, poverty and epidemics.

It is only recently that we became aware of the opposite danger, namely that of the organizational. The work of men like Kafka or Camus who lead us into a human world without contact, would never have had such impact if it did not strike a familiar chord. In Kafka the hero is faced by a humanity which, although made up by persons (civil servants, inhabitants), is a *thing*. Just as to a dictator the *I* and *Thou* is replaced by an *I* and *they* or an *I* and *it*—so for the little man at the receiving end, the man who is about to enter the castle or to be on trial, the *other* becomes the *it*. The depersonalized atmosphere of the Castle and the trial, of "America" is *unheimlich,* in the sense in which Heidegger speaks of an objectified world: *un-homelike.*

The lesson we draw from all this is that the progress in the techniques of organization which brings about such great blessings—the removal of poverty, sickness, starvation in large sectors of the world—is a challenge towards heightened interiorization of the individual life. This is the true reason why the progress in communication and organization (in itself morally neutral) evokes in many of us a kind of eschatological mood. At times Kafka uses eschatological symbolism when he speaks of human ciphers who are busy manufacturing material happiness in a mass society without content. In an original sketch for the "Penal Colony" we find a passage in which "our always cheerful commandant" exhorts the workers: "Make a path for the serpent! . . . Prepare the way for the great Madam! . . . Go to it! . . . Go to it, you serpent's fodder!." Whereupon the men take their hammers "and there was a busy knocking going on, over miles. No letdown was permitted, only a changing of hands. The arrival of the serpent was announced for the evening, until then everything had to be knocked to pure dust, our serpent does not tolerate the smallest grain of stone . . . We don't understand why she calls herself Serpent still. At least she ought to call herself Madam . . . However, that's not our worry. Our only worry is to make dust."[5] In this—that the immense machinery for the production of earthly fulfillment evokes an eschatological image—Kafka is a descendant of Dostoievsky. To me, for one, the Great Inquisitor appears only accidentally in ecclesiastical garb. He is the "commandant," the manager who sees to it that production line of terrestrial happiness, the transformation of stone into bread, proceeds without friction. And for this the presence of Christ is *the* disturbing factor. He is the sign of contradiction. He upsets the works.

Now from what we have seen, that which we call here the "sense of organism" is the feminine, and the "sense of organization" masculine. Those who are wary of the trap of clichés should study the sources of empirical observation in psychoanalysis and phenomenology which we have quoted. Woman as real or potential mother possesses the sense of creativeness by which one lets something grow, nurtures it, allows it to follow its own mysterious law of becoming. Man's sense of creativeness is that of making things work. Hence the strange "maleness" of that entire universe of the organizational. It has been pointed out that

5 *F. Kafka, Tagebücher 1910–1923,* Frankfurt: S. Fischer, 1951.

Kafka's haunting world of the "Trial" and the "Castle" is run by men, and the women who do occur are either themselves eminently phallic or masochistically submit to, and "go along with," the apparatus.

Wherever individuals become ciphers, the feminine is wounded. For on the purely natural level—apart from the question of Grace, or even apart from all theological or philosophical reflexion—the sense of the infinite importance of the single individual is rooted in the experience of pregnancy, birth, and nursing. Scripture and theology teach us that the world has been created for Man to dwell in. But while someone is reading this line, a woman gives birth, with that immediate sense of certainty that the world has been created for this particular new human being. This certainty is not the result of abstraction. It arises out of an irreducible fusion with creative being. Hence the calculus of human logistics, that horrid concept of the human "material," which can be thought of as usable and as expendable, is forever inimical to the feminine. In this, as in everything else we have been saying, the psychological transcends itself. Graham Greene, in a remarkable essay on the dogma of the Assumption, has pointed out why the era of Hiroshima and of Auschwitz is, by the strange "logic" of the eschatological drama, the time of the Blessed Virgin.

Thus we see that the regard for the human person in terms of use and disposal is the male fallacy, as it were. It is Raskolnikov's fallacy. He is obsessed by the problem of power, and as he confesses to Sonya, the murder is an experimental test case. He purposely picks on a human being whose life is "of no use." "I've asked myself one day this question—what if Napoleon, for instance, had happened to be in my place, and if he had not had Toulon or Egypt nor the passage of Mont Blanc to begin his career with, but instead of all those picturesque and monumental things, there had simply been some ridiculous old hag, a pawnbroker, who had to be murdered, to get money from her trunk (for his career, you understand). Well, would he have brought himself to that, if there had been no other means? Wouldn't he have felt a pang at its being so far from monumental and . . . and sinful, too? Well, I must tell you that I worried myself fearfully over the question so that I was awfully ashamed when I guessed at last (all of a sudden, somehow) that it would not have given him the least pang . . . He would have strangled her in a minute without thinking about it. . . ."[6] When he told Sonya, "I've only killed a louse, Sonya, a useless, loathsome, harmful creature," the prostitute's horrified response, "A human being—a louse!" could have been made by millions of mothers in countless wars and purges. Raskolnikov's murder had been an experiment in philosophy. He said so in so many words. He might perhaps have come, through intellectual argument with a man, to the conclusion that he had been mistaken. But the truth which he discovered through a woman came from an ontological *grund,* from a depth into which discursive intellect does not reach.

The uniqueness and sanctity of the human person can be grasped only by contemplation. It is elusive to discursive reasoning. "But Mary treasured up all these sayings, and reflected on them in her heart," (Luke 2, 19). Now the mystery of the *alter Christus* in everyman; the

---

[6] Fyodor Dostoyevsky, *Crime and Punishment.* Translated by Constance Garnett.

fact that each single one of the myriads of births in the world is a Nativity; that each molecule of suffering in the world is a Gethsemane—these are facts on the plane of Grace, but as immediate irreducible insights they are natural to every mother.

It is evident from all this that the errors of contemporary materialism concerning society and the person, in short the entire subject of Christian Personalism, cannot be considered apart from the charisma of womanhood.

Man and Nature.

However, what is true about Society and the Person is also true about Nature. We have touched upon this here and there, particularly in the chapters on Descartes, Schopenhauer, Sartre and Goethe. We invoked the testimony of Husserl to show how nowadays, even the person without scientific training can no longer conceive of his experience as other than fitting into a global *construct* of geometrical relationships; that the world can no longer be seen other than dressed in these clothes. "If we want to go back to experience in its deep layer and origin, then we must come to an experience of life and the world which does not yet know such idealization, but (on the contrary), represents its very fundament."[7] At first sight we are inclined to regard this as an academic matter which—contrary to the problems of Society and the Person—is devoid of moral implications. This is not so. Any image of Nature which stops where Science stops is implicitly atheistic. And wher-

[7] Husserl, E., loc. cit.

ever the scientific statement usurps global validity, it is by necessity atheistic.

Take, for example, evolution. There are working hypotheses such as the "survival of the fittest," to explain otherwise puzzling phenomena—such as the geographical distribution of plants and animals in certain areas, the extinction of certain species and the survival of others. This was the theory which the passenger of the *Beagle* originally developed. Such a theory, applied to circumscribed scientific problems, has no philosophical implications, and it is hard to see how anyone but a well-trained biologist can venture to take a stand. Out of this developed the theory of evolution, with all its vast claims about the nature and destiny of man, his being and his becoming, and his position in the universe. It is said that the faith of the common man has been weakened by such teachings as the theory of evolution. History points to the opposite: Darwin's original scientific observations expanded into a global doctrine becase there was already a depletion of faith. It was a case of *horror vacui.* We have previously remarked that the scientific-analytical method, with all its breath-taking results, cannot even be applied to such questions as Creation, the infinite variety of forms, the destiny of man, the presence of hate and corruption and their coexistence in the same world with love and beauty. As is well known philosophers of the contemporary positivist school deny the validity and genuineness of such problems. The most burning questions concerning every man are considered as "pseudo-problems." Indeed, they are, and something goes awry everytime they are posed as scientific problems. They resist objectification. There is an inwardness to the process of becoming which resists analysis. We do not need to go as far as cosmogenesis. I have a certain number of years ago been a single cell, microscopically small, and now I sit at a desk, writing. Millions of data from the cumulative sciences form a fearfully intricate net of causalities to tackle this mystery but my being and my becoming are not caught in that net. If we present, for the sake of argument, the theory of evolution in a most scientific formulation, we have to say something like this: "At a certain moment of time the temperature of the Earth was such that it became most favorable for the aggregation of carbon atoms and oxygen with the nitrogen-hydrogen combination, and that from random occurrences of large clusters molecules occurred which were most favorably structured for the coming about of life, and from that point it went on through vast stretches of time, until through processes of natural selection, a being finally occurred which is capable of choosing love over hate and justice over injustice, of writing poetry like that of Dante, composing music like that of Mozart and making drawings like those of Leonardo." Of course, such a view of cosmogenesis is crazy. And I do not at all mean crazy in the sense of slangy invective but rather in the technical meaning of psychotic. Indeed such view of the history of the world has much in common with certain aspects of schizophrenic thinking.

No better illustration could be presented for Husserl's observation about that geometrical "dress" which has become the second nature of men's thinking. To the naive beholder of nature every phenomenon—whether it be a lion or a rose, a lizard or a fir tree—conveys a sense of completion in itself. The ensemble of the things of nature conveys a sense of order, even to those who have never heard of ecology. The idea that all living things are random points of arrestation, as it were, in a blind mechanism of physical occurrences, governed by pragmatic advantages, is already an expression of a Cartesian objectification of living things, a reification of Nature which was to be the prelude and the corollary of the reification of the Person. Here creatures are thought of as *things made,* in a Universe of competitiveness which is conceived of as a vast factory.

The historical roots of the theory of evolution are quite complex. But apart from a newly awakened fascination with the "laws of history" (Herder, Hegel, Marx, Nietzsche) there was, no doubt, another ingredient: the Industrial Revolution with its concept of *advance by improved workability.* The idea that in the vast factory of nature things which do not work well are discarded for things which work better arises out of the mood of the nineteenth century. The entire universe was made to fit the drab climate of Manchester. While the epic of Genesis, with its powerful poetic form, was rejected as "anthropomorphic," an evolutionist concept of how things came about is tinged with the ephemeral of the laboratory and the market place.

Teilhard de Chardin's work is an heroic effort to baptize the evolutionary theory, and his lasting merit will be to have put the Incarnation into the centre of natural history and to have, in an involved way, re-stated the brotherhood of all creatures. But even in his work we witness the paradox of something being pressed into an objective mould which, by its nature, resists such method.

His universe is topped by a Cartesian shell of consciousness, as it were,—which is not much better than *res cogitans* growing out of a *res extensa.* (This is the reason why in Teilhard's hypothesis neither the mystery of the aesthetic nor that of the ethical are adequately treated.) The Incarnation is grafted onto natural history but it ceases to be a human story.

This is the moment when the painter's rabbit once more comes to our aid. The artist's knowledge of a creature is, contrary to the scientist's, subjective. However, it is not subjective in the sense of mood and arbitrariness, but subjective in the Kierkegaardian sense. It is an interior knowledge, not achieved by breaking-up and disassembling but by union and incorporation. It is a primary form of knowledge, related to the world which unites child and mother. Positivist thinking is so prevalent today that the latter form of knowledge is discredited. In fact, one hesitates to call it knowledge. Such a "subjective" view of nature is suppose to be regressive. However, we have seen that discursive reason, to be whole, must retain, as its soil, that form of intelligence which is derived from the world of child and mother.[8] To state our point paradoxically, we might say that the scientist knows *more* about the rabbit than the painter but the painter knows *better* about the rabbit than the scientist. One form of knowledge cannot

---

[8] Merleau-Ponty, M. *Phénoménologie de la Perception,* loc. cit., and Piaget, Jean, *La Représentation du Monde chez l'Enfant,* loc. cit., Compare also Husserl's observations on the "fundament" of experience and Heidegger's remarks on poetry as the foundation (*der tragende Grund*) of history. (M. Heidegger, Hölderlin und das Wesen der Dichtung, Langen-Müller, Munich, 1937.) The fact that in poetic knowledge we must distinguish between truth and sentimentality is no argument against its validity. The methods of scientific knowledge present also sources of error.

do without the other. The painter endows the rabbit, in that unique act of comprehension by connaturality which is the basis of all art, with the irreducible quality of *Kreatürlichkeit* (creatureliness). No matter how much the cumulative sciences may add to our knowledge of things, simple wisdom has a knowledge of Nature which flows directly from the source of love.

From all this we see that Goethe's views on science on one hand and his presentation of the Faust-Margaret tragedy on the other cannot be considered separately. Not only does the hero's moral fate have to be redeemed through the woman but his knowledge had to be tempered by hers. Faust knew a thousand times *more* than Margaret but she knew a thousand times *better* than he. Indeed, the central point of "Faust" is precisely that the noëtic and the ethical cannot be considered separately.[9]

---

9 This, I believe, explains also the puzzle of Goethe's attitude to science.

Goethe worked as a scientist in fields as diverse as mineralogy and comparative anatomy, botany and the theory of colours. There were years in which science occupied him more than poetry, and during which he regarded himself as a scientist primarily. His visual gift was so extraordinary that we are not surprised to know that his most important contributions were morphological and descriptive (e.g. the discovery of the intermaxillary bone in man). But with all this he not only kept away from, but was openly hostile towards, the exact sciences. In an intelligence so vast, this was a strange case of foolishness. There is no other word for it. Take, for instance, the following: "Physics and mathematics must be considered completely separately. The former must remain entirely independent and must try to enter into Nature and all its hallowed life with love, reverence and piety—quite regardless as to what mathematics does and achieves on its part. The latter must declare itself independent from objects of any kind (*allem Äusseren*), go its own great path (*grossen Geistesgang)* and evolve with greater purity than it does when it deals with objects (*Vorhandenes*)." (Maximen und Relexionen, 573.)

If we try to understand how a genius like Goethe arrived at such statements we must keep in mind that that simple sense of entelechy, and that metaphysical realism which lies, unwarped by analytical training at

There are trends in present day theology (*Entmythologisierung*), which want to introduce scientific positivism into the world of Faith. Not only is the gospel stripped of the miraculous. Man's upward gaze, in prayer, does not make sense anymore because in a space merely mathematically conceived there is no above. But in such a world, one is apt to forget, there is no historical time either. There is no harkening back to the message nor looking forward to fulfilment. If mathematical analysis repre-

the bottom of all views on Nature, were very strong with him. And it seems that he never realized something which is so evident today, namely that the knowledge of naive experience and knowledge by dissection are not contradictory. For example, Goethe's "Theory of Colours" is what we would today call a phenomenology of colours. Yet he regarded it as a proof against Newtonian optics. The thought, so familiar to us today, that observations may be true on two separate planes of methodology, never entered into Goethe's grotesque polemics against Newton. Behind it all lay, I believe, some kind of spiritual anguish. As a young student in Strasbourg Goethe heard the lectures of one Holbach who gave an exposition of the Universe according to Newtonian mechanics and drew from this the celebrated atheistic proof. To us today this is an old story: the infinite, drab celestial machinery, clanking along soul-lessly, with "nobody out there." For the student in Strasbourg the experience was decisive. It struck terror in his heart, a terror from which—in a sense—he never recovered. The young poet realized with immediate intuition something to which most of us have not yet caught on today, namely that a merely mechanistic view of Nature leads to an abolition of values. (The word "merely" is important because nobody denies the validity of mathematical analysis.) It seems that Rudolf Steiner was the first to see this clearly in Geothe's philosophy of Nature. Geothe's cosmology retained a medieval flavor, and his view of nature was imbued by a strong sense of entelechy all his life. Many feel that here, for once, Goethe turned his back to progress. In reality he was ahead of us. He would undoubtedly have avoided the nonsense of statements, like the one we quoted, had he known the philosophy of the twentieth century, particularly the phenomenology of Husserl. It is, in this connection, interesting that Husserl ended up by presenting a pre-Copernican view of the "Earth as an Ark," (post-humous, unpublished), and nobody should believe that he (who had begun his career as a mathematician) meant to reject Newtonian or Einsteinian cosmology. If one handed to somebody who has never seen a pebble or a tree, the results of a micro-physical analysis of the goings-on which make up pebble or tree—he would have no ideas what pebbles and trees are. I have a strong suspicion that what is true about pebbles and trees is true

sented the whole show, there would be not only no above and below, there would not only be no Ascension and no Descent, there would also not be Prophetic Time or Apocalyptic Time. We would purchase the apparent clarity of the analytic pattern with the price of inner chaos.[10] When Goethe felt the poetic reality of things threatened by the world of Newton, when he recoiled from Holbach's machinery, he remained committed to a kind of medieval universe. A reaction like this is commonly regarded as regressive, infantile. People speak in such cases of a "movement back to the mother." And they are right, only not in

---

about galaxies. In the medieval cosmology links of reference existed between the human body and the macrocosmos. No mathematical analysis has disproved this, and it is conceivable that in hundreds of years a kind of Galileo will come to prove it, and will be put in the doghouse by the clerics of a naturalist philosophy. Whitehead once remarked that, although the cosmology of Scripture and the cosmology of science look incompatible, they are not more incompatible than the corpuscular and the wave theory of light were at one time. The latter are reconciled in modern wave mechanics, and some similar entirely unforeseeable reconciliation is possible in the case of the cosmology of Revelation and of Science. (A. N. Whitehead, *Science and the Modern World,* New York, Macmillan, 1925). Goethe's and Blake's and Wordsworth's bias against the exact sciences—on the face of it so silly—is not just an expression of romantic nostalgia, a sentimental identification with the misty portrait of Mother Nature which must not be defaced by graphs. (In the context of Goethe's and Blake's thought, at least, the pigeon-holing of classic-or-romantic does not even work. The fact that the romantic in itself is not anti-scientific is illustrated in the example of Shelley who was such an enthusiastic "fan" of science.) No, far from being nostalgic, the mood of these men was premonitory. They knew that a dogmatic objectification which takes the poet's *she* and *thou* out of Nature will not stop right there at the pure *it* of neutrality. It is bound to lead to the faceless *it* of the human collective. In other words: the moral decision between *love* and *power,* between *being* and *having* begins—in a way which we can little define as yet—with Man's relationship to "animal, vegetable and mineral."

10 "Can logic give us a view of the whole?" a great mathematician once asked rhetorically. The answer was: "No; the very word which mathematicians use is enough to prove this. In mathematics logic is called analysis, and analysis means *division, dissection.*" (Henri Poincaré, *La Valeur de la Science,* Paris: Flammarion).

the derogatory sense in which they mean it. The sureness of the immediacy of experienced reality is linked with the Eternal Feminine. Henry Adams was harkening back but at the same time uncannily prophetic when he remarked of the Blessed Virgin, in a truly Goethean vein: "In the bankrupcy of reason, she alone was real."[11]

A Note on Dependence.

With these last remarks we have approached the question of faith. The theological virtue of faith, the gift of Grace, has its natural counterpart and soil in the primary relationship of the child to its mother, and in the nuptial relationship of man and woman.

Every human being has once known complete dependence and complete trust, on the level of nature—in the beginning of life. One might say that, in this sense, every mother is a natural *mediatrix* of faith. The beginning of life is also the time when our trust is tested.[12] It is no coincidence that the language of mystic union is, unintentionally, borrowed from our earliest trials in the flesh—"abandonment," "dryness," "the dark night." If one wanted to debunk the mystics he could facetiously say that "dryness," "abandonment," "the dark night," is baby talk. It is. It will be remembered what a study of the life of Francis Thompson[13] showed so convincingly: here the adult faced an alternative, as it were, between dependence and passivity in the most primitive neurotic sense, and a

[11] Henry Adams, Mont Saint Michel and Chartres. Houghton Mifflin Co., 1935.

[12] Erikson who speaks of the phases of man's life in terms of crises describes our earliest phase in terms of a polarity "trust-distrust."

[13] E. F. Sharpe, loc. cit.

life of dependence and receptiveness on the level of the spirit. In one case the poet vegetated, leech-like, sucking opium and the kindness of people; in the other he *acknowledged* his dependence—on God. I use the word "alternative" figuratively, and not to imply a wilful choice. We cannot, in this context, go into the problem of freedom in the neurosis. The observation is recalled as a crude model for a phenomenon of much wider implication. Firstly, it serves to illustrate, as we have seen, that the concept of "sublimation" is not exhausted by mechanical explanations; something of the ontological order enters. Secondly, it shows how the very rockbottom of existence already contains a hint towards being in its fullness. This is precisely what Saint Thomas meant by saying that Grace builds on Nature. In the present context this means that the relationship of utter dependence is encountered at the two ends of the human development: in the dim un-willed world of our natural start, and then again at the summit of being—as free acknowledgement, in the attitude of faith. Here *Faith* is experienced as that *trust* which arises out of a sense of utter dependence. Man has a long course of natural preparation for this because, as we have seen, he passes through that eternity of utter helplessness which enters into the history of the person. This is the meaning of spiritual childhood.

The other aspect of faith is the nuptial. The nuptial relationship is faith-ful, in the sense of trust and commitment out of love. Fidelity is derived from *fides,* and the adulterer is un-faithful.

There exists a great deal of literature on the "psychology of religion," "sociology of religion" and so on, which is diametrically opposed to all this. Such an attitude arises out of the entire climate of modern times. The anti-Christian movement is divided into many currents, so diverse that they seem incompatible with one another. There is a much greater and more essential difference between the atheism of Marx and that of Nietzsche than between Christianity and Islam. And there is again a big difference between those atheisms and a current scientific humanism which wants to assimilate "religion" to the concept of social advancement. But all these, no matter how diversified, have one idea in common: any sense of dependence in Man is an early residuum and will eventually be overcome. There is an entire trend in contemporary scientific humanism which uses sociological and psychoanalytic concepts to get that message across. The social structure of the age of faith is frequently equated with faith itself, and the liberation from the shackles of social oppression is equated with the liberation from "spiritual shackles." In one study of this kind a distinction is made between "rational faith and irrational faith."[14] "Rational faith" implies the certainty of one's own experience and the firmness of conviction in the realization of one's rational vision. It is linked with the experience of growth, it implies an active relation with man and nature and is therefore linked with *activity*. "Irrational faith"—whatever that means—can be recognized by sociological criteria: it is typical of societies in which one group submits to the power of another. Mature faith is the recognition of potentialities in me and in others, and the vision of their unfolding. A great scientific

[14] Erich Fromm, *Faith as a Character Trait* (Psychiatry, *5*, 307, 1942).

discoverer, who pursues his goal with a sense of inner certainty, has such active, mature faith.

We have chosen this example at random. It is typical of a tendency to establish the activist and rationalist mood of our time as the foundation of the human condition, and to make religious terms, hallowed by age, fit this current philosophy. Whether such "active" faith is a sign of maturity or not does not concern us for the moment. One thing is certain: such concept of faith has little to do with the Pauline idea. There is no getting away from it: the Gospel insists on our being children.

The idea that a sense of dependence is utterly dépassé, and not compatible with progress, is not so new. Feuerbach, whose atheism has so decisively influenced that of Marx, stated: "The feeling of dependence is the basis of religion, the original object of this dependence is Nature; hence Nature is the first object of religion."[15] This may historically be true. But the idea that a sense of dependence and childlikeness means acceptance of weakness and a foregoing of maleness is only the crowning of a development of centuries. For the movement of exploration and of penetration which is at the basis of science and technology is the opposite of childlike dependence. Although the scientific method is neutral, the climate of scientific materialism is more inimical to faith than anything else before. Descartes' axiom that nothing must be taken on trust was meant as a stepping stone of scientific inquiry. But, as we have seen, this Cartesian doubt has long ceased to be a neutral tool of scientific procedure. It has become a pri-

---

[15] L. Feuerbach, *Das Wesen der Religion*. New edition. (Leipzig: Kroner, 1908. Original edition, 1848.)

mordial attitude, just as much as faith has been in bygone ages. Modern rationalism does its work against faith with silent violence, like an odorless gas.

Christ who pardoned murderers reserved His word of most terrible threat for those who scandalize children. To plant the seed of doubt in a soul is worse than murder. The demoniacal is much more implied in the figure of Iago, the engineer of distrust, than in a murderer. The fact that we see a man at work who plans to destroy faith and carries his plan out in cold operation, explains the *metaphysical terror* which "Othello" strikes in the heart of the spectator. Auden,[16] in a remarkable analysis of the character of Iago, goes into that celebrated question of "unmotivated malignancy" and suggests that Iago's true motivation is his desire to *experiment.* The same could be said about Kierkegaard's Johannes. The seducer, just like Iago, tampers with faith, just for the joy of tampering. The "let's see what's going to happen" which is the basis of scientific experiment turns into the diabolical pure and simple when a soul is approached in the spirit of uncommitted curiosity. We have seen that this was the reason why Goethe made seduction the test case, as it were, of the ontological situation of Faust; and why Kierkegaard who considered the social sciences as "blasphemous" chose the story of Johannes' experiment as the prototype of evil. In the Hebrew-Christian tradition mankind is the Spouse; in the spirit of scientific humanism mankind is an object of experimentation.

It is in this same context that we have to consider

16 Auden, W. H. "The Joker in the Pack," in *The Dyer's Hand and other Essays.* Random House, New York 1962.

another phenomenon which, at first sight, seems to have little to do with it. We have already mentioned, in passing, the power of modern technology not only to still appetites but to create them. Just as Marxism has certain ascetic, spartan features (this is one of the qualities which betray that religious origin of which some observers make so much) Western materialism has openly pagan, hedonistic features. In Marxism we still hear, even today, some faint subterranean rumbling of Messianism. Hence the emphasis on sacrifice and self-discipline. Scientific humanism of the West is unabashedly geared for immediate terrestrial happiness. The complement to this is the unbelievable output, merely quantitatively, in the production of mass pleasure. Now when we scrutinize this we see the extraordinary emphasis on, or catering to, the pre-genital and the primary genital in the Freudian sense of the terms. Liberation from a puritanical morality would have been a good thing, had it led to a liberation of healthy sexuality. Instead, it is no exaggeration when we feel that future historians may look at the mass culture of today as an oral and voyeuristic form of civilization. The *panem et circenses* of previous phases of history are, compared to this, a buggy compared to a spacecraft. Instead of men being given, as in Plato's paedagogic ideal, what they *ought* to have, the masses are being scientifically studied as to what they *want* to have. And this is being poured in an unending stream, chemically into expectant mouths and electronically into expectant eyes. Thus, while the philosophers of "mid-culture" proclaim man's final liberation from the childlike dependence on faith, the managers of mass culture create forms of infantile dependence on an unheard-of scale. Jaspers[17] has pointed out that at no time in recorded history has there been such depletion of faith on such a vast scale, and we might add, as a corollary, that at no time has there existed such readiness to swallow—if we take the word to comprise all primitive forms of passivity.

With this observation we are closing a circle, as it were. For such antithesis as we are discussing here—of trust and distrust, of frenzied activism and barbaric dependence—marks the crisis of history. In that respect the present situation is in no way unique. History professors are fond of pointing out the parallel between the present time and that of the Roman Empire. As far as I can make out, they always did. The time of the Roman Empire presents, with stylized clarity, in model form, as it were, the dialectic tension of all history.[18] At the historical moment of the Incarnation Roman civilization was under the sign of power, philosophy under the sign of unaided reason, and the visible church of the Old Covenant was in danger of formalism and ossification. And this, of all times, was the hour of the poor in the spirit, the little ones, in short of all those who, power-less, acknowledge their dependence of God. All this found its highest expression in the person of the Blessed Virgin. And with a strange *fiat* of God-likeness marking the crisis of history then, it was the *fiat* of littleness which opened the curtain to the drama of the Redemption.

The Prophetic—all that which *points towards* the Incarnation—is the male. In the Hebrew Liturgy, the patri-

---

17 Jaspers, K., *Descartes*. Loc. cit.
18 C. S. Lewis speaks of it as one of the "ganglions of history."

archs are invoked, as the Blessed Virgin is in the Christian. The remote foreknowledge of that which one will neither see nor touch, is the paternal. Nevertheless, as we have seen, Israel, and mankind as a whole, men and women, represent the Bride. And it is with the Incarnation as an historical fact that the Blessed Virgin, becomes the prototype of faith. Here, contrary to the faith of the prophets, faith achieves the immediacy of certitude, in that carnal link with being which is at the core of all womanhood. In the *orans* of the Annunciation, in the nod of assent, the Blessed Virgin stood for all of us, regardless of sex. She put the final seal on holy passivity. When we say that Sacred History is "more than just a story" we are not only talking about veracity. What we really mean is that none of that which is Scripture remains imprisoned within the confine of Scripture. The facts of revelation are not *contained,* as printed words are contained between the covers of a book. Revelation is no capsule. All human lives and the process of history reflect the drama of the Redemption. Indeed, from what we have seen it appears that the so-called unprejudiced, that is to say relativist, approach of contemporary sociology and comparative anthropology to the problem is of doubtful validity. If we assume for argument's sake, that there exists a polarity "male-female" which is anchored in an absolute, then no observation of shifting social and historical contingencies can add to or subtract from that central fact. The cumulative sciences always are "up against a wall" when transcendental possibilities are under discussion, because the possibilities transcend the wall. In our present study we have chosen an interior approach to the problem, and the result makes it highly probable that there exists a sexual polarity independent of contingencies, which cannot be viewed other than against a metaphysical background. One might argue against this by saying that the people and the phenomena presented here are European and of modern times. However, our point of departure has been precisely that the "absolute" point of view is the "old" one which is shared by Greek and Hebrew, by Hindu and Chinese. There is something ubiquitous about it in time and space—and in Christian anthropology it only comes out more clearly than anywhere else. The same is true about the tradition in literature—in elements as scattered as the knowledge of the poets; the sophiology of Eastern Christendom and Dante; Novalis and Goethe; Kierkegaard and Soloviev. It is like a case of flowers widely dispersed and found in unlikely places, of which we know that they are derived from one species.

In the light of all this the insights presented here assume a meaningful pattern. Man is not only a "natural species" but also an "historical idea," to borrow a term of Merleau-Ponty. This historical idea points incessantly at the trans-historical. The personal drama reflects the dialectics of the spirit. All this makes it so important to assimilate the wealth of recent findings on the nature of Man, in psychoanalysis and in phenomenology, to a Christian anthropology. In doing so, far from succumbing to the fallacy of a reductive psychologism, we purify and enliven concepts which touch on the plane of theology. We free them from an objective heaviness which they have acquired by textbook treatment, as theological vectors. Later generations will realize that, once the fallacy of a shallow naturalism is overcome, psychoanalysis and phenomenology have helped us to regain that sense of poetic knowledge without which theology is desiccated and sterile. And if we meditate on all the data presented in the present essay, we see how the mystery of the Androgyny becomes manifest in the historical crisis.

Index